The Development of American Finance

Since the 1960s, scholars and other commentators have frequently announced the imminent decline of American financial power: Excessive speculation and debt are believed to have undermined the long-term basis of a stable U.S.-led financial order. But the American financial system has repeatedly shown itself to be more resilient than such assessments suggest. This book argues that there is considerable coherence to American finance: Far from being a house of cards, it is a proper edifice, built on institutional foundations with points of both strength and weakness. The book examines these foundations through a historical account of their construction: It shows how institutional transformations in the late nineteenth century created a distinctive infrastructure of financial relations and proceeds to trace the contradiction-ridden expansion of this system during the twentieth century as well as its institutional consolidation during the neoliberal era. It concludes with a discussion of the forces of instability that hit at the start of the twenty-first century.

Martijn Konings is a Lecturer in the Department of Political Economy at the University of Sydney. He has a PhD from York University (Toronto) and has held postdoctoral research positions at York University and the University of Amsterdam. He has published widely in the field of political economy, including several edited volumes and articles in such journals as *New Left Review*, *European Journal of Sociology*, *Review of International Political Economy*, *Politics*, *Review of International Studies*, *Critical Sociology*, and *Theory & Event*.

For Bhavani

The Development of American Finance

MARTIJN KONINGS
University of Sydney

CAMBRIDGE UNIVERSITY PRESS
Cambridge, New York, Melbourne, Madrid, Cape Town,
Singapore, São Paulo, Delhi, Mexico City

Cambridge University Press
The Edinburgh Building, Cambridge CB2 8RU, UK

Published in the United States of America by Cambridge University Press, New York

www.cambridge.org
Information on this title: www.cambridge.org/9780521195256

© Martijn Konings 2011

This publication is in copyright. Subject to statutory exception
and to the provisions of relevant collective licensing agreements,
no reproduction of any part may take place without the written
permission of Cambridge University Press.

First published 2011

A catalogue record for this publication is available from the British Library

Library of Congress Cataloguing in Publication Data
Konings, Martijn, 1975–
 The development of American finance / Martijn Konings.
  p. cm.
 Includes bibliographical references and index.
 ISBN 978-0-521-19525-6 (hardback)
 1. Finance – United States – History. I. Title.
 HG181.K68 2011
 332.0973–dc22   2011010393

ISBN 978-0-521-19525-6 Hardback

Cambridge University Press has no responsibility for the persistence or
accuracy of URLs for external or third-party internet websites referred to in
this publication, and does not guarantee that any content on such websites is,
or will remain, accurate or appropriate. Information regarding prices, travel
timetables, and other factual information given in this work is correct at
the time of first printing but Cambridge University Press does not guarantee
the accuracy of such information thereafter.

Contents

Acknowledgments	*page* vii
1. Introduction	1
2. Finance from Britain to the American Colonies	16
3. The Financial Dynamics of Antebellum America	26
4. Contours of American Finance	39
5. Contradictions of Early Twentieth-Century Financial Expansion	54
6. The United States and International Finance in the Interwar Period	69
7. New Foundations for Financial Expansion	77
8. Contradictions of the Dollar	87
9. The Domestic Expansion of American Finance	100
10. Contradictions of Late Twentieth-Century Financial Expansion	109
11. The Neoliberal Consolidation of American Financial Power	131
12. Contradictions of the Present	153
Bibliography	161
Index	195

Acknowledgments

This book started life as a doctoral dissertation at York University in Toronto. I am deeply indebted to Leo Panitch, who has been an unwavering source of support both during and after my PhD. His intellectual depth and personal generosity have been crucial at every stage of the project. Sam Gindin and Greg Albo, the other members of my dissertation committee, have been unfailingly helpful and tremendous sources of critical insight. George Comninel and Ted Winslow, as well as Eric Helleiner as the external examiner, were kind enough to read the dissertation, and their constructive comments have provided invaluable inspiration for subsequent revisions. Others who contributed in important ways to my graduate school experience include Anna Agathangelou, Rob Albritton, Stephen Gill, Steve Hellman, David McNally, and Jonathan Nitzan.

Gavin Fridell has been a great friend, and I have benefited from his sound advice on many occasions. Thanks to David Sarai for conversations ranging from social theory to American finance, and to David Friesen and Kelly Reimer for moral support. Etienne Cantin, Travis Fast, Geoff Kennedy, and Thierry Lapointe provided intellectual camaraderie, and a special note of thanks to Sam Knafo: Many of the ideas developed in this book have their origins in our discussions.

A postdoctoral position at the University of Amsterdam gave me the opportunity not only to embark on new research but also to continue work on the book manuscript. I am very grateful to Ewald Engelen for his generous support and advice. Manuel Aalbers, Rodrigo Fernandez, and Anna Glasmacher provided comments on draft chapters. My current academic home, the Department of Political Economy at the University of Sydney, has been a very congenial environment to complete work on this book. Thanks in particular to Dick Bryan, Stuart Rosewarne, and Frank Stilwell for their help over the past years.

Others from whose insights, suggestions, or help I have benefited include Scott Aquanno, Mike Beggs, Damien Cahill, David Coates, Bill Dunn, Julie Froud, Michael Krätke, Paul Langley, James Livingston, Randy Martin, Johnna Montgomerie, Michael Moran, Anastasia Nesvetailova, Eric Newstadt, Joy Paton, Chris Rude, Magnus Ryner, Leonard Seabrooke, Duncan Wigan, Karel Williams, and Alan Zuege.

I would like to thank Lewis Bateman and Anne Lovering Rounds at Cambridge University Press for their help in bringing this book to publication. Comments from two anonymous reviewers allowed me to significantly improve the argument and presentation. And I gratefully acknowledge permission from Taylor and Francis and Sage Publications to incorporate material from the following articles: "The institutional foundations of US structural power in international finance: from the re-emergence of global finance to the monetarist turn," *Review of International Political Economy*, 15 (1), pp. 35–61; and "Neoliberalism and the American state," *Critical Sociology*, 36 (5), pp. 741–765.

I am grateful for the unconditional love of my parents, Gerda and Louis. My sister, Jantine, has been a far greater source of emotional support than she knows. A fair amount of work was undertaken in the company of family – the Oklahoma branch (Jantine and John), the Ohio branch (Nandini, Ravi, Roshin, and Naveen), and the cosmopolitan branch (Raj, who will find much to disagree with in this book).

Bhavani entered my life as I was about to submit the dissertation on which this book is based. I am forever indebted to her for accompanying me from Toronto to Amsterdam to Sydney while carving out her own creative career. I dedicate this book to her, with love.

Martijn Konings
Sydney, April 2011

1

Introduction

Over the past decades, few things have been anticipated more anxiously or eagerly than the decline of American financial power. Although few doubt that the United States has benefited tremendously from the expansionary dynamics of financial markets, this advantage is often seen to have involved speculative gains bought at the expense of long-term sustainability – that is, a reckless mortgaging of the future. American finance is seen to be hugely inflated, not supported by economic fundamentals, and forever in danger of collapsing. And so, with each major crisis (the end of the Bretton Woods system in 1971, the stock market crash of 1987, the bursting of the Internet bubble at the turn of the century, and the "subprime" crisis that struck in 2007), a chorus of commentators rises to announce that the days of American hegemony in global finance are now really numbered. But American finance has repeatedly shown itself to be quite resilient. The fact that predictions of imminent decline or collapse have been made time and again over the past decades should lead us to approach such claims with a certain degree of caution. This book argues that there is considerable coherence to the construction of American financial power: Far from a house of cards, it is a proper edifice, built on foundations with their own distinctive points of strength and weakness. Even if the early twenty-first century turns out to have been the apogee of U.S. financial power, American financial actors have built up capacities that they will be able to wield for decades to come, and how the American state manages the dynamics of its financial system will remain a central question until well into the present century.

MARKET, STATE, AND POWER

The perceived threat to America's hegemonic position during the 1970s was one of the founding concerns of the field of international political economy (henceforth IPE). The approach that emerged took the Bretton Woods era from the end of World War II to the early 1970s as representing the high point of American power. In this perspective, whereas during the interwar period America's isolationist reluctance to shoulder the responsibilities of hegemony had been responsible for global economic breakdown (Kindleberger 1973), after World War II the United States committed itself to ensuring the stable reproduction of the international market economy by embedding it in regulatory institutions (Block 1977; Ruggie 1982; Gilpin 1987). The rise of economic globalization trends was seen to upset the parameters of this order of "embedded liberalism" and so to erode U.S. financial power.

Perceiving not only America's growing balance of payments deficits but also its consistent ability to attract capital to finance them, more recent IPE perspectives began to question strong claims about the decline of American power. They criticized the tendency in orthodox IPE to reduce political power to the policies of the official state and to pay insufficient attention to its socioeconomic sources. The notion of "structural power" was introduced to draw attention to the fact that control often operates in more indirect ways, that is, by influencing the institutional conditions under which actors make decisions. This concept provided the theoretical basis for a revised interpretation of the relationship between financial globalization and the American state: The reemergence of global finance, although responsible for the demise of the U.S.-dominated embedded liberal Bretton Woods institutions, also laid the basis for a more structural form of American power (Strange 1986, 1988; Gill and Law 1989; Walter 1993; Helleiner 1994; Arrighi 1994; Germain 1997; Seabrooke 2001).

However, in practice this notion of structural power has remained close to traditional notions of "the market," reflecting a persistent structuralism in IPE scholarship that has entailed a continued reliance on an external conception of the relationship between market and state. Financial expansion is consequently still depicted as a process whereby markets autonomize themselves from their institutional context and undermine political capacities: The analysis of American finance has remained centrally organized around the idea of a transition from embedded liberalism to the "disembedding" tendencies seen to be characteristic of the era of neoliberalism and globalization. The recent IPE literature has accordingly tended to develop its own thesis of American decline. Although it is recognized that the growth of financial markets has entailed considerable benefits for the United States, those are seen as primarily speculative in nature and not properly embedded in or supported by institutional structures; eventually, it is often argued, the American state will have to bow before the disciplinary imperatives of globalizing financial markets (e.g., Strange 1986, 1988; Germain 1997; Brenner 2002; Arrighi 2003). Thus, although the capacity of the American state is to some extent acknowledged, it is treated as a residual category, understood primarily in terms of the ability to defy or postpone the effects of growing economic constraints. This book is motivated by the belief that the very significant financial powers wielded by the American state deserve a less cavalier treatment, and it will argue that this requires breaking with an approach to political economy that is centrally preoccupied with the logics of state and market.

Even if one of modern-day IPE's central claims is that the distinction between politics and economics should not be mistaken for a material separation, the implications of this insight have not been pushed far enough to permit a full conceptualization of their institutional linkages (Watson 2005). This is particularly evident in the prominence of a particular appropriation of Polanyi's (1957) work, which frames capitalist development as driven by the interacting logics of market disembedding (i.e., the tendency of markets to escape from their institutional context) and reembedding (i.e., a countermovement whereby political forces seek to re-regulate the market). Such an approach conceptualizes the role of institutions primarily in terms of their ability to constrain markets and limit their reach; the expansionary logic of markets itself is seen not as constructed through the norms and rules provided by institutions but rather as driven by a presocial logic that is at odds with the regulatory effects of institutional structures (Krippner 2002; Beckert 2003; Gemici 2008; Jones 2008). This framework, premised on the idea that markets and institutions are governed by their own distinctive logics, is not sufficiently geared to the possibility that markets and their properties might, at their very core, be institutional constructions that can potentially function as vehicles of state power.

The approach adopted in this book conceptualizes market expansion as involving the creation of new social forms and linkages and so putting in place the foundations for new patterns of institutional control over the dynamics of human interaction. In recent years, several perspectives have emerged that emphasize the socially constructed nature of even the most basic and seemingly technical economic phenomena (Knorr-Cetina and Bruegger 2002; de Goede 2005; Mackenzie 2006; Aitken 2007; Langley 2008). This "social finance" literature is critical of IPE's tendency to attribute independent causal powers to markets and to give short shrift to the microlevel norms and practices that shape financial life. It views the structural aspects of power not merely as setting parameters for action but as operating through the very production of market actors' identities, capacities, and interests. This approach, however, has tended to generate its own kind of structuralism: Market processes are now seen to operate through effectively internalized financial norms. Political institutions are considered important nodal points of social relations but nonetheless viewed as being fully subject to a regime of market pressures. As a result, the portrayal of neoliberal financial expansion in the social finance literature is largely consistent with IPE's analysis of this process in terms of the disembedding of financial markets and their disciplinary effects.

It is important to approach the institutional construction of financial life as a more open process: Human agency is not exhausted or preempted by social forms and always retains an element of instrumentality in relation to them. This does not, however, imply a return to the assumption of the rational economic actor with a preexisting set of interests (Whitford 2002). Instead, the perspective advanced here emphasizes the pragmatic dimensions of the process of social constitution: Our engagement of institutional forms is motivated by the experience of problems and the aim to address those by improving our grip on the world, and it is through this process of interaction that we assemble an identity and constitute ourselves as social actors (Berger and Luckmann 1966; Dunn 1997: 695; Beckert 2002: 252; Whitford 2002: 345). Through institutions, we build up skills and capacities that allow us to navigate social life (Berk and Galvan 2009: 544). Such socialization does not necessarily entail a rigidification of agency: The development of useful habits is in fact crucial to the development of problem-solving capacities, the bricolage-like process whereby subjects recombine existing structures to expand their range of options (Berger and Luckmann 1966: 53; Dalton 2004: 604–5; Berk and Galvan 2009: 555; Engelen et al. 2010). Institutions, then, often have enabling effects (Herrigel 2010), fostering rather than constraining people's strategic and creative capacities.

That is, of course, not to deny that institutions also have constraining effects. But what a perspective centered on the interaction of practices permits us to see is that the absence of strategic flexibility is not an effect of institutional forms in and of themselves but stems from the operation of social power differentials: The growing capacity for innovative, problem-solving agency and the contracting room for maneuver available to other actors represent obverse sides of the same process of social construction (Knafo 2010). Such inequalities are organized around, yet not fully reflected in, institutions, which never exhaust the complex dynamics of human interaction (Holzman 1996; Novak 2008: 764). This element of misrepresentation is crucial to the functioning of institutions because it diverts attention from patterns of control and so promotes legitimacy (Eagleton 1991). The mediation of social connections by institutions thus facilitates the operation of power on a more systematic, structural basis than would ever be possible if control were only ever exercised directly and visibly (Lukes 1974; Roy 1997: 13). Institutions leverage particular agencies, extending their reach over wider tracts of social life.

The leveraging of the agency of some over that of others expresses itself as a process whereby institutional configurations acquire a certain degree of coherence and identity, creating a discursive context where we can meaningfully talk about organizational forms (e.g., the Treasury) as possessing agency and capacities. This context sets the stage for subsequent interactions: Elite actors' privileged access to institutional mechanisms of control allows them to play a dominant role in shaping the development of social life (Savage and Williams 2008). As a consequence, inequality often has a cumulative character: Social constructions tend to become layered, with new ones built on top of existing ones, thus allowing power to sink more deeply into the basic modalities of social life and to take on more structural qualities. What this amounts to is a picture of society as a pyramidal constellation of institutional mechanisms, where interaction channeled through the forms of everyday life results in the creation of networks of structural power that form the basis for the construction and legitimation of higher-level institutions (Abrams 1977). It is through these processes that public authority is constructed: Statehood, as the public sanctioning of relations of control, can be found at all levels of social life. The official state, rather than being a substantive entity in and of itself with merely external connections to the social realm, sits at the pinnacle of this constellation (Bratsis 2006), deriving capacity and leverage from its linkages to social institutions. We need a conception of the "integral state" (Gramsci 1971), that is, an understanding of power that does not confine its view to the institutions of the formal state but examines its internal connections to processes situated at different levels of social life.

It bears emphasizing that this process of hegemonic socialization is only poorly captured through concepts such as "entrenchment" or "stabilization." The dynamics of human interaction do not slow down or become less complex: The layering of social constructions is not a result of gradual, default accretion but occurs through ongoing strategic adjustments. At no point does the pragmatic disposition give way to a lifeless submission to norms, and as actors exploit the leeway available to them, they generate new interdependencies that existing institutions do not afford much grip on (i.e., new contradictions and problems that put pressure on the integrative capacity of existing institutions). In such situations, elite actors can often avail themselves of considerable latitude pursuing reforms aimed at institutionalizing the new social effects in ways that are consistent with existing mechanisms of structural power. Thus, the construction of the integral state involves a dynamic process of continuous institutional adaptation and elaboration through which dominant actors build their capacities vis-à-vis subordinate actors.

In capitalist societies, the integral state expands dramatically. The modern polity, organized on principles of legal equality (Wood 1995), can tap into sources of legitimacy that were not available to more traditional forms of rule. It is precisely this projection of neutrality that permits power relations to become layered to an unprecedented extent and life in modern society to become shot through with institutional rules and norms (Mitchell 2005), resulting in the build-up of an elaborate, intricately interconnected constellation of control mechanisms. In this way, the modern state comes to have access to what Mann (1984: 189; 1993: 59) has called "infrastructural power," that is, a capacity to implement projects through a social sphere characterized by a high degree of connectivity. Compared to more traditional forms of rule, infrastructural power is indirect, diffuse, and crucially dependent on the kind of legitimacy that secures cooperation (Calhoun 1992). The capacity of the modern state can be highest when it is organically allied to social networks of control and leveraged by an infrastructure of lower-level institutions and norms (Mann 1993; Ansell 2000; Hobson 2000; Novak 2008; Bell and Hindmoor 2009; Konings 2010).

However, modern power is a contradictory affair: The proliferation of institutional forms in social life lays the foundations for, but does not automatically translate into, a higher degree of effective political capacity. Because structural power relations are constituted through the limits on more direct forms of authority and regulation, the immediate effect of their expansion is often precisely to complicate and jeopardize existing institutional capacities. The mediated nature and complexity of modern power means that its operation is often not transparent to its participants,

Introduction

making it difficult to wield even for those who are positioned favorably in its networks and derive a great deal of leverage from them. Dominant actors are likely to have considerable strategic leeway and room for experimentation, but they are not above the contradictions and confusions of power: They must still fumble around for the right switches and levers and learn how to manipulate them (i.e., work their way, through trial and error, toward the more subtle skills required for the navigation of indirect social relations).

This conceptual framework permits us a new vantage point from which to examine the dynamics of capitalist development. The systemic logic and expansionary qualities of capitalist markets arise through processes of institutional construction that establish the conditions for more far-reaching, structural forms of control over the dynamics of social interaction; but these complex patterns of new connections generate their own problems, which have to be maneuvered, negotiated, and managed. The tensions that characterize capitalist development, therefore, are not best seen in terms of the clash of an economic market logic with its institutional surroundings but should be viewed as contradictions internal to the processes whereby our practices become institutionalized and modalities of control are built. Whereas IPE has typically taken the financial instability of the modern era as evidence for the idea that capitalist markets tend to destroy institutional capacities for the coordination of socioeconomic life, this book interprets the tensions faced by the modern American state as inherent aspects of the processes through which financial power develops, reflective of the difficulties involved in navigating indirect modalities of power and managing increasingly complex and interwoven networks of social relations. Thus, the narrative laid out in this book traces how institutional innovations create mechanisms of control and so enhance the structural basis of political authority yet how, at the same time, the creation of such indirect power relations is responsible for new contradictions and challenges that need to be handled and negotiated and prompt further institutional reform and innovation.[1]

---

[1] The primary objective of this book is to elucidate the nature of modern financial power through an engagement with political economy themes; it does not aim to contribute to the rich literature on American political development. But because I will draw on this literature to place the analysis of finance in its historical and social context (and will do so without explicit consideration of the many important issues that it raises), it seems appropriate to briefly situate the approach adopted in this book with respect to the main conceptual perspectives employed in that field (for an overview, see Orren and Skowronek 2004). The modern study of American political development is dominated

THE DEVELOPMENT OF AMERICAN FINANCE: TOWARD A NEW INTERPRETATION

The rest of this chapter offers an outline of the interpretation of American financial development that this book presents, giving an overview of the central arguments concerning the sources of U.S. financial power and highlighting the respects in which the narrative differs from the conventional account. We begin this outline by drawing attention to a sense in which modern finance can be said to be "American" that is generally not sufficiently appreciated. The IPE literature typically locates the origins of modern-day financial markets in the breakdown of the Bretton Woods system in the early 1970s – and it views the dynamics that resulted as an amplified reemergence of the liberal financial structures that prevailed under British hegemony. This book advances a different perspective: It traces the origins of the financial practices and relations that have shaped financial life over the past decades back to the transformation of the American financial system from the late nineteenth century. The direct descendants of the distinctly American institutional forms that emerged in that context would profoundly shape the nature of present-day finance.

Chapters 2 and 3 are devoted to sketching the contours of the pre–Civil War financial landscape out of which those new institutions would arise. One key objective here is to question the usefulness of taking the notion of a liberal market economy as a conceptual starting point. This is

by perspectives that place a great deal of emphasis on the autonomy of the institutional structures of the state. This institutionalist turn, led by authors such as Skowronek (1982) and Skocpol (1979, 1985), was motivated by a concern that overly society-centered approaches – which include views of American history as governed by a consensual culture of classical Lockean liberalism (e.g., Boorstin 1953; Hartz 1955) as well as the New Left's rediscovery of social conflict (e.g., Countryman 1967; Domhoff 1967; Bernstein 1968; Weinstein 1968; Henretta 1974, 1979; Gutman 1976; Nash 1976; Clark 1990, 2002) – tend to give short shrift to the constitutive role of institutions and to assume that the institutional level is a somewhat passive manifestation of social life. The literature that has emerged from the institutionalist turn tends to analyze the process of state building in terms of the internally generated dynamics and expansion of bureaucratic structures and executive agencies (e.g., Finegold and Skocpol 1995; John 1997; Carpenter 2001). Although many authors seem to acknowledge that especially Skocpol's (1985) criticism of society-centered approaches might have bent the stick too far in the other direction and emphasize the mutual interaction between state and society (e.g., Bensel 1990, 2000; Orren 1991; Sanders 1999), even they tend to work with an overly narrow conception of political authority and state capacity, which are seen to derive primarily from the state's internal cohesion and organizational integration. In recent years, several authors (e.g., King and Lieberman 2007; Novak 2008) have argued for the need to look behind the state's formal framework and to conceptualize the constitution of its infrastructural capacities through its institutional linkages with social life.

Introduction

important particularly because – contrary to the idea that the U.S. financial system should be comprehended as an instance of the Anglo-Saxon market-based model – the United States did not follow in the tracks of financial modernization laid down by Britain. The highly dynamic and liquid financial system that emerged during the late nineteenth century did not represent a variation on a general model of liberal finance but can only be understood as a complex and highly specific historical construction, driven by its own institutional logic. That construction emerged out of a pre–Civil War system that had greatly limited financial integration and the infrastructural mechanisms that elites and public authorities could deploy. Although many of the elements of British finance were transported to the New World, for various reasons early America did not reproduce the systemic dynamics of British finance. In particular, the absence of a nationwide market for well-secured short-term obligations made the American banking system consistently illiquid and crisis-prone. Political strife, in which agrarian interests played a key role, time and again thwarted attempts to construct a more integrated financial system.

During the last decades of the nineteenth century, this fragmented financial structure prompted the development of practices and strategies that set American finance on a qualitatively new path, giving rise to a system that was much more dynamic, expansionary, and integrative than the British system had ever been. Chapter 4, covering the postbellum era, traces the emerging contours of this new system of financial intermediation. Central to this account is the fact that, as banks' need for liquidity intensified, they responded by pioneering a distinctive form of "financial banking" (Youngman 1906: 435) based on the investment of funds in the stock market and associated speculative markets. American banks' ability to practice securitization *avant la lettre* had major consequences. The development of these new financial networks meant that financial elites were able to leverage their stock market dealings with the savings of ordinary Americans. In addition, banks' newfound access to liquidity meant that they were now in a much better position to create liquidity and extend credit for a variety of purposes.

The emergence of this much more expansionary institutional basis gave a highly significant twist to the role of finance in American society. Whereas throughout the nineteenth century the relationship between financial institutions and the American lower classes had been fraught with antagonism, the new framework was capable of integrating a wide variety of popular interests and ambitions. Consequently, the period saw the rapid proliferation of institutional connections between the realm of high finance and everyday life. Moreover, this dramatic financial growth did not occur through a retreat of the state but precisely through the expansion of public and civic authority. These observations point toward a portrayal of the late nineteenth and early twentieth centuries that differs in key respects from the conventional characterization of this period as the classic age of liberal high finance. Chapter 5 examines the contradiction-ridden expansion of these new networks of financial power. The foundation of the Federal Reserve system in 1913 was a response to recurrent crises brought on by the sudden evaporation of market liquidity. But as it left fully intact the web of techniques and connections that stood at the basis of America's distinctive pattern of financial expansion, the presence of a lender of last resort served to fuel rather than dampen the unstable growth of new forms of credit. The systemic risks entailed by America's trajectory of financial growth were recognized only when it was too late.

The Crash and the Great Depression affected not just the United States but also the world at large. IPE interpretations of the interwar period revolve around the idea that the forces of instability could have such dramatic global consequences because of America's irresponsible foreign policies. According to this perspective, after World War I the United States had replaced Britain as the world's preeminent financial power, yet its politics and policies remained mired in myopic unilateralism and failed to provide the international economy with stabilizing institutional foundations. Chapter 6 argues that this interpretation relies too much on a cyclical model of capitalist history, which sees hegemonic powers as successively taking responsibility for the reproduction of the international market economy. The United States' inability to stabilize the dynamics of its financial system was a significant factor in the making of the global economic depression of the 1930s, but this is not best understood in terms of America's failure to discern its true hegemonic interests. America's financial interest in the world was simply still relatively limited: The challenge to Britain's position in international finance resulted from the intergovernmental debts incurred by European countries during World War I and the dollar's growing role as a reserve currency, but an infrastructure of dollar-centered private credit relations linking American finance to the international economy in an organic way remained largely absent. When, decades later, a dense web of connections between American finance and the world economy developed, its operational mechanisms reflected not an abstract image of liberal world order but rather the specific institutional mechanisms that American finance had developed at home.

Introduction

The New Deal further reorganized the operations of the state around America's reconfigured landscape of financial relations and institutions. IPE has conceptualized the post–New Deal and post–World War II era in terms of the American state's commitment to "embedding" financial markets – that is, to shielding the population from the vagaries of markets and building an international regime that permitted other nations to do the same. However, the overall tendency of New Deal policy making was not to suppress the expansionary dynamics of American finance but rather to put them on a more stable footing. Chapter 7 outlines how American elites and policy makers, when faced with widespread popular discontent, discerned ample opportunity for pursuing regulations that would promote the further integration of the American population into the financial system. The state's efforts to extend the use of securitization techniques were accompanied by an awareness that the volatility generated by financial expansion should and could be managed through policies of macroeconomic stabilization. In this sense, New Deal policy making reflected a growing awareness of the potentially symbiotic relationship between capitalist expansion and regulatory capacity, that is, a conception of organically embedded, infrastructural state power associated with a conception of the economy as sufficiently institutionalized and systemlike that it could be regulated through the manipulation of key institutional parameters.

The New Deal reorganization of the state also ushered in a new conception of foreign economic policy: Connections between American financial capital and the international economy were decreasingly viewed as a threat to the capacity and autonomy of the United States, and an awareness emerged that such linkages could in fact increase the leverage of American actors and policy makers. Although this new approach came too late to prevent the collapse of the world economy during the 1930s, it became important in informing the U.S. approach to the post–World War II reconstruction of the world economy. Chapter 8 offers a reinterpretation of America's financial engagement with the world after World War II. The central point is that IPE's organizing concept of embedded liberalism offers little conceptual purchase on this era. Although America's plan for the post–World War II international economy envisaged a multilateral system of trade and payments, the relative weakness of Western European economies greatly limited the extent of financial liberalization during the late 1940s and 1950s. Initially liberalism was not so much embedded as nonexistent: The problem was less how to suppress than how to resuscitate international finance. Hence, it was not through prudent stewardship of a liberal world order but virtually by default that New York – as the only open financial center – became the world's financial capital and the dollar the new international currency. The United States made full use of the dollar's status, spending freely on national security and foreign aid. However, such seigniorage privileges were not organically embedded in networks of private international relations. This became apparent during the 1960s, when, in the context of a restored international payments system, a growing dollar overhang put considerable pressure on the position of the dollar. The decade saw a series of largely unsuccessful attempts to contain capital outflows and stem the deterioration of the balance of payments. But toward the end of the 1960s, the Nixon administration abandoned such attempts, turning to a policy of "benign neglect" that allowed the balance of payments deficit to grow unchecked.

This policy turn, which culminated in the abandonment of Bretton Woods system and gave a huge boost to the growth of global financial markets, has traditionally been viewed as signaling the decline of America's financial hegemony. More recent work in IPE has done much to reconsider this interpretation by drawing attention to America's continued centrality in international finance and the ability of U.S. public and private actors to benefit from the system's new dynamics. But what has generally not been sufficiently appreciated is the extent to which financial globalization was in fact centrally driven by the growth of American finance and how its specific dynamics were shaped to the core by institutional forms and practices of specifically American origin. This book, therefore, seeks to understand post–World War II financial globalization not as a reemergence of international finance but rather as a process whereby the long-standing dynamics of American financial expansion began to assume global dimensions.

To that end, Chapter 9 shifts the focus from the international arena back to the domestic dynamics of American finance following the New Deal. From this perspective, too, embedded liberalism is a misnomer: The development of American finance was hardly embedded in the Polanyian sense of "contained" or "suppressed." Even if the New Deal reorganization of the financial sector had placed particular restrictions on banks' room for maneuver, it had created many more new opportunities, particularly in the sphere of mortgage and consumer lending. Over the course of the post–World War II period, the American working classes became ever more fully integrated into the financial system, both as investors and savers and as borrowers and consumers.

This process generated new contradictions, which are explored in Chapter 10. By the late 1950s, American banks were running up against

Introduction

the limits to their credit-creating capacities, and during the following decade they pursued a range of innovations designed to circumvent regulatory restrictions. Introducing new forms of securitization, they further transformed the institutional basis for financial intermediation in such a way as to dramatically enhance their capacity to create liquidity. When the Federal Reserve sought to curb these innovations, banks turned to the overseas Eurodollar markets (the pools of dollars that had formed as a result of the dollar overhang), in the process reshaping the institutional framework for international financial intermediation.

This dynamic had contradictory effects. On the one hand, it propelled the institutionalization of a transnational infrastructure of financial relations governed by American rules for the trading of dollar debt, serving to loosen external constraints on the United States. It was the Nixon administration's emerging awareness that America's debt to the world was no less the world's problem than it was America's that motivated the turn to a policy regime of benign neglect. On the other hand, the same mechanisms of financial innovation that served to entrench the dollar as international currency also posed a major challenge to the control of American financial authorities. The internal expansion of American finance now existed in a mutually reinforcing relationship with its external expansion, and the 1970s saw a spectacular acceleration of the pace at which financial relations in American society proliferated and deepened. The contradictions of monetary management became ever more pronounced, and by the end of the decade they came to a head.

Thus, the problems of the 1970s (such as high levels of inflation and pressure on the dollar) were contradictions internal to the modalities of American financial expansion: The projection of U.S. financial power abroad occurred through the very same structures that complicated the control of American financial authorities at home. This theorization contrasts with the IPE perspective, which analyzes the developments of the 1970s in terms of the growth of external constraints. Accordingly, IPE views the political turn to neoliberalism as a series of policies whereby the American polity submitted itself to the pressures of disembedded international finance. The interpretation advanced in Chapter 11, by contrast, emphasizes that neoliberal policies, by resolving some key contradictions at the heart of the modalities of financial expansion, laid the foundations for a more coherent expansion of the network power of American finance and so allowed the American state to regain a considerable degree of institutional control over financial markets.

Key here is the realization that we cannot critically comprehend neoliberalism in its own terms, as a victory of markets over states and their policies. The Federal Reserve's turn to monetarism, in particular, had little to do with the subordination of public or private actors to the constraints of global markets. Indeed, American finance exploded: Government, corporate, and household debt grew at unprecedented rates, supported by an extraordinary capacity of American intermediaries to attract and create liquidity. In other words, neoliberal policies embedded the mechanisms of financial expansion in a new institutional regime that served to enhance the infrastructural capacities and policy autonomy of the American state. This certainly did not mean that financial markets had become immune to instability. But even as predictions of decline abounded, the American state displayed considerable agility in constructing more effective institutional linkages between its regulatory authority, innovation strategies of intermediaries, and the financial aspirations of ordinary Americans. The result was the rapid widening and deepening of networks of credit and debt, overseen by a public framework that actively and effectively managed the contradictions generated by the progressive erosion of the extant boundaries between high finance and everyday life.

But financial expansion did not just produce the kind of instability that could be efficiently addressed within the institutional parameters of the regime that had been consolidated during the neoliberal era. Chapter 12 discusses the growth of American finance during the first decade of the twenty-first century and the new contradictions it generated. Those culminated in the subprime crisis, which struck in 2007 and subsequently assumed momentous proportions. Predictions of imminent collapse once again abounded, and IPE authors rushed to analyze the crisis as the result of how several decades of market expansion had undermined the institutional sources and coherence of American financial power. However, there was never much compelling evidence that the crisis had dealt a decisive blow to the networks of organically grown practices and relations, constructed over the course of more than a century, that make up the edifice of American financial power. Although the novelty of the tensions that American authorities were dealing with meant that they were forced to apply the fullest extent of their regulatory capacities, these policies were sufficiently effective to preserve the integrity of America's core financial institutions and the infrastructure of power they organize.

This is not to make any substantial predictions about the future of American finance, but rather to insist that such questions are better studied through a focus on contradictory processes of institutional construction

Introduction

than in terms of the corrosive and constraining effects of market expansion on political agency. Although over the next few years American elites will enjoy considerable latitude in developing new institutional capacities to address new contradictions, finding effective policy solutions is an inherently uncertain process. But if we are currently witnessing the beginning of the end of American financial power, we won't know that until some time from now, when we will be able to look at things with the benefit of hindsight. Either way – whether the current conjuncture represents the further rise of American finance or the start of its fall – how the United States will manage the myriad institutional linkages through which it is connected to the domestic and global sprawl of American finance will remain a central question for those seeking to understand the dynamics of contemporary capitalism for some time to come.

2

Finance from Britain to the American Colonies

INTRODUCTION

One of the key sources of American financial power is that it has developed, through complex and contradictory historical processes, an extraordinary capacity for the creation of liquidity. It is common in IPE scholarship to make a distinction between money liquidity as reflecting real economic value and credit liquidity as created in speculative anticipation of the production of such value. But it is important to appreciate that all forms of liquidity represent relations of credit and debt in the sense that they are only valuable if they can be socially validated as such (Dodd 1994; Ingham 2004). This is the case even for what may appear to be the most "naturally" liquid forms of value like gold: Accepting gold in payment for a good or service is to assume that society is taking on a debt that will be discharged in the future. But of course it is only plausible to claim that all forms of liquid value represent relations of credit and debt if we also reject commonsensical interpretations of the latter as easily created and extended in a financial sphere governed by the wish to escape the allegedly more complex and demanding imperatives of real-world production. Contrary to the commonsense notion that credit is an easy means to provide people with "free lunches," there is nothing simple or straightforward about its creation. Of course, credit relations are often created without being properly embedded in a wider network of stabilizing relations, leaving them with insufficient support in the foundations of social life and so rendering them unstable and prone to losing value (i.e., suffering inflation); but this is no different from how things work in the more tangible world of manufacturing or, indeed, any other sphere of human action. The successful creation of credit and liquidity is an inherently complex process characterized by a multitude of institutional mediations.

What this means is that we should not – as is common in IPE approaches – view the fluidity and dynamism of modern-day American finance as the outcome of a liberal logic inherent in Anglo-American societies, often seen as entailing the relative weakness of substantive social bonds and public institutions and the consequent prevalence of market principles. We should instead work to grasp the liquidity-creating capacities of modern finance as itself an institutional construction. For the purposes of this book, it is useful to think of the credit-creating capacities of modern finance as having been produced in two stages: first through the British and then through the American transformation of financial relations. The former was responsible for the creation of a specific set of institutional linkages that conferred a high degree of systemic coherence on banks' attempts to create credit by issuing obligations. The latter occurred in an institutional landscape that in some respects resembled that of Britain but was configured in a very different way and lacked many of its underlying networks and causal mechanisms. The result was the somewhat truncated development of early American finance. Yet eventually the socioeconomic fabric of nineteenth-century America evolved to produce its own logic, subsuming the inherited institutional forms into a new set of relationships characterized by practices of liquidity creation that were much more flexible and expansionary than the techniques pioneered in the British context. This chapter and the following two chapters trace the effects of what was essentially an attempt at selective institutional transplantation, the dynamics of partial acceptance and rejection by the socioeconomic body, and the contradiction-ridden emergence of financial relations characterized by their own distinctive systemic properties. The present chapter begins by giving an account of the origins and nature of British finance and then proceeds to examine American attempts to reproduce aspects of that system, the obstacles such efforts encountered, and the strategic responses that this triggered.

CONTOURS OF BRITISH FINANCE

During the late Middle Ages and the Renaissance, the minting of coins was typically a public monopoly (Kohn 1999a), giving rulers access to seigniorage privileges (i.e., the ability to reduce the gold or silver content of coins) (Spufford 1988). It was difficult for authorities to benefit in similar ways from private credit relations that did not involve the use of coin, and rulers therefore sought to make trade and commerce dependent on the supply of specie. But economic actors, experiencing a consistent shortage of liquidity, continued to develop a range of private credit relations (Wray 1990). The result was a tension between public and private mechanisms of liquidity production (Boyer-Xambeu, Delaplace, and Gillard 1994; Ingham 2004).

Banks played a major role in this private credit system, intermediating the financial obligations generated in transactions (primarily bills of exchange but also promissory notes).[1] They held funds deposited by merchants and transferred them to other merchants to settle their debts (Kindleberger 1993: 45). Over time, banks began to make loans on the basis of idle deposits. In doing so, they functioned on the principle of "fractional reserves": Their outstanding liabilities were exceeded by their holdings of specie (de Roover 1963: 2). But the creation of credit in this way was risky and unstable (Ingham 1999: 88): Once depositors learned that a bank's obligations exceeded its specie-holdings, they would withdraw funds and so trigger a run on the bank, usually resulting in bankruptcy. From the fifteenth century, bank crises became a serious problem (Kohn 1999b: 21). Authorities in Southern Europe responded by tightening control and transforming private deposit banks into public banks whose ability to extend credit was highly regulated (Usher 1943; Avallone 1997). In much of Northern Europe, deposit banks were banned (Kohn 1999b: 22).

Under these circumstances, merchants began to look for ways to settle debts that would not be dependent on banks. In international commercial centers (and, in particular, Antwerp), financial obligations were made transferable (Kohn 1999c: 24): The debt represented by an instrument became payable "to bearer" (van der Wee 1997: 182). To prevent this new method from developing into an incentive to accept bad debt and pass it on to someone else, the transferrer was required to assume responsibility for the bill's settlement by endorsing it. The principle of endorsement meant that the more often a financial instrument was passed on, the more secure it became (Quinn 2004: 154). Financial instruments now became negotiable and this created a foundation for the

---

[1] Promissory notes were general confessions of debt, whereas the bill of exchange was the more typical instrument used in commercial credit extension. The bill of exchange had originally been an instrument to remit funds and convert them from one currency into another, but in the context of the papal ban on usury and interest payment it proved a convenient means of extending credit: Through manipulation of the rate at which funds were converted into other currencies, bills allowed for interest charges to be hidden in an exchange transaction (Usher 1914; de Roover 1974: 212).

"discounting" of debt: the purchase of a financial obligation before its date of maturity for a price below its nominal value (Kohn 1999c: 27). The spread of discounting served to promote the circulation and liquidity of financial instruments (van der Wee 1977: 332; Kohn 1999c: 28).

It was in England that these new financial techniques articulated with a resurgence of banking to produce a new set of financial dynamics (Davis 1973: 248; van der Wee 1997: 184).[2] In rapidly commercializing England, deposit banking had been banned for a long time (Kerridge 1988), motivating the absorption of the instruments and techniques pioneered in Antwerp and the subsequent emergence of a domestic money market (Rogers 1995; Munro 2000). When deposit banking was permitted from the middle of the seventeenth century, fractional reserve banking emerged as a systemically viable practice for two reasons. First, instead of personal deposit certificates, banks issued impersonal promissory notes that could be transferred (i.e., bank notes payable to bearer) (Quinn 2004: 154). This meant that people could make payments using bank obligations without the bank being directly involved. Banks' obligations began to circulate. As the note issue of a bank developed a reputation for soundness, the bank was able to enter more notes into circulation on the basis of a constant amount of specie reserves (van der Wee 1977; Quinn 2004: 155). Second, banks typically issued their notes by discounting bills of exchange, which were short-term and secured both by the commercial transaction from which the bill had arisen and by the endorsers of the bill. Consequently the bank's asset portfolio was highly liquid, which greatly reduced the possibility that it would be unable to redeem bank notes. This liquidity further promoted the reputation of a bank's note issue, allowing it to put more notes into circulation. The idea that banks should only discount short-term bills of exchange arising from commercial transactions was formalized as the "real bills doctrine" (Santiago-Valiente 1988), which would provide the main conceptual foundation for commercial banking until the twentieth century.

Financial innovation produced an institutional framework that made available to banks a greatly heightened capacity to create credit without

---

[2] This role in advancing financial practices is often ascribed to Amsterdam, which was developing as a center of international commerce. However, Amsterdam authorities were particularly mistrustful of the uncontrolled proliferation of private financial instruments that Antwerp merchants brought with them, and the Amsterdam Exchange Bank was supposed to replace all endorsed private paper with drafts on the Bank (Neal and Quinn 2001: 10). That is, its function was to control, and assume many of the functions previously performed by, the private circulation of financial obligations (Davis 1973: 247).

generating serious instability or inflation. As the British economy developed, the private creation of liquidity through the issuance of bank notes grew rapidly (Davies 2002: 279; Knafo 2008: 185), and by the early nineteenth century bank notes had replaced coins as the largest component of the domestic circulation. This development implied an extension of the structural basis for the creation of credit that drove a proliferation of financial relations throughout society, well beyond the direct control of public authorities. The British state's response consisted of attempts to curb banks' note-issuing practices by imposing strict convertibility requirements (i.e., the gold standard). But the result was not a restoration of public control over the volume of liquidity in the economy: Private credit creation continued undiminished. Instead, it involved a more complex realignment of political authority with expansionary economic processes. The decline of traditional, direct modalities of state power found its counterpart in the growth of infrastructural capacities: As the mint lost its institutional centrality, the Bank of England learned to manipulate some key institutional parameters of money creation (Wray 1990: 53; Knafo 2008) and the Treasury could borrow large sums.

It is against this background that the prevalence of liberal ideology during the heyday of British finance should be understood. Whereas IPE scholarship has tended to interpret liberalism in terms of the subordination of the state to markets, this book views liberal discourse as an ideological expression precisely of the growing coherence of the state's infrastructural capacities. Liberalism as an official ideology only becomes plausible in a context where private and public institutional connections have assumed a sufficient degree of coherent alignment and density that regulation can accomplish political objectives largely unobtrusively, without the need for highly visible ad hoc interventions implemented by authorities whose purposes seem to be forever at odds with social interests. The prevalence of liberal ideology expressed a (temporary and provisional) resolution of institutional tensions and the availability of organizational devices that permitted the British state to harness banks' growing financial capacities to public purposes.

FINANCE IN THE AMERICAN COLONIES

If the attitude of the British state toward the transformations of the domestic financial system had evolved through contradiction and ambiguity, its colonial policies were much more implacably repressive. The colonies were plagued by consistent coin shortages (Ferguson 1953;

Brock 1975): The lack of economic development meant that there was very little opportunity to earn coins while most of the money that immigrants had transported from the Old World quickly flowed abroad again (Nussbaum 1957: 3). Colonial Americans' efforts to relieve the liquidity scarcity focused most centrally on the creation of a supply of paper currency – a feature of economic life that many had been familiar with in their native England.[3] But British policies sought to preserve the dependence of the colonies on the mother country and therefore imposed all manner of constraints on the colonists' ability to create an indigenous monetary circulation (Nettels 1952).

To understand the dynamics around paper money schemes, it is important to appreciate that colonial America's monetary scarcity was not considered a problem by all of its inhabitants. Upper-class merchants were predominantly engaged in the trans-Atlantic trade and financed their business through bills of exchange drawn on London (Michener 2003). These merchants generally held hostile attitudes toward attempts to promote the internal development of the colonies and reduce its dependence on trade with England (Riesman 1983: 140).[4] Paper money schemes found a high degree of support among two other social groups – what Matson (1998: 4) calls "middling merchants" and farmers. The scarcity of liquidity especially affected the merchants of modest background who were engaged in domestic trade and whose livelihood depended on the extension of internal commercial relations and the ready availability of means of payment. They formed the driving force behind the most important source of paper money – the "bills of credit" issued by the colonial legislatures. Such bills were not redeemable into specie on demand, but they were supposed to be retired in the future on the basis of tax revenues

---

[3] Other media included commodity moneys and informal credit. Commodity moneys (such as wampum and tobacco) found considerable application but suffered from serious disadvantages. Because they were often freely obtainable, their supply rapidly expanded, triggering inflation. Some were hard to transport and hence of limited use for long-distance trade (Nussbaum 1957; Studenski and Krooss 1963: 14). More significant was the use of informal bookkeeping credits (Riesman 1983: 118–9; McCusker and Menard 1985; Flynn 2001; Wright 2005: 51–2). These procedures were sometimes at the basis of localized clearing systems, but commercial networks in colonial America were insufficiently dense to allow them to evolve into coherent institutional solutions to the shortage of currency.

[4] The viewpoint of the upper classes found expression in the continued prominence among American elites of traditional mercantilist ideas (Crowley 1992, 1993) – which contrasted with the intellectual scene in Britain where mercantilist theory was generally considered to have been superseded by Adam Smith's discovery of the origins of national wealth in the domestic economy (even if Britain's foreign policies were still highly mercantilist in nature).

(Nussbaum 1957: 18; McCusker 1976). In many colonies, however, tax collection was consistently problematic, jeopardizing the value of the bills.

Farmers had a more complex relation to monetary matters. On the one hand, farming was often primarily for subsistence (Kulikoff 1989, 2000: 206): By diversifying their crops and only increasing productivity through specialization as a supplementary strategy (Bushman 1998), farmers sought to remain self-sufficient and to avoid becoming overly dependent on market relations. On the other hand, to the extent that farmers did use local marketplaces to trade their excess production, they had an obvious need for means of exchange. More important, however, was the fact that farmers' financial needs were highly distinctive: What they needed was long-term credit to acquire a farm and land, the key ingredients of yeoman independence. Land banks and loan offices were set up specifically to meet the credit needs of farmers (Sparks 1932; Ferguson 1953; Nussbaum 1957). Essentially, these institutions were publicly sponsored credit unions of farmers. Their notes were not supposed to circulate outside the restricted community of those who had a personal stake in the bank, and to the extent that this did happen land banks were unstable and prone to failure. For while their notes were redeemable on demand, these banks held the most illiquid of assets – that is, mortgages (Thayer 1953).[5]

Thus, when it came to matters of money and finance, colonial American society was dominated by a concern with how, and indeed whether or not, to create a monetary circulation based on paper currency. Banking was understood primarily in terms of its note-issuing function (Miller 1927: 11–3; Hedges 1938; Redlich 1968: 12),[6] and this was viewed as a matter of public policy (Hammond 1957: 68). This perspective contrasted with the situation in England, where the idea of banking had been most fundamentally associated with the practice of holding deposits and only gradually become associated with the issuing of notes (Mints 1965). American banking had not experienced the more gradual and organic development that British banking, always closely bound up with the expansion of commerce, had undergone (Sylla 1999: 262). In other words, while the

---

[5] In addition to governmental issues of bills of credit and land banks, there were notes issued by banks with a charter from the colonial government. During the colonial period these were negligible in quantitative terms, but they nonetheless presaged an organizational form that would prove central to American financial development after the Revolution (Studenski and Krooss 1967: 14).

[6] Indeed, the word "bank" referred primarily to an issue of notes. "To the colonists, 'banking projects,' and 'paper money schemes' were the same thing" (Eliason 1970 [1901]: 8).

institutional form of paper currency itself was transplanted, the underlying socioeconomic mechanisms through which it had functioned in England were not. In particular, America lacked a discount market for bills of exchange, which had been a crucial precondition for the viability of English commercial banking: The density of commercial relations was just not such as to give rise to the requisite volume of trade-generated "real bills." Colonial financial intermediaries were therefore not commercial banks in the classic sense of the word (i.e., private institutions receiving demand deposits and making short-term commercial loans) (Hedges 1938: 12ff), but public institutions putting notes into circulation in ways that were often directly shaped by political interests and objectives.

During the second half of the eighteenth century, the English state grew increasingly intolerant toward colonial paper money schemes (Brock 1975). The circulation of paper money had begun to foster a degree of internal commerce that, it was feared, would reduce the dependence of the colonies on the mother country. In addition, the depreciation of American paper money harmed the interests of English merchants, who were creditors to the colonies. During the three decades leading up to the Declaration of Independence, the English undertook a series of attempts to demolish American financial institutions that culminated in the complete prohibition of bills of credit through the Currency Act of 1764 (Krooss 1967; Perkins 1994: 50). Yet British measures failed to achieve a structural reduction in colonial economic activity: Rapid population increases, as well as the growth of wheat and grain production and trade, increased the size of the American market (Riesman 1983, 1987). As a consequence, the shortage of currency was felt with growing intensity, triggering great hostility toward British policies. The discontent sparked by England's financial policies fed into the broader tide of anti-English sentiment and so contributed to the revolutionary uprising (Greene and Jellison 1961; Ernst 1973).

TOWARD INDEPENDENCE

Mobilization for the Revolutionary War served to further reinforce Americans' concern with the internal economy (Riesman 1983: 298). Crucial to the war effort was the issuance of large amounts of paper money (known as "continental bills") by the Continental Congress. However, popular aversion to centralization and taxation meant that the Continental Congress had only limited powers to levy taxes (Ferguson 1961; McNamara 2002: 135) and as a consequence the continental bills became subject to rapid depreciation (Studenski and Krooss 1963: 28;

Baack 2008). Policies at the level of the states did much to exacerbate this situation (Nussbaum 1957: 40; McGuire 2003: 16). Faced with huge quantities of depreciated paper, they sought to bestow value on these bills through governmental fiat by passing private legal tender laws. But this exercise of public authority had little support in social practices: Attempts to force people to accept bills at face value sparked considerable popular discontent and social unrest.

The Bank of North America was chartered in an attempt to stabilize the American financial system: It was set up to issue notes on the basis of specie holdings and expected to provide support for the public finances (Studenski and Krooss 1963: 32). Its short life provides a window on the kind of contradictions that would plague American attempts to create a coherent financial system for some time to come. The on-demand convertibility of bank notes into specie provided a more stable basis for note circulation (Perkins 1994: 118) but also made it imperative for the Bank to hold liquid assets with a high rate of turnover. In keeping with the real bills doctrine, therefore, the Bank only extended short-term mercantile credit, with exceptions made only for government loans (Hammond 1934). In an important sense, the Bank functioned as a credit union for the local merchant population: Philadelphia merchants held the Bank's stock, sat on the board of directors, and were the primary beneficiaries of its credit facilities. Yet despite this close association with mercantile interests, the Bank still had insufficient access to short-term financial instruments, rendering attempts to emulate English banking methods precarious. But the difficulty that the Bank experienced in finding short-term assets did not translate into a willingness to provide long-term credit to the agrarian classes, which constituted a rapidly growing proportion of the population. When the Bank boycotted a land bank opened by the Pennsylvania legislature, it confirmed the farmers' view that the bank represented an elite project aimed at the production of unnatural concentrations of wealth, and the swift agrarian retaliation consisted in the repeal of its charter (Hammond 1957: 54; Nettels 1962: 85; Perkins 1994: 132).

By the time of the Constitutional Convention in 1787, the new republic was in dire financial straits. American attempts to adopt English banking methods were fraught with difficulties, and the Bank of North America had faltered on the strength of agrarian resistance. In light of the disaster with the continental bills, the Constitution (authored by many of the elites who had always viewed public paper money schemes with considerable concern [McGuire 2003]) forbade note issues by either the federal government or the states (Schweitzer 1989; Sylla 1999: 263). One of the first acts of sovereignty was thus to prohibit Americans from developing the mechanisms of credit creation that had originated on American soil and functioned with some, albeit limited, degree of coherence.

CONCLUSION

This chapter has outlined the nature of the British transformation of financial relations and argued that it laid the foundations for the extension, in complex and contradictory ways, for the infrastructural capacities of the British state. If the British state had viewed the proliferation of credit relations at home with considerable concern, it was fundamentally opposed to such developments in the colonies. While this would become an important factor in motivating Americans to challenge British authority, it was only one of the problems that colonial subjects faced. American colonists tried to re-create a paper currency, but their economic structure did not supply the organically grown configurations that might have permitted them to reproduce the systemic dynamics of British finance. Such institutional forms were of course connected to *different* patterns of social relations; yet the resulting configuration, not having evolved through a more gradual development of finance and banking, nonetheless lacked density and coherence. That the issuance of public bills of credit was ultimately not sufficiently embedded in and supported by the socioeconomic fabric became especially clear toward the end of the colonial period, when federal and state authorities unsuccessfully sought to extend their infrastructural capacities through the legal imposition of paper money schemes. By the time the American Constitution was drawn up, public bills of credit had become so discredited that they were banned altogether.

3

The Financial Dynamics of Antebellum America

INTRODUCTION

The demise of the American institution of governmental issue of paper money did not usher in a pattern of financial development on the English model. This point is significant, because the persistent notion of a general Anglo-Saxon path of liberal financial development is one of the most serious obstacles to an accurate understanding of the distinctive institutional dynamics of American finance. Although the idea that America's economic development represents the unfolding of market principles has been widely challenged in historical literature, the notion that a laissez-faire attitude governed freely after the colonial yoke had been thrown off has remained highly influential (e.g., Lemon 1980; Bruchey 1990; Rothenberg 1992; Wright 2001, 2002; Buder 2009). The assumption in IPE scholarship that American finance is best understood as having evolved through largely unregulated markets and relatively weak regulatory institutions has similarly proved tenacious (e.g., Zysman 1983; Vitols 1997; Hall and Soskice 2001). As this chapter will demonstrate, the significance of the antebellum period for our understanding of American finance lies precisely in the fact that it did *not* develop according to the model of economic liberalism. It was the highly politicized configuration of financial relations in the early American republic that would later, from the midnineteenth century, generate the strategic innovations out of which a qualitatively new institutional basis for financial intermediation would arise.

The objective of this chapter is to give an account of that antebellum institutional landscape. The achievements of English finance continued to provide a standard to emulate, but the broader conditions under which such transplanted practices might have grown organic roots failed to materialize. The antebellum period did not witness the gradual emergence of a system of private intermediaries connected through broader networks of trade, and the organization of the nation's financial affairs remained highly politicized. The rapid growth of the agrarian population during the first decades of the nineteenth century was crucial in this respect, because it created a number of obstacles to the reproduction of British financial dynamics. Farmers' objectives were profoundly shaped by the republican ideal of the independent yeoman farmer, connected to but not dependent on markets (Henretta 1974, 1988; McCoy 1980; Headlee 1991; Clark 1990, 1997, 2002). The sheer economic weight of agrarian interests meant that the American economy did not develop a sizeable discount market for mercantile bills of exchange, which represented a major problem for banks. Furthermore, farmers resisted policies oriented toward the creation of a more coherent and integrated financial system (Goebel 1997). To be sure, agrarian sentiments were not just important in their own right. Farmers' susceptibility to different and often opposing ideological pulls (at different times, American farmers supported such opposing ideologies as easy money and hard money, no banks and free banking) tended to make them a political "masse de maneuvre," the "raw material for manipulation" by political and financial elites (De Cecco 1984b: 4). This political dynamic was especially significant because interelite struggles remained a pronounced feature of the American political–economic landscape (Domhoff 1967: 12; Fink 1988; Beckert 1993: 4–5):[1] As different elites took turns recruiting parts of the agrarian population to foil the designs of rival factions, the effect was to destroy any possibility of an integrated financial system.

THE EARLY GROWTH OF AMERICAN BANKING

The Revolution was followed by a surge of popular unrest and demands that served to draw American elites together in defense against the masses (Countryman 1976; Nash 1976; Egnal 1988) and so was a significant factor in the emergence of the Federalist coalition (Schlesinger 1957; Ferguson 1983). Alexander Hamilton, the first Secretary of the Treasury, aimed to establish the public credit of the American state

---

[1] For the development of different kinds of socioeconomic elites and their political orientations over the course of the nineteenth century, see Albion 1939; Pessen 1973; Wilentz 1984; Doerflinger 1986; and Beckert 1993.

(Sylla 1999: 257) and to bind the interests of the nation's financial and mercantile elites to its policies (Fraser 2005: 15). This program involved the creation of a permanent national debt through the transfer of states' debts to the federal government (Sylla 1998: 86) and the founding of a national bank modeled on the Bank of England (Morgan 1956; Klubes 1990; Cowen 2000). The First Bank of the United States, chartered in 1791, was supposed to set in motion a dynamic whereby its assistance to the federal government would enhance the quality of public obligations (Davies 2002: 474), which would in turn lubricate the mechanisms of commercial banking and so allow the Bank's notes to form the basis of a uniform national stock of money (Taus 1943: 17; Redlich 1968).

The Federalist financial program was short-lived. The immediate post-Revolution period was characterized by large additions to the population, the overwhelming majority of whom settled in the West (Van Fenstermaker 1965). As the Federalist program had little to offer the agrarian classes, its social basis grew increasingly tenuous. Southern elites sought to exploit farmers' anti-Northeastern sentiments for their own purposes (Burch 1981a: 69). The rise of Republicanism, which sought to decentralize financial authority and to limit the growth of banks, seen to be associated with the speculative rentier activities of Northeastern financiers, meant the death knell for the Hamiltonian financial program. The Jefferson administration began paying down the national debt and severed all government ties to the First Bank.

However, the federal government's disavowal of responsibility for the regulation of the nation's financial affairs turned out to have very different effects than intended: States began to charter large numbers of banks (Dewey 1972; Klebaner 1990: 11). Several factors were responsible for the growth in the number of banks under Republican hegemony. First, Republicanism may in principle have been opposed to banks, but in practice even many of its adherents were dependent on access to credit in ways that overrode political allegiance or calculation. Second, Republicans' own decentralization policies meant that these issues now got decided at the state level, where corruption was rife and local politicians were under intense pressure to charter banks (Bodenhorn 2003: 15). Third, once some states began chartering banks, an element of interstate competition was introduced. That is, if a state refused to charter banks, it lost business to a neighboring state that did. The dynamic at work here was reinforced by the fact that the conditions associated with bank charters provided an important means for states to raise funds for public infrastructural works (Van Fenstermaker 1965: 17), themselves a key means through which interstate competition was conducted (Bodenhorn 2003: 227). Fourth, once a few banks were chartered in a state, the political calculus of their opponents changed: Given that a charter could often not easily be revoked, continued opposition effectively came down to giving monopoly positions to existing banks (which were often in the hands of local elites). Consequently many opponents of banks reasoned that it made more sense to strive for their "democratization" (Bodenhorn 2003).

It bears emphasizing that these developments did not represent a "deregulation" of banking. In contrast to England, private commercial banks were virtually unknown in the United States. Banking was a particularly risky business, and prospective bankers were unlikely to take such a leap while being subject to unlimited liability. Furthermore, given the absence of a tradition of note issue by private entities, new banks needed public sanction to have their bank notes accepted and circulated as liquid means of payment. But the public chartering of banks was not just a matter of expediency: Banking was considered as inherently a question of public policy (Davis 1900, 1901; Novak 1996), to be regulated through corporate charters that induced private parties to undertake the provision of a public good by offering monopoly privileges and limited liability but at the same time set conditions for the activities that the corporation was allowed or required to engage in. The right of note issue was exclusively for incorporated banks (Bodenhorn 2000). On the rare occasions that private persons tried to break into commercial banking, they were generally prohibited from doing so.

Of course, the actual practices of commercial banking diverged from the prescriptions of such public-spirited doctrines. Because charters conferred monopoly positions, they were much sought after, and bribing state legislators to obtain a bank charter was a widespread practice (Bodenhorn 2003: 14). Moreover, banks were often in the hands of local mercantile factions who ran them as their own credit unions, excluding rival factions and the lower classes. Lamoreaux (1986) has described early American banks as investment pools established on kinship-based networks; their loan facilities were reserved for insiders (Van Fenstermaker 1965: 20; Krooss 1967: 124). This insider character was crucial to banks' stability. For the illiquid nature of their asset portfolio meant that the more banks relied on deposits (redeemable on demand), the more vulnerable they were to a bank run. Insertion into insider networks meant that the bulk of a bank's funds came from the capital (not subject to withdrawal on demand) paid in by its owners (Lamoreaux 1986: 654).

During the following decades, the insider character of banks began to erode, entailing significant financial instability. As the economy grew and states granted more charters outside the main commercial centers, banks began issuing notes to people who did not own any of their stock, and their deposit base grew (Redlich 1968: 50). As a result, a growing share of their liabilities became subject to withdrawal on demand while banks experienced as much difficulty as ever making short-term loans. As the number of banks grew and competition for short-term assets increased, banks found themselves forced to invest ever more funds in longer-term assets (Redlich 1944, 1968: 44; Krooss 1967). Financial instability became particularly serious after the Republicans' refusal, in 1811, to renew the First Bank's charter. The number of state banks grew quickly (Studenski and Krooss 1963: 107) and, because of laws prohibiting branch banking, these were all separate institutions without any formal institutional linkages. Government policies contributed to the growth of banking. With the outbreak of the War of 1812, the federal government found itself in need of a fiscal agent just at the moment when the First Bank had been destroyed. It was forced to turn to the state banks, and its deposits gave a huge boost to their business.

CONTRADICTIONS OF EARLY AMERICAN BANKING

The key problem faced by the banks was the lack of liquid assets – that is, the absence of a discount market for bills of exchange. America's economy was highly agrarian and had not been boosted by an industrial revolution on the scale that England's had (Pred 1966a, 1966b). Markets for commercial financial instruments were consequently not nearly as well developed as in England. The credit needs of farmers were diametrically opposed to the idea of short-term, self-liquidating bills: They wanted mortgages, long-term credit secured by immobile real estate (Sparks 1932). The American short-term money market was small and composed chiefly of promissory notes (Redlich 1970), which were longer-term and less liquid than the bill of exchange (Myers 1931: 47). Whereas a bill of exchange was considered self-liquidating because the commercial transaction from which it arose was supposed to furnish the funds for the payment of the bill, a promissory note was not connected to a specific transaction and secured only by the personal creditworthiness of the promissor and that of any endorsers.

The state of the money market meant that banks were forced to invest a large part of their funds in longer-term assets. Although banks in the commercial centers were still able to acquire a certain amount of short-term bills, they made many longer-term loans, held government securities and corporate stock, and were involved in a variety of speculative activities (Hedges 1938: 102). The countryside was entirely deprived of short-term paper. Therefore, country banks, which became an ever more important part of the system as U.S. economy expanded westward, had no choice but to make highly illiquid loans on real estate. The mismatch between the maturity structure of their asset portfolios and liability portfolios became highly pronounced (Golembe 1952: 239–40). In other words, American banks were faced with contradictory imperatives, on the one hand forced to make long-term investments and on the other hand required to maintain the on-demand convertibility of bank notes (Hammond 1934: 94). They consequently were structurally illiquid, making the American financial system consistently prone to financial crises (Hedges 1938: 22; Van Fenstermaker 1965).

To a significant extent, American banks were dependent on the market for long-term securities.[2] The capital markets grew steadily because of the increase of public borrowing requirements,[3] but even here commercial banks experienced growing competition. The United States did not have a tradition of institutions that had started out as merchant bankers and gradually branched out to engage in the raising of funds and placement of securities for states, incorporated enterprises, and wealthy individuals (Hidy 1941; Katz 1968; Chernow 1990: 4). But the growth of the securities business occasioned a more formal organization of the New York Stock Exchange and gave a boost to the number of private bankers who subscribed to the debt with a view to selling it on to others (Chandler 1954; Carosso 1970: 1; Roy 1997: 125). The consequences were significant for commercial banks, who found themselves being gradually squeezed out of the securities business, leaving them in an ever more precarious situation.

---

[2] This market was composed chiefly of government obligations and stock issued by corporations. The vast majority of public corporations were enterprises engaged in the construction of infrastructural works. Manufacturing enterprises were generally not incorporated. Hardly any industrial securities were listed on the New York Stock Exchange until the very end of the nineteenth century (Roy 1997).

[3] Initially, the War of 1812 gave a boost to the capital market (Myers 1931: 17). From the late 1820s, during the Jacksonian period of states' rights and anti-Federalist sentiments, federal finances were governed by austerity (McFaul 1972). But the decline in federal debt was offset by the large increases of debt issued by states and public corporations engaged in the competitive construction of transport networks to capture a share of the growing East–West trade in agricultural products (states either undertook these tasks themselves and issued debt or they chartered companies that issued stock [Myers 1931: 29; Haeger 1981: xii; Larson 2001]).

THE SECOND BANK OF THE UNITED STATES AND ITS DESTRUCTION

The Second Bank of the United States, which existed from 1816 to 1836, did much to bring some order to America's financial system (Catterall 1902; Dewey 1968). The growing instability of state banking during the 1810s had resulted in a decline of public confidence in banks' ability to redeem the chaotic hodgepodge of notes that made up the circulation, touching off a panic and forcing banks to suspend specie convertibility. The Republicans, who had opposed the renewal of the First Bank's charter a few years before, realized that it had had effects that ran directly counter to their aims (Hammond 1957: 236). The Second Bank made a point of redeeming all the bank notes of small state banks that it received, thus gradually draining those banks of their specie and restricting their basis for note issue (Johnson 1998: 112; Davies 2002: 477). As a result, by the late 1820s the United States was making significant strides toward a uniform national currency (Walters 1945; Fraas 1974). In addition, the Second Bank took on market-making functions, accepting and discounting bills of exchange (Myers 1931: 49; Knodell 1998; Davies 2002: 477) and so giving a boost to the use of these instruments in domestic trade (Shulz and Caine 1937: 195; Smith 1953). The result was a gradual expansion, formalization, and integration of the market for commercial credit. The Second Bank also assumed lender-of-last-resort functions (Hammond 1957: 324), standing by to lend funds to banks under pressure.

The reorganization of the American financial system was cut short by the rise of the Jacksonian movement. Agrarian interests had grown disillusioned with Republicanism, which they viewed as having slowly bared its elitist nature and come to resemble the Federalist program that it had initially been designed to replace (Ferguson 1983: 35; Egnal 1988; Ellis 1996: 150–1): It had issued countless charters and created a second national bank no sooner than the first one had been destroyed (Schlesinger 1945; Silbey 1991; Larson 2001; Henretta 2002). Moreover, despite this rapid growth of finance, the supply of long-term credit in agrarian areas had remained precarious. The Second Bank became a focal point for this ire. When it decided to put an end to long-term credit extension altogether, farmers took this as proof of its corrupt nature (Dewey 1968).[4] It is important to note that by this time the relationship of farmers

---

[4] Agrarian dislike of the Second Bank was also fueled by the fact that a large proportion of the Bank's stock was held abroad, especially by English investors. "In 1839, on the eve

to paper money had undergone a significant transformation: Whereas in the past farmers had supported public schemes for the issuance of bills of credit, by now paper money had become synonymous with the notes issued by banks that had little concern for their financial needs. According to "hard money" doctrines, all money in circulation should be specie, with no place for bank notes (Goebel 1997).

Farmers' discontent was again a critical *masse de maneuvre*. From the late 1820s, the beginnings of an independent manufacturing sector (Sellers 1991; Ellis 1996; Wilentz 1997) had produced a new set of elites whose interests were at odds with those of the "cotton alliance" between Northern merchants and Southern planters that had come to dominate Republicanism (Williams 1961; Pessen 1973; Burch 1981a). Many of these ascendant elites were based in New York and saw the Second Bank, located in Philadelphia and associated with older mercantile elites, as an impediment to the ongoing expansion of their business (Wright 2005: 149–50). They were able to play on popular discontent to undermine the power of the Republican party. The Jacksonian coalition that resulted was heterogeneous (Hammond 1957: 329; Holt 1996): Its binding element was a demand for the destruction of the Second Bank.

THE INDEPENDENT TREASURY

Ahead of the expiration of the Second Bank's charter in 1836, Jackson prohibited the Treasury from depositing government funds with the Second Bank, forcing it to place its funds with state banks instead. Because a large share of government revenue derived from the sale of public land, many of the Treasury's funds ended up being held in Western banks, where they served as the basis for the extension of long-term credit and the growth of poorly secured note issues (Knodell 2006). The government responded by imposing strict convertibility conditions on banks holding government deposits and ordering the Treasury to redistribute its funds. These actions were followed by the Specie Circular, which stipulated that henceforth only specie would be acceptable in payment for public lands (Taus 1943: 37) and so triggered a scramble for specie just at a time when Western banks were suffering from the redistribution of funds to Northeastern banks (Timberlake 1960b; Rousseau 2002). Thus, although Jackson's policies had sought to hasten the demise of

---

of its final liquidation, one-half of its capital stock was held abroad and one-fourth of all the stockholders were resident in the British Isles; forty-two of them, to the horror of the Congress which was investigating the subject, bore titles of nobility" (Myers 1931: 20).

the "paper money system" (Scheiber 1963: 200), their main effect was to make paper money less safe (Macesich 1960). The situation deteriorated further when in 1837 the Bank of England restricted its discounting of trans-Atlantic bills of exchange and the domestic scramble for specie liquidity became compounded by a foreign drain on American specie (Temin 1969). These developments triggered a run on the banks, forcing them to suspend convertibility (Myers 1931: 67). They consequently were ineligible to hold government deposits, and the Treasury withdrew its funds, transferring them to the mint and other improvised places (Studenski and Krooss 1963: 111), thereby making an already serious situation even worse. The consequences of the 1837 panic were significant: The number of banks began to fall for the first time since the birth of the republic, and the amount of bank notes in circulation declined dramatically (Hedges 1938: 21–2).

Jackson and other hard money Democrats took the financial turmoil as yet further evidence for their belief in the fundamentally flawed and immoral nature of bank credit. Reasoning that the government was only to blame insofar as it had allowed the public finances to become entangled with the creation of paper money in the first place, they used the events as arguments for a further separation of government funds from the banking system, in effect seeking to formalize and make permanent the situation that had arisen. This push for an "Independent Treasury" had the effect of alienating powerful business interests in the Jacksonian coalition (Scheiber 1963: 212–4), who were concerned it would mean a further contraction of means of payment. Contributing to a wider process of political polarization that increasingly coincided with sectional divisions and so laid the basis for the Civil War coalitions (Silbey 1991; Holt 1999), they now aligned themselves with the Whigs, who advocated a developmental program that sought to reverse many of the Jacksonian policies (Studenski and Krooss 1963: 111).

Yet at no point would the separation between the public finances and the banking system be as clean or complete as hard money Democrats might have wished (Kinley 1910). This was true of the antebellum era,[5]

---

[5] Although the federal debt had been paid off in 1835, from 1837 the economic downturn and declining land sales combined to significantly reduce the government's revenues, leading the Treasury to start issuing debt again. The Treasury needed Congress's approval for the issue of notes, but it was free to determine the rate and used this discretion to alleviate tightness in the money market, issuing substantial amounts of debt at low interest rates (Timberlake 1960a: 93–4). This played a significant role in counteracting the effects of the monetary contraction brought on by the dramatic decline in the bank note circulation

but the Independent Treasury would throughout its existence (until 1921) be deeply connected to the organization of the nation's financial system through the channel of public debt. Indeed, over the next decades authorities increasingly sought to tie banks' note-issuing capacities to their holdings of government debt, a procedure that was expected both to ensure a steady demand for public debt and to provide a more secure basis for note issue than the practices that banks themselves had evolved. This logic was evident in the "free banking" system that emerged in Northern states during the last decades of the antebellum period, and it would subsequently become a central feature of the postbellum banking system. Thus, the Independent Treasury, far from being materially divorced from the nation's banking system, developed new procedures for exercising a modest degree of control over the American financial system (Taus 1943; Timberlake 1960a). If such mechanisms would be significant in shaping the development of American finance over the next decades, they would ultimately also prove to be limited: The connection between public debt and banks' note issues was not sufficiently finegrained or far-reaching to permit the Treasury to effectively stabilize the dynamics of American finance, especially as the latter underwent drastic transformations.

FREE BANKING AND BANKERS' BALANCES

State-level responses to the panic of 1837 significantly shaped the subsequent development of American finance (Huston 1987: 2–3). Some Southern states responded by imposing strict limits on the number of banks they chartered (Green 1972; Schweikart 1987), but in the Northeast the configuration of political forces (the weight of business interests) and economic conditions (even agrarian areas were significantly dependent on banks) were such that a general repression of banking was never in the cards. Increasingly dependent on mechanisms of financial intermediation, many reasoned that the excesses and abuses of banking had more to do with its monopolistic nature than with the institution

(Cohen 1971: 8). Similarly, during the second half of the 1840s the Treasury needed to place sizeable loans to finance the Mexican war. The Treasury required significant assistance from bankers, and, to obtain this, relaxed its rules requiring specie payment and extended an informal commitment to relieving conditions of money market stringency (Cohen 1971: 41–2). When, during the 1850s, the surplus rose again, the Treasury began buying significant amounts of government debt (Timberlake 1960a: 100; Wood 2005: 141), which served both to infuse specie into the banking system and to make government debt more liquid.

as such, and that addressing this required not the restriction of banking but precisely the opening up of access to bank charters (Bodenhorn 2003: 190). Meanwhile, those who remained opposed in principle to the proliferation of banks were caught in the same dilemma that we have highlighted before: To oppose the deregulation of banking came down to supporting the oligopolistic position of existing banks. Many of them therefore bought into a political strategy that aimed at the full-blown "democratization" of banking. In 1938, the state of New York adopted the Free Banking Act, and during the 1840s and 1850s it would be copied by many other Northern states (Beckhart 1922; Rockoff 1975a). After the Civil War, it would form the basis of the National Banking System (Shade 1972). On the one hand, the system transformed the decision to charter a bank from a legislative act into an administrative procedure: Any individual or group of people able to meet certain minimum requirements would automatically be entitled to a charter. On the other hand, the free banking law was firmly part of a trend toward stricter regulation when it came to the charter provisions (Rockoff 1975b). In particular, the note issues of banks were to be fully secured by government securities deposited with the state comptroller.

New York's free banking legislation was followed by a wave of new banks. One crucial consequence of this development was the growth of so-called bankers' balances, that is, deposits held by one bank with another bank. Given the prohibition on branch banking, every new banking establishment was a new, autonomous bank without any formal linkages to other banks. As economic connections between different areas grew and bank notes began to circulate more widely, the need for interbank transactions grew. Because financial markets were not efficient enough to function as a vehicle for the conduct of interbank business, such integration could be achieved only through interbank deposits. In practice, this meant that smaller country banks held balances with banks in the main commercial and financial centers, especially New York (Myers 1931; Gische 1979: 27; Weber 2003).

Bankers' balances were demand liabilities and hence their growth resulted in intensified competition for the liquid short-term assets that were in permanent short supply. It was the development of the market for "call loans" – loans to stock market brokers on security collateral that were callable on demand – that gave the banks new options. The rapid growth of the railroads was responsible for an increase in the number of stock issues and an expansion of the stock market (Fishlow 1965), offering plenty of opportunities for speculative trading and motivating brokers to borrow large amounts of funds to trade with (Hidy 1951: 272; Michie 1986, 1987). The expansion of the stock market and the call loan market became mutually reinforcing: The growth of the stock market drove the demand for call loans, and the call loan system in turn facilitated speculative trading and so promoted the rapid growth of the stock market. In this way, the operations of the American banking system became connected to and dependent on speculative processes that involved considerable instability (Myers 1931: 135–6). In times of financial distress, liquidity in the call loan markets was prone to drying up precipitously. Whenever the railroad sector got into trouble and stock prices fell, this set in motion a complex process of deleveraging and vanishing liquidity that typically resulted in a systemwide credit freeze and banks being forced to suspend convertibility. The crisis of 1857 was the first crisis that was deeply shaped by the new structure of institutional connections between the banking system and the stock market (Huston 1987; Calomiris and Schweikart 1991).

CONCLUSION

This chapter has discussed how the antebellum period saw a number of attempts to create a more coherent and centralized financial system and how such efforts faltered on the strength of populist and republican sentiments among the growing agrarian population of the United States as well as the ways in which these forces were exploited by political elites. Questions of finance and banking were highly politicized, producing a system of strict and detailed financial regulation. This in turn meant that the proliferation of financial relations in early America assumed the form of a fragmented patchwork of localized practices and subsystems. During most of the antebellum period, therefore, the mechanisms of American finance were marked by a low degree of integration and network power. What remained absent were the kind of comprehensive institutional linkages that leverage the reach of financial agency, transmit its effects across a wider socioeconomic terrain, and so create effective mechanisms of control. The infrastructural power of the American state remained very limited.

Toward the end of the antebellum period, this picture began to change in two ways. The creation of a link between banks and public debt permitted authorities to exercise some limited degree of control over bank strategies, and this institutional connection would become a significant factor in the subsequent evolution and reorganization of

American finance. Moreover, American banks began to create a system of interbank balances that had the effect of centralizing reserves in New York banks. This system would prove of momentous consequence to the financial development of the United States, as during the postbellum period it would become a source of pressures and opportunities that spurred American elites to pursue entirely new financial strategies, creating a qualitatively new institutional framework of credit relations and rules for financial intermediation.

4

Contours of American Finance

INTRODUCTION

It is common, for both IPE scholars and other commentators, to trace the origins of modern-day finance to the globalization trends of the 1970s, when the Bretton Woods system broke down and financial markets began to globalize. The assumption that typically accompanies such interpretations is that late-twentieth-century finance represents a reemergence of the financial relations and principles that had prevailed during the late nineteenth and early twentieth centuries under British hegemony. Such perspectives, however, fail to recognize the extent to which the nature of present-day global finance has been shaped by institutional forms of distinctly American provenance. This chapter begins to trace the emergence of the institutional forms that would stamp the twentieth-century development of American finance and that would come to shape the character of financial globalization during the late twentieth century. It gives an account of financial transformations during the postbellum era, outlining the processes through which a new pattern of financial intermediation emerged that differed in crucial respects from the British financial model.

As the previous chapters have shown, the colonial and antebellum eras had been characterized by attempts to copy the key institutional features of British finance (above all a noninflationary circulation of paper money) and the political resistance to such attempts as well as the more technical contradictions engendered by procedures of selective institutional transplantation. But during the last decades of the nineteenth century, American finance evolved its own distinctive set of organizing principles, organically rooted in privately originated practices and held together by intricate networks of domestically grown institutional mediations. Organized through a complex set of linkages between banks and the stock market, American finance was marked by capacities for liquidity creation and a degree of dynamism that had never been available to British banks. This model set the development of American finance on a qualitatively new path. These American transformations had little impact on the world of international finance of the late nineteenth and early twentieth centuries, which during this time was fully shaped by British forms and techniques. For most of the twentieth century, the development of American finance was predominantly internal. It was over the course of the post–World War II period that these expansionary dynamics began to externalize and became the driving force behind trends of financial globalization.

Some of the developments that are pertinent to the American transformation of finance have already been briefly discussed at the end of the last chapter. But it was especially the postbellum configuration of financial institutions that drove key actors to pioneer qualitatively new financial practices. Although the war served to affirm the authority of the federal government (Moore 1966; Keller 1977; Bensel 1990, 2000), attempts to create a more coherent national financial system were still heavily constrained by the force of agrarian movements and populist programs. Civil War legislation essentially incorporated institutional fragmentation and decentralization into the structures of the national financial system. As a result, during the postbellum era banks were still faced with the same structural constraints that they had experienced during the antebellum period. Under these circumstances, they began to develop new forms of financial intermediation, turning to a distinctive form of "financial banking" (Youngman 1906: 435). While the instability that this development entailed became a major focal point for the clash of political interests, this was not simply a replay of the conflicts of the antebellum era. Although financial elites were still faced with major political obstacles that they could not tear down at will, they were now much more capable of finding ways around them through a range of innovations, in the process creating an intricately interwoven web of financial connections that gave them access to new capacities for the creation of credit. The financial dynamic that resulted was an important factor in the consolidation of American capitalism at the end of the nineteenth century (Livingston 1987; Ferguson and Chen 2005).

THE CONSTRUCTION OF A NATIONAL FINANCIAL SYSTEM

On the eve of the Civil War, the Treasury's vaults were empty, and its control over the nation's banks was tenuous (Patterson 1952: 35; Studenski and Krooss 1963: 138). When the government took a loan from a consortium of major banks, this weakened their balance sheets so much that they were once again forced to suspend convertibility (Gische 1979: 33).[1] In this context, financial reform came to be seen as a necessity (Trescott 1963). The National Bank Acts, modeled on the New York free banking system, established a system of federally chartered banks, to exist alongside state banks (Sylla 1969).[2] Charters were granted through an administrative procedure: Anyone fulfilling the stipulated requirements was entitled to a charter, and in this sense entry was free. National banks were required to buy Treasury bonds and deposit them as collateral for the uniform national bank notes that they issued – which was intended as a way both to promote a steady demand for government securities and to secure the value of bank notes (James 1978; Sylla 1999: 267). In addition, the Act required banks to hold a percentage of their deposit liabilities in reserve – that is, as deposits with other banks (Feinman 1993). The result of this was a three-tiered reserve system with New York as the central reserve city. As we have seen in the previous chapter, there already was a voluntary system of correspondent banking in place whereby banks held substantial deposit balances with money center banks, and the Act essentially formalized and extended these arrangements (Myers 1931: 222; Smiley 1973; James 1978).

The National Bank Acts were very much pieces of war legislation, passed to shore up the fiscal position of the federal government and to improve the country's economic and financial infrastructure (Sharkey 1959: 226–7). But even though the Acts were not primarily designed to bestow financial benefits on this or that private interest, they still had to carefully maneuver the various social groups of which the war coalition

---

[1] The government's debt-funding problems were compounded by the difficulties that the government experienced selling bonds: Private bankers and the large private fortunes in Northeastern cities had enjoyed strong connections to the South and vigorously opposed the war (Katz 1968; Berk 1994). The government managed to partly compensate for this lack of financial support by hiring the firm of Jay Cooke, who did not limit his attempts to raise funds to elite circles but sent his agents all around the country to actively market governments bonds (Larson 1936; Hidy 1951; Gaines 1962).

[2] Hitherto the only federally chartered banks had been the First and Second Banks of the United States.

was composed. A prima facie view of the most important elements of the National Bank Acts would suggest that they heavily favored the large Northeastern banks in industrial and commercial centers at the expense of Western banks, as the reserve system centralized large amounts of funds in the hands of city banks (Gische 1979). And of course the very creation of a national banking system represented a setback for those populist forces that had spent the previous three decades campaigning against anything that smacked of federal involvement with financial affairs.

However, it is crucial to appreciate the various ways in which populist and agrarian forces shaped the new system. The need to placate such interests had ruled out any plans for a central bank. The fact that the National Banking System was based on the principle of free banking went against the wishes of the New York financiers, who had preferred a more selective system based on legislative discretion. The National Bank Acts did nothing to prevent states from chartering and regulating their own banks. The prohibition on branch banking was incorporated into the new federal system (Mason 1997; Redenius 2007). Banks were prohibited from accepting bills of exchange. And to check financial and industrial concentration, banks were not allowed to hold industrial stock, and limits were imposed on the size of loans that banks could make to any single borrower. All in all, even though the war required and effected a centralization of financial authority at the federal vis-à-vis the state level, this occurred very much under the constraints imposed by popular pressure, and in a number of respects the legislation actively promoted a decentralized, fragmented banking system.

The new system did of course contain a major boon for city banks: They were at the apex of a pyramidal system of reserve balances and were thus assured a steady supply of deposits without any effort on their part. But this benefit came with its own challenges: Bankers' balances were liabilities that were redeemable on demand. Although the bankers' balances tended to be somewhat more stable than before (because they were held for the purpose of fulfilling reserve requirements), they were still subject to the vagaries of the economy at large. Fluctuations in the public's willingness to hold bank notes and deposits and its demand for cash were rapidly reflected in banks' need for reserves. The growth of bankers' balances, therefore, spawned an increased concern with bank liquidity and this had major consequences for the strategies banks pursued and the interaction patterns they created in doing so.

BANKS AND FINANCIAL MARKETS IN THE POSTBELLUM ERA

The years preceding the Civil War had seen the hesitant development of a discount market for bills of exchange, but this was choked off by events during and after the war (Hedges 1938). The bulk of bills of exchange had been generated by the cotton trade, and this had been dealt a serious blow by the severance of commercial connections with the South. In addition, the war had engendered high rates of inflation – reinforced by the issuance of several tranches of public bills ("greenbacks") that quickly depreciated after their convertibility was revoked (Studenski and Krooss 1963: 145). As a result, merchants sought to minimize the length of credit terms: Instead of creating a bill of exchange, they made increasing use of open-book accounts, which they encouraged their debtors to settle in cash as soon as possible by offering a significant discount (Myers 1951a: 572). The spread of this practice brought about a sharp decline in the volume of bills of exchange (James 1978: 56). At the same time, it occasioned an increase in the volume of promissory notes (Klein 1911–12): The high cash discount in commercial credit made it tempting for debtors to borrow money to immediately settle their debts, and they did so by issuing their own promissory notes (James 1995: 221). In a break with antebellum practices, these new promissory notes were "single-name," that is, not endorsed (Myers 1931: 317; White 1998: 18–19).

It is important to appreciate the historical significance of this growing market in "commercial paper" (Agger 1914; Myers 1931; Greef 1938; Selden 1963: 1; James 1995: 219).[3] Hitherto, directly issuing and selling debt on the basis of nothing other than their personal credit was a privilege reserved for states or publicly chartered corporations (Baskin and Miranti 1997; Michie 2003). Single-name promissory notes made the direct access to credit more widely available. Of course, this privilege remained reserved for the propertied class; purely consumptive personal debt would remain unavailable to ordinary people for some time to come. But these developments nonetheless produced a facility with new, more flexible mechanisms of credit creation. In this way, the single-name promissory note also laid the basis for "disintermediation," the bypassing of financial intermediaries in favor of direct borrowing or lending in

---

[3] The commercial paper market would for the longest time be a specifically American institution. A similar market was not to be found in any other country until more than a century later (Kahn 1993; James 1995: 249).

financial markets. The National Bank Acts had imposed strict limits on the size of loans that banks could make to any single borrower. Initially, borrowers tried to obtain loans from several banks at the same time, but as the postbellum economy took off many corporations and large enterprises outgrew banks' lending capacity to such an extent that they chose to have recourse to the commercial paper market (Agger 1914; Phillips 1921; Foulke 1980 [1931]; James 1995).

American banks became increasingly dependent on commercial paper as the basis of their asset portfolio (Jacobs 1910; James 1995). However, single-name commercial paper was far removed from the idea of self-liquidating "real bills," as it was unsecured, unendorsed, and longer-term (typically four to six months). In addition, the secondary market remained undeveloped: Issuers typically objected to having their paper shifted around as this created the impression that their credit was in doubt (Goodhart 1969: 22; Broz 1997: 43). Banks naturally considered the purchase of single-name commercial paper more prudent if they were familiar with the issuers and had found them to be creditworthy in the past, and their methods for evaluating the safety of an investment increasingly focused on borrowers' credentials and reputation. In this context, lending criteria gradually shifted from traditional ones (such as the nature of an underlying transaction or endorsement) to borrowers' personal credit (Greef 1938; Foulke 1980 [1931]; James 1995). American banks set up specialized credit departments that developed sophisticated methods for gathering and evaluating financial information concerning the creditworthiness of potential borrowers (White 1998).[4]

Despite these adaptations in banks' strategies, commercial paper was still considered a relatively risky investment. Consequently, what became ever more important as a source of liquid bank assets was the market for call loans (McCaffrey 1938). As we have seen in the previous chapter, already in the antebellum period the concentration of deposits in New York and the growth of the call loan market had established a network of relations between the banks and the stock market, and during the postbellum era the growth of this market accelerated dramatically (Myers 1931: 270). It is important to appreciate that, at this time, bankers did not consider call loans to be risky or speculative but as quite prudent forms of investment. A typical investment strategy was to buy large

---

[4] Such activities were both facilitated by, and gave a further boost to, the development of financial accounting statements that allowed the evaluation of issuers' creditworthiness to go beyond merely ascertaining a good reputation (Miranti 1986; White 1998: 20).

amounts of slightly higher-yielding commercial paper as the basis of a bank's asset portfolio and to invest in call loans those funds that it could not afford to have tied up for any significant length of time (Myers 1931: 274–5). Just as the way in which American banks adapted to the reality of the commercial paper market led to new ways of thinking about the security of an asset, so their engagement with the call loan market laid the basis for changing conceptions of liquidity: Although traditional notions of liquidity related primarily to the maturity match between assets and liabilities (i.e., because deposits and bank notes were demand liabilities, assets were supposed to be short-term and self-liquidating), the new banking methods conceptualized liquidity not so much as the property of an asset itself but as the product of wider institutional structures, in terms of the ease with which an asset could be disposed of in financial markets (James 1978: 48). Although it would retain considerable theoretical prominence in intellectual and policy circles, the prescriptions of the real bills doctrine became increasingly irrelevant to banks' investment decisions (James 1978: 57).

RAILROADS AND FINANCIAL INSTABILITY

It became increasingly apparent that the market for call loans was characterized by major instability. Funds being poured into the call loan market fueled speculation, driving up stock market prices and so further increasing the demand for call loans. But of course this self-reinforcing dynamic also worked in the opposite direction. When a number of banks simultaneously called their loans, brokers were forced to sell off parts of their portfolios, thereby exerting a further downward effect on the level of stock prices and prompting other banks to call in their loans as well. This would spark a scramble for liquidity, with all banks calling their loans and brokers even less capable of meeting their obligations. Thus, when banks collectively called their loans, the market quickly froze up: Even though call loans seemed perfectly liquid from the perspective of the individual bank, they turned out to be much less so on an aggregate level. Throughout the postbellum period, this mechanism functioned to amplify the effects of financial shocks to cause full-blown crises (Myers 1951a: 577).

Instability during the postbellum era was especially pronounced because of the dramatic growth of the stock market as a result of the westward extension of the railroad sector. Owing to the high fixed costs of construction and operation, overinvestment and overproduction are more or less inherent in a competitively organized railroad sector (Tufano

1997). Competitive imperatives did not result in marginal adjustments to the growth of demand but occurred through one line outcompeting others, resulting in huge overcapacity.[5] The massive overproduction of railroads gave rise to price wars and high rates of failure (Berk 1994: 36), making the sector consistently crisis-prone (Dobbin 1994). Private bankers played a crucial role in fueling this process (Berk 1994: 28). When incorporated enterprises were unable to pay their debts, the public interest demanded that they nonetheless continue to operate (instead of being closed down and having their assets sold off) and a "receivership" would be organized to negotiate the different financial interests involved (Kirkland 1961: 72). Investment bankers, as the representatives of the railroads' creditors, were usually appointed as receivers (Martin 1974). But they were of course hardly perfect agents of the public interest: They tended to reduce fixed costs by eliminating undesirable debts, make their own positions permanent, and pursue reorganizations that benefited their own financial prospects rather than the operation of the railroads. Bankers became involved in the reorganization of one railroad after the other, merging roads and creating huge trusts while reducing fixed costs at the expense of railroads' creditors (Chernow 1990: 57). The oligopolization of the railroad industry, while reducing the number of new entrants, did little to actually decrease the intensity of competition (Kolko 1965); in fact, it merely fueled the overproduction of railroad mileage that lay at the root of the vigorous competition between gigantic enterprises. The railroad sector had entered a cycle of "overcapitalization, failure, reorganization, failure, reorganization, and merger" (Roy 1997: 108).

These developments entailed ever greater instability in the market for railroad stock. And these shocks reverberated through the financial system at large, from the stock market through the market for call loans into the banking system. Nor did the effects of a shock stop at the large New York banks that had funds invested in the call loan market: It impaired their ability to redeem obligations to other reserve city banks, in turn leaving the latter unable to meet their obligations to country banks. The postbellum financial system as a whole was structurally unstable, and violent crises occurred during the 1870s, 1880s, and 1890s. During such financial crises, both the Treasury and the New York Clearing House (established in 1854 by New York banks) would intervene to counteract the effects

---

[5] Of course, railroad enterprises needed a public charter, but this did not form much of a guarantee against wasteful investment. States were in competition with each other (Dunlavy 1991; Holt 1996: 249), each seeking to capture as much railroad track and future business as possible.

of vanishing liquidity (Myers 1970: 189; Wood 2005). The Treasury did so not only by buying and selling public debt but also through more direct measures that strained against the prohibitions of the Independent Treasury Act. But it lacked the power to convert bank credit into fully liquid assets, and hence its ability to function as a lender of last resort remained very limited (Taus 1943: 70). The New York Clearing House issued certificates that could be used to settle interbank debts during crises (Cannon 1910; Gorton 1985). Although these certificates played a more significant role with each crisis (Timberlake 1984), they never came to function as fully liquid means of payment (White 1983: 79).

STRUGGLES OVER REFORM

Widespread concern with the state of the American financial system and calls for financial reform were first sparked by the 1873 crisis, which ushered in a major depression. Critiques and proposals were advanced by different economic interests and their content varied accordingly (Nugent 1963). After the Civil War it had become increasingly apparent that the Republican program for industrialization posed a threat to the way of life of independent farmers (Mayhew 1972), rendering implausible its claim to the ideology of "free labor" (which had formed a crucial ideological underpinning of the Northern war coalition) (Foner 1970; Ashworth 1996). As a result, other political movements experienced a rapid resurgence, the effects of which were reinforced by the emergence of new divisions among elites (Benson 1955; Burch 1981b; Ferguson 1983: 48). The Democratic Party experienced a revival, but the postbellum period also saw the rise of a variety of populist movements, often originating in rural areas (Goodwyn 1978; Hattam 1993; Ritter 1997; Sanders 1999). These movements took a keen interest in (what from a present-day perspective would seem to be) "technical" financial questions.[6]

---

[6] It is instructive to contrast this with the concerns of European working classes, whose minds have rarely been preoccupied with financial questions. To them, the institutional makeup of the financial system and exchange relations was of secondary importance: Of more immediate relevance were the terms of the wage relation (Geary 1981; Sassoon 1996). In the United States, however, the ideal of the independent farmer continued to exercise huge ideological influence on the lower classes until the very end of the nineteenth century (Beckert 1993: 73). Given that the exact composition of markets and exchange relations was so crucial to their ability to reproduce themselves as independent farmers, the kind of financial questions that were largely depoliticized in Europe were at the heart of political struggle and debate in the United States.

Populist forces demanded public but decentralized control over money and credit. This involved a significant shift in their position on the question of paper money (even if this was underlain by "a continuing distrust and hatred of bankers and bank-notes" [Sharkey 1959: 220]): They realized that "hard money" policies would have the effect of further depriving the West of credit and increasingly viewed such Jacksonian concerns as a distraction from the root causes of financial instability – namely, the speculative practices fostered by the structures of the National Banking System (Berk 1994: 39).[7] Populist ambitions for financial reform therefore centered on changes to the reserves system, the return of decisions on bank charters to the states, and the public issuance of bills of credit (for which the greenbacks provided a rallying point). Financial elites, by contrast, advocated a more centralized but private control over financial markets. Ideally, New York financiers would have wanted to leave intact the existing structures of financial markets and supplement them with a privately controlled central bank that would check speculative excesses and function as a lender of last resort.[8] Essentially, their solution to recurrent instability was the further extension of New York's control over centralized reserves (Berk 1994: 45).

---

[7] As one populist put it, "it will be seen that our present difficulties are the result of an inordinate and uncalled-for expansion of the railroad system; a vicious custom of banks paying interest on deposits, thereby imposing on them the necessity of lending those deposits to brokers and speculators 'on call'; certification of checks when no funds were on deposit, thus affording an improper credit to the drawer without any substantial foundation; and a resulting deficiency in the reserves so great that the slightest panic drove the banks into suspension for want of ready money to meet a run upon them. This was inflation, speculation, an expansion of the credit system to an unnatural extent, in short, a financial bubble; and when the credit of the great corporations and banking houses had been stretched to its utmost tension, and when the touch-stone of demand of payment came to be applied, by the withdrawal of country bank balances and merchants' deposits, the bubble collapsed and the distress we now experience ensued" (Washington Townsend, quoted in Berk 1994: 39).

[8] This stance on financial questions was allied to a distinctive theory of the causes of and solution to overproduction, which needs to be understood as part of the broader views on economic development held by America's corporate and financial elites. Although from a present-day standpoint industrial development and economic competition often seem inseparable phenomena, for late-nineteenth-century American elites it was the progressive organization of economic activity in ever larger units that was the key to development and modernization (Galambos 1983; Perrow 2002). Competition was often seen as precisely destructive – as vividly demonstrated by the railroad sector. As a key cause of excessive competition, overproduction and instability they saw the fact that poorly organized, decentralized financial markets made capital available for entry into markets that could be adequately served by a limited number of large enterprises (Livingston 1986). Infusions of greenbacks or silver currency were seen as only reinforcing these trends.

The upshot was a political deadlock that lasted for several decades (Berk 1994). Because the institutional core of the banking system and credit creation was out of reach for both sides, public debate focused above all on the currency (Unger 1964). This was a more indirect way of addressing the same issue: The question of the official monetary standard was about whether public authority would be applied to concentrate financial capacities in the hands of New York elites or to make available alternative bases for the creation of liquidity. Whatever their official rhetoric, elites' fundamental concerns were not with "easy credit" as such, but rather with the possibility of socially valid mechanisms of credit-creation situated outside the New York axis between the banks and the stock market. Whereas populists saw the greenbacks as the potential basis of a republican regime of public credit (Carruthers and Babb 1996; Ritter 1997), elites viewed bank notes convertible into specie as the only acceptable kind of paper money and demanded an official gold standard. During the 1880s and 1890s, the corporate and populist programs continued to clash. As the prospects for a soft money regime based on greenbacks grew increasingly dim, populist coalitions of farmers and workers came to advocate an augmentation of the money supply through the monetization of silver, but the idea of a bimetallic regime was only marginally more palatable to elites' sensibilities. The battle over the monetary standard would be decided only during the last years of the nineteenth century, and the gold standard was formally adopted in 1900.

In the meantime, the political stalemate permitted the continuation of the financial dynamics that had triggered the debates and struggles over reform in the first place. Two developments were crucial here. First, over the course of the postbellum era manufacturing firms grew rapidly, as a result of the general trend of economic expansion but also owing to the concentration and cartelization of the manufacturing sector (Kirkland 1961). The financing requirements of these enterprises began to outgrow the financing capacity of national banks (which was limited by regulation), and they turned to the commercial paper market as well as state banks and trust funds (which were under no such regulatory restrictions). The loss of custom pushed banks to become ever more heavily involved in speculative financial markets. Second, as a result of investment bankers' activities in the railroad sector, over the course of the postbellum era the corporation had gradually changed from a legal form granting conditional and temporary monopoly privileges into an institution entitled to the same constitutional protections as individual persons (Roy 1997). From the late 1880s, manufacturing enterprises began to adopt the "privatized" corporate form, allowing for an acceleration of concentration and resulting in the birth of a market in industrial securities that entailed a huge expansion of the stock market. Private bankers shifted their focus and became involved in the management of industrial enterprises in much the same way as they had been in the railroad sector. The relationship of banks to the manufacturing industry now came to resemble their relationship to the railroads sector: it became mediated by the stock market. We shall examine these developments in turn in the following two sections.

FINANCIAL BANKING

The two most consequential restrictions on national banks under the National Banking System were the prohibition on branch banking and the restriction on loan size. As the American economy grew and the average size of enterprises increased, banks were unable to provide these enterprises with sufficient funds. This situation triggered disintermediation tendencies: Large enterprises and corporations with substantial borrowing requirements increasingly raised funds in financial markets (Robbins and Terleckyj 1960: 13). In addition, the restrictions on national banks fueled the growth of state banks (White 1982b) and trust funds (Barnett 1911; Neal 1971), whose conditions of operation were much more permissive.[9] These challenges meant that national banks were under great pressure to look elsewhere for business opportunities (White 1992b). They poured ever more funds into the call loan market, and during the 1890s they moved into the securities business in a more direct way by setting up securities affiliates (Peach 1941) and by linking up with large investment banks (Cleveland and Huertas 1985: 33). National banks' strategies were sufficiently successful that they were able to stem the tide of decline. However, they also gave a massive boost to the very processes that had been responsible for the chronic instability plaguing the American financial system. This was the case all the more because the growth of state banks and trust companies rendered the interventions of the New York Clearing House even less effective, as the latter was organized by the large national banks on a fairly exclusive basis (Tallman and Moen 1995: 6).

[9] State banks had no restrictions on the size of their loans, were allowed to hold stock, were under lower reserve and capital requirements, had no bond-security requirement, and were allowed to establish branches within a city (Cleveland and Huertas 1985: 58–9). Trust companies were under even fewer restrictions than state banks, because they did not require a charter. Of course this also meant that they were not allowed to engage in note issue, but this represented ever less of a serious constraint due to the development of checking accounts (Kroos and Blyn 1971: 103; James 1978: 39–40).

Thus, disintermediation and the intense competition among different financial institutions had sparked a wave of financial innovation that further deepened the connections between the banking system and financial markets (De Cecco 1984b) – what Youngman (1906: 435) termed a trend to "financial banking." In present-day language, banks were "securitizing" their asset portfolios, that is, replacing more traditional assets with money and capital market instruments. There was an important flipside to this development: Banks' ample access to liquidity meant that they were now in a much better position than ever before to extend credit across the board, including longer-term, unsecured, and personal debt. Their involvement in relatively illiquid forms of credit now came to seem less problematic. In other words, the new framework of financial intermediation created a much more expansive basis for credit extension than had been provided by more traditional commercial banking practices. This would be of momentous significance to the financial development of twentieth-century America.

THE "MONEY TRUST"

The transformation of the functions of large New York banks was reinforced by a broader transformation of the American political economy that occurred during the last decade of the nineteenth century (Williams 1961). During most of the nineteenth century, manufacturing firms did not operate under a public charter (Seavoy 1972, 1978; Smith and Dyer 1996; Roy 1997: 54) and could not issue stock (Sobel 1965; Krooss and Blyn 1971: 130; Werner and Smith 1991; Mowery 1992). This situation changed drastically during the last decade of the nineteenth century. During the preceding decades, industrialists had responded to crises of overproduction through attempts to reduce competition, setting up pooling arrangements and trusts. Such developments triggered political and regulatory action to enforce more competitive market structures, which culminated in the Sherman Antitrust Act of 1890, prohibiting all industrial combinations restraining trade and commerce (Sklar 1988). Trying to find new ways to organize their industries on a less competitive basis, manufacturers looked to the privatized corporate form (Fligstein 1990; Roy 1997: 191). This trend interacted with investment bankers' shift in business focus (Prechel 2000: 43): By the early 1890s, the situation in the railroad sector had reached new depths (Kolko 1976: 3), leading bankers to look elsewhere for opportunities. They now turned their gaze to the manufacturing sector (Navin and Sears 1955; Bensel 2000: 304). The new corporate ownership structures facilitated financiers' attempts to wrest control from industrial leaders, and they continued to merge companies where the latter had left off. Between 1890 and 1905, American industry experienced an unprecedented wave of mergers and incorporations (Lamoreaux 1985; Roy 1997). A market in industrial securities developed for the first time, giving a tremendous boost to the call loan market, financial innovation, and speculative activities (Navin and Sears 1955; Smiley 1981).[10]

The incorporation wave triggered a convergence of financial and industrial interests: Many investment bankers took positions on the boards of large corporations, and interlocking directorships became a prominent feature of the American economic landscape (Bunting and Barbour 1971). Populists came to refer to the New York financial establishment as the "Money Trust" (Rochester 1936). To be sure, competition was by no means absent from these new financial structures: The frantic pace of financial innovation can be understood only against the background of the continued competition among financial intermediaries, including the competition from smaller and regional institutions that were not fully integrated into the structures of the New York Money Trust. The competition engendered by the decentralizing effects of regulation remained a crucial factor, and the system of unit banks was sustained by a substantial entrepreneurial sector (Kolko 1963: 140, 1976: 3; Piore and Sabel 1984; Berk 1991; Scranton 1997).

The alignment of elite interests was a major factor in breaking the political stalemate that had prevailed for several decades and it received its clearest expression in the presidential elections of 1896: The defeat of William Jennings Bryan by William McKinley left the Republican Party free to crucify the prosperity of ordinary people on a "cross of gold" (the expression Bryan used in his nomination speech) and meant the fatal blow to populist hopes for a producers' republic based on a soft money regime. The defeat of the populist program ushered in a long period of Republican political hegemony – the "System of 1896" – that would end only with the onset of the Great Depression (Burnham 1981; Ferguson 1981). Nevertheless, the end of populism as a movement did not mean an end to the hold of populist and republican sentiments on the consciousness of the American working classes (Goebel 1997: 147; Johnston 2003).

---

[10] The expansion of the stock market gave rise to the first independent credit-rating activities: In 1900, John Moody published the first *Manual of Industrial Statistics* (Sinclair 2005: 23–4).

Although hopes for a producers' republic had been dashed, the ideal of economic independence would reemerge in a different guise and give rise to new aspirations that would need to be accommodated. Populist sentiments became increasingly bound up with issues of consumption and would gradually morph into the ideal of privatized consumption and suburban homeownership (Kazin 1998) – in which capacity they would become pillars of the American financial system.

CONCLUSION

The antebellum period had been characterized by a high degree of institutional fragmentation. The government's regulatory capacity was sufficient to effect a reorganization of the financial system in the context of the Civil War, but the new system nonetheless incorporated the power of populism and the states and essentially institutionalized regulatory fragmentation at a higher level. As a central bank or branch banking was a political impossibility, the new system extended the use of bankers' balances as the primary means of financial integration. This concentrated huge amounts of funds in the hands of New York bankers. They needed to invest these funds, and, in the absence of a discount market for bills of exchange, they began to develop alternative investment strategies, turning to the stock market and call loan market for liquid assets. The ever-present threat of disintermediation further fuelled banks' willingness to explore the opportunities offered by financial banking. In this way, the savings of ordinary Americans ended up leveraging the speculative strategies of New York financiers. The incorporation of American industry at the end of the nineteenth century meant that the relations between the banking system and the American economy at large became mediated by speculative financial markets, laying the foundations for the further growth of the new system of financial intermediation. What had evolved by the beginning of the twentieth century was a highly distinctive pattern of structural power relations, characterized by close connections between banks and financial markets that promoted continuous financial innovation and liquidity production.

5

Contradictions of Early Twentieth-Century Financial Expansion

INTRODUCTION

The IPE narrative of financial development tends to portray the early twentieth century as the classic age of high finance, when states were committed to a liberal financial regime based on the gold standard. Although this picture captures some aspects of the international financial relations that pivoted on London, it does little to clarify the development of early-twentieth-century American finance – which was driven precisely by mechanisms of financial intermediation that were very different from those that underpinned the rise of British finance. This is especially clear when it comes to the significance of the American gold standard. The victory of gold was hardly an expression of financial discipline and was in no meaningful way allied to an institutional commitment to external financial openness. Instead, it served to consolidate the organization of liquidity creation around the institutional axis of New York banks, the call loan market, and the stock market, thereby withholding public sanction and social validity from other potential bases of credit creation. Even if advocates of the gold standard presented their case in terms of the "discipline of gold," there was nothing contained or disciplined about the pace at which credit creation and financial innovation accelerated after the turn of the century. The transformation of financial intermediation that had begun in the late nineteenth century made available to American banks an unprecedented capacity for the creation of liquidity and they exploited this to open up new lines of business. The start of the twentieth century consequently witnessed the growing penetration of financial principles and relations into American life.

This chapter examines the expansion and deepening of domestic financial markets as well as the contradictions that this process gave rise to. Recurrent crises culminated in the panic of 1907 (Poole 1951a), which saw bank runs, a scramble for liquidity, a freezing up of the market for call loans, a stock market meltdown, and, ultimately, the suspension of convertibility. The Treasury and the New York Clearing House were unable to fundamentally alter the dynamics of the American financial system or remedy its problems (Myers 1971: 245–6). The effects of the crisis rippled through all sectors of the economy and so imbued the idea of far-reaching political reform with a sense of necessity that it had hitherto not possessed (White 1983: 63). The way in which plans for a central bank came onto the political agenda was illustrative of how the operation of social power was changing: Whereas during the nineteenth century the recruitment of popular interests by elite factions had resulted in the continuous creation of new obstacles to coherent institutional solutions, during the twentieth century financial elites would display an exceptional capacity to turn crises into opportunities for the further integration of the population into the financial system.

Moreover, this process of financial integration and expansion did not occur through a process of market disembedding or state retreat, but precisely through processes of detailed public and civic regulation. The push for financial regulation should be placed in the broader context of the spirit of reform that permeated the Progressive Era (Wiebe 1962; McCraw 1984). To a significant extent, Progressivism represented a response to the "social problems" to which the modernization of the United States had given rise. Although they had lost the political initiative, the more everyday resistance and discontents of the lower classes had by no means disappeared (Weinstein 1968: 3–5; Ewen 1976: 15). At the same time, corruption and collusion among corporate and financial elites were increasingly common, and the concentration of financial power in the New York Money Trust, with J. P. Morgan as the central figure, bred considerable popular discontent (Rochester 1936). Civic-minded middle-class reformers sought to address these problems by giving America an infusion of morality through the reorganization of some key institutions and the thoroughgoing regulation of socioeconomic life (McCormick 1981, 1986). Recognizing in particular the integrative capacities of financial institutions, the Progressive reform movement sought to ensure that ordinary people would not be excluded from their benefits (Jacobs 1999; Cohen 2003; Ott 2007). In this way, Progressivism expressed an incipient awareness of the infrastructural dimensions of modern power, viewing the proliferation of financial connections in terms of the emergence of new mechanisms for controlling the dynamics of social life, as providing points of leverage for public policy.

What Progressive reformers did not fully appreciate, however, were the contradictions embedded in the construction of these public capacities: They tended to underestimate the selectivity and bias of institutional forms as well as the more technical difficulties in realizing potentialities for new mechanisms of control and coordination. They often failed to recognize that the institutions of modern life were composed of relations of power and control and that the inclusiveness they advocated amounted to incorporation into networks of inequality (Stromquist 2006). As a result, Progressivism became allied to the ambitions of America's corporate and financial elites as these pertained both to the reorganization of the legal frameworks regulating their business (Kolko 1963, 1976; Livingston 1986) and to their ability to follow up their defeat of the Democratic and populist political programs with a victory over the more everyday social and economic resistance of the lower classes (Ewen 1976; Lustig 1982). The spirit of technocratic reform was instrumental in the creation of bureaucratic and administrative structures that penetrated deep into American economic and social life (Wiebe 1967; Skowronek 1982; McCormick 1986: 178; McGerr 1986, 2003; Silbey 1991: 240). Their apparent neutrality made them efficient vehicles for the extension of infrastructural mechanisms of elite control (Kolko 1968: 58; Weinstein 1968: ix; Kantor 1990: 260; Roy 1991: 151).

FOUNDATIONS OF THE FEDERAL RESERVE SYSTEM

In the wake of the 1907 crisis, Congress instituted the National Monetary Commission and charged it with preparing a report on the problems of the financial system and recommending a long-term solution. New York bankers, who were closely involved in the writing of the plan, had initially advocated the creation of a central bank on the model of the Bank of England, but as it became clear that this would arouse intense popular hostility, the proposals shifted toward a less centralized reserve association, presented as an adaptation of existing clearing house arrangements (Timberlake 1978: 187). In addition, the Commission's plan sought to placate Midwestern banks by proposing the replacement of the existing system of note issue on the basis of government bonds with a currency issued on the basis of commercial banks' assets (Broz 1997: 177).

The idea of an asset-based currency was closely associated with the real bills doctrine, which would provide one of the main ideological pillars of the Federal Reserve System as it was eventually created (Burgess 1936; West 1973; Timberlake 1978, 1993). There was something paradoxical about this, given the fact that banking practices had already become significantly dissociated from the doctrine's prescriptions (White 1998). The real bills doctrine, however, had come to be espoused by Western interests. In the new context of the formal gold standard, to continue advocating greenback doctrines would have played right into the hands of elite reformers, who sought to centralize a range of monetary functions. Populist sentiments were deeply concerned about the prospect of an activist central bank with ample room for elitist cooperation and discretionary interventions. But, they were potentially willing to tolerate a reserve association that functioned according to fixed, clearly laid-down rules for credit extension – such as provided by the real bills doctrine (Wheelock 1991: 13) – and passively accommodated the credit demands generated by the real economy by discounting bank assets. In subsequent years, the real bills doctrine would prove an important factor in facilitating the compromise that would eventually emerge (Wiebe 1962). These negotiations took place against the background of the probing efforts of the Pujo Committee, charged with investigating the practices of the New York Money Trust (Weldin 2000: 4). Under great public interest, the committee uncovered ample corruption and collusion,[1] thus contributing to a public climate that worked to the advantage of those seeking substantial revisions to the original plan.

The Federal Reserve Act that was ultimately passed in 1913, although very much a project of financial elites, contained important compromise features reflecting the political force of agrarian interests and populist sentiments (Johnson 1998; Sanders 1999; Weldin 2000).[2] As a result of its compromise features, it was not entirely clear how it would operate, and the tensions generated by these "internally contradictory foundations" (De Cecco 1984b: 20) would be a key driving force behind the dynamics

---

[1] The committee had no difficulty naming the main players involved: "the most active agents in forwarding and bringing about the concentration of control of money and credit ... have been and are: J.P. Morgan & Co., First National Bank of New York, National City Bank of New York, Lee Higginson & Co., Kidder, Peabody & Co., and Kuhn Loeb & Co." (quoted in Geisst 2001: 122).

[2] As Sanders (1999: 258) puts it, "The capitalists had finally gotten the central banking system that all other industrial countries had and that the farmers had denied them for eighty years. But they got it on the farmers' terms, and the old anxiety about a politically controlled banking agency was still current in New York financial circles."

of the Federal Reserve System over the next decades.[3] The Act created a new currency and a system of fairly autonomous regional Reserve Banks overseen by a Federal Reserve Board (Wood 2005), although the division of power between the Board and the Reserve Banks was not in all respects clear (Weldin 2000: 5). Membership of the Federal Reserve System was compulsory only for banks with a federal charter, and few state banks joined the System because it came with more restrictive reserve requirements. Reserve Banks were to guarantee bank liquidity by purchasing bank assets through the discount window, but the Act, aiming to placate different interests, was vague about the definition of "eligible paper," just stating that credit extension should be aimed at "the maintenance of sound credit conditions, and the accommodation of commerce, industry and agriculture" (Greider 1987: 283). In keeping with the real bills doctrine, Federal Reserve Banks were expected to promote the creation of an American market for bills of exchange, but it had been clear all along that rediscounting practices would not be limited to those assets narrowly defined as "real bills" but would have to accommodate American conditions and include commercial and agricultural paper (Agger 1914).

The Federal Reserve, then, was not formally founded as a close ally of the financial markets.[4] But an emphasis on the populist constraints on financial reform should not blind us to the fact that the Federal Reserve System has not exactly gone into history as an institution of, or accountable to, the American people. Perhaps the most crucial aspect of the Federal Reserve System was to be found not in its formal institutional makeup and operating procedures as such, but in what it did *not* do: It did little to undermine the institutional structures of financial intermediation that had evolved during the previous decade (Cleveland and Huertas 1985; Zweig 1995: 36–7). The Federal Reserve System did not

---

[3] The rest of this paragraph highlights some of the most important provisions in the Federal Reserve Act. For a more complete overview, see the table in Broz 1997: 51–3.

[4] Sanders quotes the opinions of two Congressmen. Representative Lenroot commented as follows on the passing of the Federal Reserve Act: "[It] takes the reserves of the banks of the country that are now piled up in the city of New York and used to aid stock speculation upon the New York Stock Exchange and distributes those reserves back to the different parts of the country from whence they came" (Irvine Lenroot quoted in Sanders 1999: 236). Representative Ragsdale commented, in a similar vein, that "we have before us a currency bill that we can all safely hand to the people of the United States and say the power of the Money Trust is broken and that the people have come into their own. [Applause on the Democratic side.] . . . Mr. Speaker, the time has come, and it has been written into this statute for the first time in this country, that farm lands are a basis for credit in America, and that the owners of them who produce the wealth of this country shall share in that financial system" (J. Willard Ragsdale quoted in Sanders 1999: 237).

reorganize the capital markets or limit commercial banks' access to them (Myers 1951a: 582), nor did it challenge the core structures of the Money Trust. One reason for this was that agrarian and populist forces had primarily been concerned with the formal administrative structure of the system, and this had given financial elites the opportunity to divert attention toward the minutiae of reform proposals and away from the structural basis of their power (Myers 1951b). Ironically, it would be this very power base that would later allow New York financial elites to gradually assert control over the Federal Reserve System: In typically Progressive fashion (Roy 1991), the control that financial elites failed to get through the legislative process, they would achieve through a less conspicuous conquest of the institutional structures and operational mechanisms of the Federal Reserve System (Kolko 1963: 247).

THE FEDERAL RESERVE SYSTEM DURING ITS EARLY YEARS

The outbreak of World War I meant that the question of what constituted "eligible paper" became an issue even before the Federal Reserve had had the time to establish basic procedures. War finance required the use of financial obligations that were long-term and unsecured. Although the Federal Reserve Board initially objected to the idea of discounting such paper, when the United States entered the war in 1917, all governmental bodies were instructed to lend their full cooperation to the war effort (Roberts 1998). In addition to standing by to discount the non-standard types of paper involved in the financing of European countries, the Federal Reserve was responsible for supporting the Treasury's debt-funding efforts (Anderson 1965: 11). The Treasury sought to fund the war debt by selling short-term debt to commercial banks in anticipation of revenues from long-term bonds or taxes, and the Reserve Banks' willingness to discount Treasury government debt at a preferential rate made it attractive for banks to purchase government securities.

These policies were "a far cry from the real bills doctrine" (Degen 1987: 35). Moreover, they proved sticky: The years during and after World War I saw a progressive relaxation of the eligibility requirements. The Federal Reserve's discounting policies afforded banks easy access to liquidity and so enabled them to extend credit freely (Degen 1987: 33–4). Of course, the Federal Reserve policies were intended to encourage the banks to lend liberally only to the government, not to other borrowers; but the discount mechanism offered no way to control what kinds of loans banks would make. Furthermore, the Federal Reserve's support for the government's borrowing did not cease with the end of the war: The Treasury opposed moves to raise the discount rate or to abolish the preferential rate as it would have driven up the yield on government securities and so undermined its ability to fund the debt. When the Treasury, aware that inflationary and speculative tendencies were getting out of hand, abandoned its opposition to higher interest rates, the Federal Reserve Banks raised the discount rate, but did so just at a time when the economy had passed the peak of the upturn, thus reinforcing the effects of recession (Degen 1987: 39).

The key to understanding such seemingly erratic policy-making behavior lies in the fact that the Federal Reserve was born with a mandate not for *monetary* policy but for *credit* policy (Hardy 1932; Chandler 1971: 10–1). The distinction may seem scholastic, but its implications are profound. The Federal Reserve was primarily a bankers' bank, a bank responsible for keeping the banking system liquid by functioning as a lender of last resort – that is to say, "a central bank *was* a bank, not just another regulatory body" (Grant 1992: 155). The concept of monetary policy as it is practiced today presupposes an appreciation of the infrastructural characteristics and network properties of the financial system: Considerations of how financial policies can be used to affect general business activity and price levels are at its heart. During the 1920s, however, modern macroeconomics had not yet been born: The understanding of the linkages between different parts of the economic system was still inchoate and rudimentary, and a developed conceptualization of the relevant transmission mechanisms was absent (Mehrling 1997). "The Fed's objective, as frankly stated in records of its own deliberations, was the restoration of 'sound financial conditions', not the restoration of economic growth" (Greider 1987: 290). To be sure, sound financial conditions were in part understood in terms of the needs of the real economy, but only insofar as these needs expressed themselves on the financial level, in terms of money market indicators (i.e., as a demand for credit) (Wheelock 1991: 114). The Federal Reserve followed what would later come to be known as a "money market strategy."

More concretely, the real bills doctrine prescribed passive accommodation of banks' demand for credit in the money market. Although this principle may seem innocent enough, upon closer inspection it is rather contrary to what we nowadays consider to be basic principles of monetary management. For its effects were procyclical. During an economic upturn, banks would try to meet the increased demand for credit; this would translate itself into an increased demand for bank reserves, which

Early 20th Century Financial Expansion

the Federal Reserve perceived as an indication of monetary tightness that it would seek to loosen by discounting the assets offered by the banks; and vice versa. Thus, during an upturn the Federal Reserve would pursue expansionary policies and credit would be liberally available, and during a recession it would restrict credit expansion and it was hard to obtain credit for anything. This was all the more problematic given the fact that much of the excess credit generated during upturns was used for speculation; the real bills doctrine in no way guaranteed that the proceeds from a discounted asset would be used for productive purposes.

THE DEVELOPMENT OF BANKING DURING THE 1920S

The contradictions of monetary management were further reinforced by the impact of the creation of the Federal Reserve on the nature of banking, especially on the behavior of the large New York commercial banks. The institutional foundations of the system of financial intermediation that had evolved over the previous decades were fully intact, and the presence of a lender of last resort, an ever available source of liquidity, meant that banks felt they could now take greater risks than before and exploit the opportunities offered by financial markets with even greater vigor (Phillips 1921; Baster 1937). The high degree of integration of banks and financial markets, backed up by a passive, accommodating lender of last resort, laid the basis for the financial dynamics of the 1920s.

The first years after the war saw a growth in banks' corporate finance business (Cleveland and Huertas 1985: 73). But corporations' credit needs in fact quickly outgrew banks' financing capacity. The result was a wave of disintermediation, with corporations relying increasingly on new stock flotations (De Cecco 1984b).[5] Banks could not replace this lending business with holdings of commercial paper (as they had done in the past), because the latter market shrank significantly (White 1992b) – due not only to the corporations' preference for issuing stock (James 1995) but also to the Federal Reserve's policy of promoting the use of bills of exchange (Greef 1938).[6] Banks' strategies therefore focused even more centrally on

---

[5] Whereas in 1920 58 percent of banks' assets were in commercial lending, by 1929 this had come down to 37 percent (White 1990: 70).

[6] Potentially, banks could have compensated for the declining supply of commercial paper by buying larger amounts of bills of exchange. However, precisely because they were so well-secured and safe, the yield on bills of exchange was lower than that on other money market instruments, and banks remained reluctant to invest a large amount of funds in the discount market. At no point before 1929 did banks hold more than five percent of the total volume of bills (Balabanis 1980 [1935]: 39).

the stock market than in the past. Their involvement in the market for call loans grew further, and through their security affiliates they speculated in the stock market more directly and took on investment banking functions for the corporations that used to bank with them (Osterweis 1932; White 1992b), underwriting and placing stock issues as well as assisting companies in an advisory capacity.[7] Thus, banks fully exploited the opportunities offered by the financial structure that had been constructed over the previous decades, developing a range of strategies that led them further away from traditional commercial bank activities.

Banks also drew new economic actors into these financial dynamics, promoting the widespread holding of securities by the public (De Cecco 1984b; Cleveland and Huertas 1985: 135–9; Perkins 1999; Morrison and Wilhelm 2007: 203, 216). The extraordinary deepening of the public's involvement in financial markets during the 1920s was very much the result of attempts by commercial banks and brokers to carve out a niche independent of large investment banks like J. P. Morgan, who remained aloof from retail activities (Zweig 1995). In this regard, their ambitions were fully in line with Progressive attempts to make access to the stock market available to all American citizens. Reformers promoted and facilitated the New York Stock Exchange's (NYSE's) attempts, following the revelations of the Pujo Committee, to profile itself as an essentially democratic and accountable institution, offering American citizens access to the prospects of ownership they had lost with the demise of programs for a republic of independent producers (Ott 2009). Thus, the 1920s became the decade of the rise of a stratum of ordinary investors (De Cecco 1984b; Geisst 1990: 4). Commercial banks transformed themselves into "financial department stores" offering a wide range of services to an ever larger public and holding a wide range of financial assets (Greef 1938; De Cecco 1984b; White 1992b).

To some extent, banks also sought to counter the decline in domestic corporate business by developing their international activities (Poole 1951b). Before World War I, commercial banks' international business had been negligible, but during the interwar period large banks began to open foreign branches, following American corporations investing abroad. Banks' main motivation for pursuing overseas commercial business was domestic in nature: They wanted to be able to engage in international transactions to

---

[7] Security affiliates often made use of call money to leverage their investments. Essentially, "banks extended loans to themselves that were used to fund security market operations" (Geisst 1990: 7).

attract corporate custom at home (Cleveland and Huertas 1985: 122). Large commercial banks also entered into alliances with private investment bankers who were involved in the financing of European governments (owing to the U.S. government's intransigent stance on the question of Europe's war debts). Toward the end of the 1920s, as the American stock market took off, banks gradually lost their interest in international activities (De Cecco 1984b: 21).

THE GROWTH OF CONSUMER DEBT

The American public participated in the financial system in their capacity not only as investors, but also as borrowers. The emergence of the commercial paper market after the Civil War had made direct access to credit more widely available, but it had still been restricted to well-established enterprises and individuals whose personal creditworthiness was not in doubt. The only kind of more formal credit that ordinary people could hope to obtain was credit secured by real estate (i.e., mortgage credit), and even this had been consistently problematic.[8] Ordinary people in need of credit for purposes of consumption were often forced to turn to pawnbrokers or loan sharks (Grant 1992: 79). Progressive reformers took offense at the injustice of workers falling prey to the exploitative practices and extortionate rates of illegal lenders and embarked on a campaign to give ordinary people access to formal credit. We should be careful not to read present-day understandings of consumption, shaped by post–World War II consumer culture, back into the past: During the first decades of the twentieth century, questions of consumption and consumer credit were highly politicized (Donohue 2005; McGovern 2006), often seen as the potential basis for a new easy money regime and as representing a continuation rather than an abandonment of republican sentiments. Consumer credit, it was believed, was unlikely to bring full economic independence, but by loosening budgetary constraints it might allow workers to create a certain distance from the pernicious imperatives of the market and wage labor.

It was precisely for this reason that the financial establishment remained critical of the idea of widely available consumer credit, seen as

---

[8] Regional state banks were the main source of mortgages, but the illiquid nature of these loans meant that their ability to extend such credit was still limited. The difficulties associated with obtaining mortgages gave an impetus to the growth of thrifts, or savings and loan associations: credit unions with an explicit civilizational purpose, promoting saving habits and financial prudence and using the funds generated to promote the independence and dignity that comes from owning one's own home.

undermining financial discipline and promoting idleness and indolence.[9] The period following the end of World War I consequently saw the growth of a new group of financial intermediaries specializing in various forms of consumer financing (Flam 1985; Calder 1999: 19). Especially installment credit (i.e., a loan repaid in parts) grew rapidly: In the past the principle of installment credit had been applied only to mortgages, but now it was extended to a whole range of durable consumer goods (Olney 1991).[10] It was during the second half of the 1920s that the nation's financial establishment became more accepting of consumer credit (Calder 1999: 235). Crucial to this change of heart was the observation that consumer credit imposed many more obligations on the debtor than popular myth would have it: It turned out to be a fairly good disciplinarian, locking workers into a schedule of repayments that increased rather than reduced their dependence on the labor market.[11] Thus, by the late 1920s banks abandoned most of their misgivings about consumer credit and began to make up for lost ground (Geisst 1990). In this way, "Lending and borrowing entered the social mainstream" (Grant 1992: 145), and consumption and consumer credit were transformed from an arena of political contestation into a source of potentially endless business opportunities.

THE DEVELOPMENT OF FEDERAL RESERVE POLICIES DURING THE 1920S

Over the course of the 1920s, the way in which the Federal Reserve's procyclical policies facilitated financial expansion and speculative practices became cause for concern. It was increasingly realized that premising monetary

---

[9] Indeed, the words used were not "consumer credit" but "consumptive credit," a term that "smelled of disease. It prejudged a loan of money or goods as destructive and socially wasteful" (Calder 1999: 250).

[10] The item that most prospective buyers could afford only on the basis of installment credit was, of course, the automobile (Calder 1999: 184).

[11] In 1927, Edwin Seligman published *The Economics of Instalment Selling*, which offered a new understanding of the ingredients of a productive lifestyle characterized by discipline and thrift, establishing a direct link between consumer credit and saving: "he argued that installment credit increased not only consumers' capacity to save but also their desire to save. This had always been recognized as true for home ownership. Give a man a home mortgage, it was held, and he will work twice as hard. Now Seligman applied the same reasoning to credit for furniture, automobiles, and other durable goods.... The family with car payments to make would be forced to work hard to make the payments and, through the new leisure opportunities provided by the car, enabled to work hard. Presumably, they would also be less likely to fritter away paychecks on frivolous, nondurable expenditures. The result would be increased savings" (Calder 1999: 252).

policy on automatic control mechanisms guaranteed little concerning the uses to which credit would be put and that a more active approach to credit policy was required (Wicker 1966; Bach 1971; Degen 1987: 44; Wheelock 1991), involving, among other things, a shift in orientation from procyclical to countercyclical policies (Degen 1987: 47; Wheelock 1989). This, however, was still a long way from modern monetary policy. For although the Federal Reserve's policy orientation was now more active and directed toward broader macroeconomic indicators, its interpretation of these trends was still fully filtered through the money market. It was not guided primarily by considerations concerning economic growth or monetary aggregates, but by banks' demand for credit. Moreover, the Federal Reserve's primary policy lever was still a passive instrument. The Federal Reserve could raise and lower the discount rate, but manipulating the price of bank reserves did not allow for effective control over the behavior of banks: In good times, banks would present paper for discount to be able to extend new credit regardless of the discount rate, and during a recession there was little demand for new loans so that banks had no reason to seek advances from the Reserve Banks, no matter how low the rate.

To be sure, the 1920s saw the invention and development of "open market operations," which in principle allowed for precisely the kind of active interventions that were needed in a more discretionary orientation to financial policy (Meltzer 2003: 141). But the effectiveness of this new policy instrument, as well as the general growth of the Federal Reserve's governing capacities, was hampered by divisions within the Federal Reserve System itself. Open market operations were a more or less accidental discovery: When the Reserve Banks began trading government securities for their own account and saw the significant effects that this had, they realized that, when properly coordinated, it could potentially be used as a policy instrument (Anderson 1965; Wheelock 1991: 113). Benjamin Strong, the governor of the Federal Reserve Bank of New York (FRBNY), successfully proposed a centralization of the System's open market operations, with policies formulated by the new Governors Conference – which later became the Federal Open Market Committee (FOMC) – and executed by the FRBNY (Roberts 2000a). The Federal Reserve Board initially did little to oppose these changes, assuming that it was just a matter of technical innovation, but with time it became clear that a powerful policy instrument had come under the control of the FRBNY, which was closely associated with Wall Street interests. For financiers, the new organizational setup "provided the arrangement of power they had originally wanted in the new central bank" (Greider

1987: 293). Financial elites had managed to bypass the legislative framework of the Federal Reserve System and to establish their own power base – which was shielded from public scrutiny precisely because it operated under the institutional cover of the Federal Reserve Act.

Although the 1920s saw a considerable sophistication of the procedures for open market operations (Chandler 1958), in quantitative terms they remained secondary to the discount window. More importantly, their use was significantly shaped by the fact that the FRBNY's concerns were not confined to the state of the domestic economy: The New York financial establishment, to which it was closely connected, had made significant loans to European governments and therefore had a strong interest in the stability of the international financial system. The FRBNY often seemed to pay closer attention to its relations with the Bank of England than the concerns of the Federal Reserve Board. Britain's return to the gold standard (in 1924) was heavily dependent on its ability to attract large flows of short-term capital. Hence, it was essential that London interest rates remain above New York rates, and the FRBNY saw it as its task to assist the Bank of England in this objective (Clarke 1967). Thus, FRBNY policies were often expansionary for reasons that had little to do with the state of the domestic economy, and monetary policy came to be infused with an inflationary bias. Much of the excess credit thus created found its way into speculative channels.

THE CRASH AND DEPRESSION

From the mid-1920s the level of speculation began to set off alarm bells. What raised particular concern was the combination of runaway speculation and lackluster business activity (Anderson 1965: 56–7). This concern, however, was not complemented by any serious tightening policies: For a long time the FRBNY kept up its expansionary policies. After 1925 the American economy was weakened so much that all the additional liquidity created by the Federal Reserve's policies went straight into the stock market. It was only from late 1927 that the FRBNY and other Reserve Banks began to advocate tighter policies. However, by that time the Federal Reserve Board had become opposed to aggressive attempts to curb speculation, considering that that such policies were likely to adversely affect the provision of productive credit (Degen 1987: 54). It was only in August 1929 that the Board gave its approval to discount rate rises, but by then it was already too late to halt the stock market from spinning out of control (Minsky 1986; Bierman 1998).

When the stock market crashed in October 1929, the effects rippled throughout the economy (Kindleberger 1973). It now became clear how deeply the stock market had become interwoven with the rest of the financial and economic system (Fearon 1987). Banks were battered from all possible sides: The value of their stock investments collapsed, brokers defaulted en masse on call loans, and many corporations and individuals defaulted on their bank loans. The presence of a central bank did not suffice to halt bank panics, as had been hoped. All this resulted in a wave of bank failures in 1930 and a sharp contraction of the money supply (Wicker 1996).

Whereas before the crisis the Federal Reserve had failed to pursue contractionary policies and in effect fueled speculative tendencies, now the Federal Reserve refused to counteract the consequences of the crisis through expansionary policies (Friedman and Schwartz 1963; Temin 1976; Meltzer 2003). Decisive here was the judgment that the crisis represented a necessary correction of the excessively speculative and inflationary tendencies that had plagued the American financial system during the late 1920s (Chandler 1971: 114; Wood 2005: 191–2). Ultimately, then, the Federal Reserve saw its role still very much as one of accommodating the demand for credit so that the volume of currency could vary according to the demands of industry and commerce. Federal Reserve policy still took its cue primarily from the demand for credit generated in the economy and expressed in the money market – and in the years after 1929 the demand for credit was, of course, virtually non existent (Chandler 1971; Wigmore 1985). The American economy now descended into the Great Depression (Kennedy 1973).

CONCLUSION

The foundations of the Federal Reserve System were complex and contradictory. Charged with controlling the instability and excesses generated by the configuration of financial institutions and relations that had emerged by the early twentieth century, it lacked the requisite interests and instruments. The presence of the Federal Reserve as a lender of last resort in fact served to promote the kind of practices that were at the root of financial instability. Financial elites now operated within an institutional structure that made available unprecedented capacities for the creation of liquidity and the network power embedded in the dynamics of the American financial system continued to grow. The financial architecture that had emerged over the course of the postbellum era and had received official confirmation at the very end of the nineteenth century was now being consolidated and its associated mechanisms of control extended throughout socioeconomic life. Yet the authority that the Federal Reserve could exert over these processes remained limited: It had been inserted fully into their contradictions and did not possess a magical regulatory formula allowing it to stabilize the expansion of financial networks. The growth of structural power, in other words, did not automatically translate into enhanced infrastructural capacities for the federal state. The proliferation of institutions promoting financial expansion was not functionally part of the formation of integral statehood but rather complicated the state's exercise of its formal authority – as became all too clear with the Crash and the Depression.

6

The United States and International Finance in the Interwar Period

INTRODUCTION

The Crash and Depression meant the collapse of not only the American financial system, but also the world economy at large. In the previous chapters, international dimensions featured only insofar as they affected the domestic development of American finance. It is now time to look at the relationship between American finance and international finance in a more systematic way. IPE scholars, as well as other international relations scholars and historians, have traditionally taken the period between World War I and the collapse of the world economy as a key point of reference in theorizing the making of the American century. The key claim here is that, although after World War I economic and financial international power passed from Britain to the United States, the latter failed to perform its role as guardian of liberal world order in the way that Britain had done before the war (Costigliola 1977, 1984; Burk 1992; Wilkins 1999): Because of the isolationist ethos that prevailed in the United States, the increase in American international capabilities and power resources was not accompanied by a willingness to assume the responsibilities of hegemonic leadership (Kindleberger 1973; Gilpin 1987; Nye 1990). The United States, in other words, was a reluctant "heir to empire" (Parrini 1969). In this interpretation, it was the American reluctance to shoulder its hegemonic responsibilities that allowed for the ruinous expansion of the self-regulating market, which would be at the root of the collapse of the interwar economy, the subsequent rise of economic nationalism, and the fragmentation of the world economy. This narrative provides the backdrop for the conventional IPE conceptualization of the form that

U.S. international power took after World War II: Having learned its lessons and cognizant of the havoc that the disembedding tendencies of capitalist markets would wreak, the United States now shed its isolationist stance and was not only capable but also willing to assume the mantle of hegemony. That is, it committed itself to "embedding liberalism," to providing the institutional supports and collective goods that are needed to hold together a liberal world economy.

The interpretation of interwar America as a reluctant imperial heir carries problematic conceptual implications: It implicitly relies on British financial power as a template for the rise of American power (O'Brien 2003; Ingham 1994), assuming a certain degree of structural similarity in the relationship between hegemons and international orders. As Ingham has argued, "the model of Britain's nineteenth-century role is an inappropriate one for understanding the nature of American dominance and, in particular, is the source of some confusion in assessing the USA's role in the postwar international monetary system" (Ingham 1994: 41). The eventual international expansion of American finance would precisely not occur on the comparatively restrictive British model of international high finance; rather, it would be driven and shaped by the much more dynamic and expansionary financial techniques and institutions that had emerged within the United States.

It is certainly the case that American policies played a significant role in producing the global depression and that (as we saw in the previous chapter) those policies were characterized by considerable misapprehension of the processes they sought to regulate. But the suggestion that America failed to appreciate its "true" interests and that the inward focus of its policies essentially represented a "major blunder" (Hybel 2001: 45) is questionable: American policy makers were hardly "mistaken" in their focus on domestic processes. The expansion of American finance during the early twentieth century was predominantly internal and had only a very limited international dimension: Relatively few banks had overseas operations, the role of New York as an international financial center remained limited, and the dollar did not decisively displace sterling as the international currency. The challenge to Britain's position in international finance was a result not of an outward expansion of the new system of American finance but rather of the intergovernmental debts incurred by European countries during World War I. This highly politicized structure of public credit relations was not accompanied by the construction of organic linkages between the dynamics of American finance and the sphere of international finance (Arrighi 1994: 271–2).

The United States in the Interwar Period

Thus, the idea that the United States was capable but unwilling to assume hegemonic responsibility seems a poor way of capturing the constellation of forces during the interwar period. In one sense, due to the absence of an international infrastructure of dollar-centered private credit relations, the United States was not just reluctant but unable to provide organic hegemonic leadership (Ingham 1994: 32). In another sense, the United States was quite willing to pursue its own interests; it was just that those interests were not bound up with the stable reproduction of an international financial order along the lines of British nineteenth-century liberalism. This chapter offers an alternative interpretation of developments during the interwar period.

THE CONTOURS OF BRITISH FINANCIAL LEADERSHIP

Although British financial hegemony is often associated with the gold standard regime, it is important to appreciate that the bulk of world trade was already financed in sterling bills before the gold standard was instituted. The pre–World War I international system is therefore best considered a gold-sterling standard (Williams 1968; Lindert 1969; Ingham 1994). Britain had become the most advanced manufacturing economy and established its global dominance as a trading nation from the late eighteenth century, and sterling took on the role of international transactions currency in the wake of this. By the early nineteenth century, a political bloc of financiers and merchants had consolidated that demanded liberal external economic policies to boost Britain's position in international commerce. This coalition also had considerable control over the (privately owned) Bank of England, which concentrated its policies on maintaining currency stability (Sayers 1936; Bloomfield 1959; De Cecco 1984a; Scammell 1985). Through a regime based on the convertibility of sterling into gold at a fixed rate and unilateral free trade policies (Plat 1968; Barkin 2003), Britain increasingly became an entrepot, performing all manner of commercial and financial services not directly related to its manufacturing strength. London already possessed a large domestic discount market of well-secured trade-related paper, and foreign merchants could do no better than make use of the London market (Scammell 1968; Nishimura 1971; Cottrell 1991).

This edifice began to show cracks during World War I. The war disrupted trade patterns, and the role of sterling as an international currency took a major hit. Britain suffered a large drain of gold and found itself forced to abandon the gold standard. Central banks began to diversify out of sterling, increasingly holding dollar reserves (Eichengreen and

Flandreau 2008). During the period from the end of World War I until the return to gold in 1924, Britain sought to counteract such trends by promoting the adoption of a formal sterling standard, but such moves were blocked by the United States. In addition, Britain had been forced to obtain large American loans and now found itself entangled in a structure of debt with the United States as the main creditor. However, the pace at which British financial power declined during the interwar period should not be overstated. It managed to reduce some of the pressure on its currency by creating a sterling bloc, walled off from the rest of the world through tariffs. Moreover, the abandonment of the gold standard (and the failed return to gold between 1924 and 1931) did not destroy the totality of international credit relations on which Britain's financial leadership rested: As a private transactions currency, sterling retained considerable strength (Ingham 1994: 43). And despite major liquidations during the war, Britain was still the main foreign investor (Barkin 2003: 100). Most importantly, however, during the interwar period the United States offered little in the way of alternative structures for commercial international intermediation. Britain's financial position was grounded in its position in world trade, its overseas investments, and the London discount market – the United States possessed none of these to a similar extent.

THE U.S. AND INTERNATIONAL FINANCE BEFORE THE CRASH

Until World War I, the role of American markets, institutions, and intermediaries in international finance was minor (Carosso and Sylla 1991; Walter 1993: 121). To be sure, private bankers played a role in government policies designed to promote the overseas interests of America, offering foreign governments loans in exchange for the opening up of markets (Rosenberg 1985, 1999; Hybel 2001: 39; Mitchener and Wiedenmier 2005). But the participation of private bankers in such Dollar Diplomacy was as far as America's financial prowess went internationally. The prohibition on national banks establishing branches was a factor here, but the main institutional reason for the marginal role of the United States in pre–World War I international finance was the absence of an American discount market for bills of exchange (Carosso and Sylla 1991; LaRoche 1993: 79). In previous chapters, we have seen the differences between America's commercial paper and the bills of exchange on which the British financial empire was based. Commercial paper – unsecured, unendorsed, and without any self-liquidating features – was entirely unsuitable for the financing of international trade (Goodhart 1969).

In some respects, the decade of the 1910s represented a turning point (Phelps 1927). First, the Federal Reserve Act allowed American banks to establish overseas branches and some of the large New York banks made use of this. But they expected limited benefits from this international business by itself and were interested in doing so only to the extent that their ability to arrange international transactions would help them to attract corporate custom at home (Cleveland and Huertas 1985: 122). Of greater significance was the fact that the newly created Federal Reserve System was charged with the task of creating an American market for bills of exchange to make New York more competitive as an international financial centre (Broz 1997). Although this market grew considerably during the 1920s and so gave a boost to the role of the dollar as an international currency (Battilossi 2002a), it remained highly "artificial," that is, dependent for its maintenance on the Federal Reserve buying and selling bills. The discount market never rivaled its London counterpart in size, and it failed to push out the commercial paper market. Furthermore, it only existed for a good decade: It was annihilated during the crash of 1929 and the Great Depression and afterward only recovered to a very limited extent (Burgess 1936; LaRoche 1993: 80).

Thus, the American challenge to the position of England in international finance during the interwar period was not based on the competitive emulation of English financial practices: The rise of American finance during the interwar period had relatively little to do with the expansion of commercial banking or the role of dollar-denominated debt in financing world trade (Germain 1997: 78–9; Hudson 2003: 53). Much more consequential than either of these were developments at the level of government. Central banks began to diversify their holdings of foreign exchange, and over the course of the 1920s the dollar overtook sterling as an official reserve currency (Eichengreen and Flandreau 2008). More importantly, during the war European countries had incurred huge debts, making the United States a net creditor for the first time in its history (Meter 1971). Much of the fate of international finance during the interwar period can be explained as a function of how the United States managed the European war debts.

Although European countries argued that the question of war debts should be seen in conjunction with the large losses they had sustained and the issue of reparation payments, the United States refused to acknowledge any such connection and demanded repayment. The isolationist or mercantilist ethos that characterized the Republican administrations of the 1920s played a major role here (Becker 1982; Barber 1993). The economic interests that underlay the "System of 1896," predominantly oriented toward the domestic market, were generally wary of involvement in international affairs. The Open Door policies of the 1920s were primarily concerned with ensuring adequate supplies of raw materials to the domestic economy and opening up selective export markets. And Europe was neither an important export market for these corporations nor a place where they had many investments. To be sure, the interwar period also saw the buildup of significant international interests by American capital, which tended to favor a more lenient approach to the question of war debts and a more constructive involvement in European affairs (Ferguson 1984). But such demands fell on deaf ears.

While the U.S. government demanded repayment, it was unwilling to allow European countries to earn the required funds by opening up its markets, continuously raising tariffs to shield American businesses from competition (Hudson 2003: 65). This stance meant that the European allies were forced to put tremendous pressure on Germany to make its reparation payments. Because the latter far exceeded Germany's capacity to pay, it was forced to turn to the United States for loans. The U.S. State Department, concerned about Germany's predicament, interceded with private banks, applying moral suasion to direct capital flows in accordance with political objectives. That way, the world economy could be stabilized without the American government being seen as getting itself entangled in European problems (Chernow 1990). The United States came to be at the center of a convoluted triangle of international payments: The bulk of the loans went to Germany, from there to England or France, and then back to the United States (Fisk 1924). No special conditions were attached to America's interwar lending to European countries – and in this respect, it was quite different from the kind of Dollar Diplomacy that the United States had applied to non-European countries from the beginning of the century, as well as from the loans that the United States would make to Europe after World War II.

During the late 1920s, the domestic stock market boom began to reorient the interests of investors toward speculative opportunities at home, cutting European borrowers off from credit. The stock market crash was followed by America's descent into the Great Depression, which quickly spread across the Western world. When the Macmillan Report revealed that Britain's short-term foreign liabilities were many times larger than its short-term foreign assets and so triggered a run on sterling, Britain was forced to put an end to convertibility. As governments scrambled for gold, they sold dollars no less than sterling: The dollar suffered a significantly greater setback than sterling as international reserve currency, and the effects of this would last until the end of the 1930s (Eichengreen and

Flandreau 2008: 22). Although the Roosevelt administration understood the long-term benefits of a more constructive engagement of Europe's problems, the Depression meant that domestic recovery took precedence over any other considerations. Democrats had much higher hopes for the potential benefits of national regulation in combating the economic malaise than the Republican administrations of the 1920s (Hudson 2003: 86), and their overriding concern was therefore to maximize the degree of domestic policy leeway available to pursue reflationary policies. Roosevelt not only opposed debt reduction and lower tariffs but also abandoned the gold standard and devalued the dollar to effect a domestic reflation, further restricting the ability of European countries to export and thus triggering a wave of protectionism (Hudson 2003: 110). European countries suspended their debt payments and Britain stepped up its efforts to create a trade bloc based on Imperial Preference. International finance collapsed along with the international economy and would have to be reconstructed virtually from scratch after World War II.

Thus, America's role in international finance during the interwar period was more destructive than constructive. The publicly created credit relations of debt organized around the dollar were not part of the formation of an organic set of connections between American finance and the world economy (Stern 1951): They did not replace but were rather "superimposed" on private credit relations based on the sterling system (Brown 1940: 138; quoted in Langley 2002: 62). The dollar's role as a private transactions currency was limited, and as a result sterling retained a considerable degree of strength in international trade and its financing, also enhanced by the fact that for a long time Britain still adhered to free trade policies while the United States was already becoming increasingly protectionist (McKercher 1988: 435).

The relative resiliency of Britain-centered financial structures seems to have been better understood by some contemporary authors than recent accounts (e.g., Patterson 1916; Wyse 1918). Writing in 1916, Patterson predicted that, unless America fundamentally changed the course of its financial policy making, hopes that its assumption of international creditor status would entail a smooth transition of financial hegemony were bound to be disappointed. America's role was not supported or leveraged by the kind of financial relations that had propelled Britain's rise to financial preeminence: The United States lacked a discount market and a banking system that could play a significant role in international trade financing, and it had high tariffs, relatively little foreign trade, and small foreign investments. For the United States to acquire a more sustainably prominent position in international finance, Patterson argued, it was to reform its financial system in the direction of the English system and, in particular, resist the temptation of continuous political interference. However, such reshaping of American finance in the British mould remained a distant prospect – during the interwar period, and even during the first decades after World War II. The United States would not become the kind of open, liberal clearing house thriving on unilateral free trade that Britain had been (Silver and Arrighi 2003). But although Patterson acutely discerned the obstacles to a simple passing of financial power from one liberal hegemon to another, what he could not foresee was that, several decades later, the very non-British dynamics of American finance would produce their own brand of international power. That global expansion would not be driven by the emulation of British financial practices and would assume a qualitatively different form than British financial hegemony. The next chapters will trace the specific ways in which American finance internationalized to reshape the world of global finance.

CONCLUSION

During the interwar period, the structural power embedded in the mechanisms of American finance remained largely confined to domestic affairs. Although the configuration of intergovernmental war debts posed a significant challenge to Britain's ability to maintain its pre–World War I leadership in international finance, and although the dollar rivaled sterling as an international reserve currency, U.S. international power was not leveraged by a system of private credit relations and financial techniques, which were still largely organized on the basis of sterling credits and bore the stamp of British banking methods. As a consequence, the United States did not decisively displace British intermediaries and financial markets from their central position in international finance. Thus, the interpretation offered in this book breaks with the idea that the United States was a reluctant hegemon during the interwar period: Such a perspective is framed too much by a cyclical model of hegemonic succession that does not view socioeconomic sources as constitutive aspects of state power. Instead, the account advanced here emphasizes the limited organic connections between American and global finance during the interwar period and hence the limited embeddedness of the international power of the American state in private financial mechanisms.

7

New Foundations for Financial Expansion

INTRODUCTION

The New Deal reconstitution of the American state in the wake of the Great Depression was an important episode in the making of modern American finance. IPE scholarship tends to depict the New Deal reforms in terms of a Polanyian reembedding of the financial system. From such a perspective, the laissez-faire ethos of the early decades of the twentieth century had, with disastrous consequences, permitted financial markets to become disembedded from social and political institutions, and the New Deal was motivated by the aim to prevent this from reoccurring by restoring regulation and constraining the growth of markets. The present chapter argues that this is a problematic interpretation. The early twentieth century had seen a proliferation of financial connections and their penetration into new layers of social life, and the New Deal reforms did not reverse this process but precisely promoted its continuation: Their effect was to further integrate the American population into the financial system. If New Deal policy makers were acutely aware of the volatility and contradictions that such financial expansion had entailed, they discerned ample opportunity to manage this through modern policies of macroeconomic stabilization. That is, regulation was not viewed as something externally imposed on and constraining markets, but as organically allied to and facilitating their expansion. The real significance of the New Deal was not to be found in the reassertion of government against markets, but rather in the emergence of an awareness that the pursuit of public objectives could be leveraged by enlisting those market forces (Hyman 2007). In this way, the New Deal represented a significant step in the direction of a more developed conception of infrastructural state capacity. This orientation evolved through the further alignment of the Progressive reform agenda with business interests: If before the Depression corporate and financial elites had already been able to use the Progressive reform ethos to defuse the radical potential of social and industrial resistance (Bernstein 1968; Weinstein 1968; Gordon 1994), from the New Deal onward it would allow them to make the aspirations of the working classes positively serviceable to the exigencies of capital accumulation.

More specifically, the understanding of the New Deal as the civilization of American capitalism is misleading or one-sided in several respects. First, although very much a response to the surge of popular discontent (Gourevitch 1984; Vittoz 1987), the New Deal's financial program enjoyed considerable support among corporate and financial elites. Second, the New Deal involved not a Polanyian rebalancing of market and state, nor did it represent a mere policy shift motivated by a changing balance of social power: Rather, the American state began to redefine the very nature of economic policy, aiming to adjust the infrastructure of its government apparatus to the systemic properties assumed by financial life since the late nineteenth century. The conception of economic policy that emerged in this configuration of political forces was a qualitatively new one that cannot be captured in terms of Keynesianism and laissez-faire liberalism as basic types of capitalist order. Third, the new configuration of interests shaped a new approach to economic and financial foreign policy that was oriented not so much toward confining capitalism within the regulatory frameworks of nation-states but rather toward the multilateral liberalization of trade and finance (Lacher 1999). These points will be taken up in turn.

THE SOCIAL FORCES UNDERLYING THE NEW DEAL

The New Deal program could count on the support of a significant part of the American business and financial establishment. The incorporation of American industry around the turn of the century had not only created the large, labor-intensive corporations predominantly oriented toward the domestic market that formed the core of the System of 1896, but also laid the foundations for more capital-intensive forms of investment. Especially World War I gave a boost to the growth of more technologically advanced American corporations. Europe's high tariffs furnished a major incentive to establish overseas subsidiaries, and because of their technologically advanced nature those companies were in a better position to pursue foreign investments. During the 1920s, foreign direct investment by American corporations in Europe increased substantially (Wilkins 1974; Lipsey 1988). Multinational corporations often found themselves at the margins of the existing structures of financial intermediation, and this offered opportunities for investment bankers whose relations to the J. P. Morgan–dominated structures of the Money Trust had remained instrumental and whose affinity with the Republican Party had remained tenuous (Ferguson 1981).

Multinational interests advocated lower tariffs, open world markets, and a more forgiving attitude toward Europe's war debts (Ferguson 1981: 337). But such demands were ignored by the Republican administrations of the 1920s and the result was a disjunction between the growing economic power commanded by the multinational interests in American capital and the political influence they wielded (Frieden 1988). Republican domestic policies were considered equally troublesome: While the relatively gentle methods of Progressive reform increasingly gave way to a repressive clampdown on labor, the approach to the regulation of competition in industry and finance was very passive, limited to the encouragement of business efforts at voluntary regulation. As the Depression deepened, the limits of such voluntarism became increasingly apparent and led to calls for a more comprehensive program of state regulation and enforcement (Vittoz 1987). Industrialists with multinational interests stood much to gain from an end to a depression that had originated in the United States but was rapidly spreading around the globe. They could also afford to be more favorably disposed to such a program of massive state intervention because their capital-intensive nature allowed for a conception of capital's relation with workers that stressed not only their costs but also their role as consumers. Fordism as a mode of production went together very well with the Progressive emphasis on the reform of state and social institutions oriented toward the citizen-as-consumer (Aglietta 1979). The Republican reluctance to consider implementing a comprehensive program for state-led recovery led many of these industrialists to shift their allegiance to the Democrats (Ferguson 1984; Cox and Skidmore-Hess 1999).

Similar developments can be found in the financial sphere. This is not to detract from the extent to which the New Deal's financial legislation was motivated by widespread animosity toward financiers: Politicians and the public had wasted no time in pinning the blame for the crisis on the financial establishment. Just as the Federal Reserve Act had been heavily influenced by the way in which public opinion was shaped by the investigations of the Pujo Committee, the New Deal legislation was passed against the background of the investigation of the Pecora Commission, which uncovered a range of shady financial practices and connections (notably between the FRBNY and private investment bankers) (Carosso 1970; Weldin 2002: 11). This was the context in which elites waged their struggles. Investment houses such as Kuhn, Loeb & Co. saw the popular hostility toward the Money Trust as an opportunity to loosen Morgan's grip on American finance. These bankers were more alert to new business opportunities and less averse to joining commercial banks in exploiting the opportunities associated with the expansion of "low finance" during the 1920s (Perkins 1999). To them, the situation represented a way to dissolve the Morgan-owned glue that held together existing financial networks and so to open up the field to new players (Ferguson 1981). In the Democratic Party, they were able to strike up an unlikely alliance with Western banks.

A NEW CONCEPTION OF ECONOMIC POLICY

However, as Panitch and Gindin (2005) argue, there is some danger in overemphasizing the impact of interelite conflicts on the reconstitution of the American state during the New Deal. This process was not a matter of multinational elements in American capital gaining control of the existing apparatuses of the American state in an instrumental way but was about the ways in which they facilitated and promoted a shift in the structural basis, conceptual orientation and practical operation of economic policy. The New Deal is often interpreted as an example of a "double movement," the phase in which a market economy run amok is reembedded in and contained social and political institutions. But, as we saw in Chapter 5, the development of American finance during the early twentieth century cannot be accurately grasped in terms of laissez-faire or market disembedding; instead, it was driven by the incorporation of ever wider swathes of social life into networks of financial institutions and norms. The New Deal did not reverse this process but put in place the conditions for its further deepening. Policy makers recognized that the growing connectivity of socioeconomic life was not just responsible for intense contradictions but also opened up new possibilities for public policy. The significance of the New Deal lies in this (partial) realization of the potential for infrastructural power. Its public policy innovations represent more novelty than can be captured through the Polanyian emphasis on the periodically recurring advances of the market and society's reaction to it. The New Deal involved not a quantitative rebalancing of the logics of state and market but rather a qualitative transformation of the uses of public authority.

The Keynesian notion that aggregate demand cannot be taken for granted presupposes a modern, "macro" conception of the economy as more than the sum of individual acts of production and exchange. That is, it presupposes an appreciation of capitalism's systemic properties. One of the traditional rationales behind reflation was classically populist: Rising prices worked to the advantage of debtors. But what developed in the context of the Great Depression was the notion that inflationary policies did not merely redistribute income from one class or region to another but could also positively affect aggregate macroeconomic indicators. The new conception of economic policy saw the benefits of reflation as potentially redounding not only to indebted farmers but to the American economy as a whole.

The New Deal was an expression of the new idea that a national economy could be regulated by adjusting some of its key institutional parameters through state intervention. Before the early twentieth century, national economies just did not exhibit a sufficient degree of uniformity and predictability or enough systemic properties to give rise to the idea that such institutional regulation was possible (Mitchell 2005).[1] Of course, regulation existed before the 20th century. But in more traditional societies, political regulation was itself directly constitutive of the economic activity in question. The birth of Keynesian regulation in the mid-twentieth century was different in the sense that it respected the limits imposed on state intervention by the state's constitutional form – that is, the limitation of the reach of the state by the demarcation of a private sphere of noninterference (what we have come to think of as the "economy") (De Brunhoff 1978). Although the state has only a limited number of points of entry into the economy available for the purpose of intervention, the growth of structural power due to the proliferation of socioeconomic institutions means that those points of entry have become highly leveraged.

---

[1] As Hudson (2003: 118) points out, the idea of a national economy that was not subject to mob rule deliberately pursuing inflationary policies was so far removed from traditional common sense that the Europeans were genuinely befuddled as to why the Roosevelt administration was willing to wreck the London Economic Conference in 1933 so as to be able to persist in its inflationary policies. Interestingly, it was Keynes (whose *General Theory*, first published in 1936, would become the most well-known articulation of these new economic conceptions) who defended Roosevelt's decision to take the dollar off gold and his refusal to stabilize the exchange rate of the dollar (Hudson 2003: 109).

THE NEW DEAL REORGANIZATION OF THE AMERICAN FINANCIAL SYSTEM

For all the opposition that the New Deal's labor legislation elicited from capitalists, in the financial sphere the New Deal institutions were all along oriented more toward promoting than reducing the working classes' integration into and dependence on the financial system. They sought to restore popular faith in the financial system by compartmentalizing it (addressing, in particular, the overly cozy relations between banks, financial markets, and the FRBNY seen to be at the root of instability [Burns 1974]), fortifying sectors with populist appeal (such as the market for mortgages, with its strong links to the American dream) and through policies favorable to pension funds and insurance companies. Compared to the hopes for hegemonic integration put on the mechanisms of private credit, the extent of statist redistribution was very limited – and, moreover, came under attack during the second half of the 1930s (Brinkley 1995) and World War II (Waddell 2001). Such restructuring was accompanied by the strengthening of the public oversight of each of the segments and the system as a whole. This reflected a conception of enhanced state capacity that laid the foundation for the emergence of modern forms of monetary management (Greider 1987: 313).

The Glass-Steagall Act separated commercial banking and investment banking: Banks were to choose between the business of taking deposits and making loans or the dealing in long-term capital (Benston 1989), preventing institutions holding the public's deposits from using those funds to speculate on securities. Subsequent legislation created a regulatory body for the securities markets – the Securities and Exchange Commission (SEC) – that was to prevent the reemergence of the kind of practices brought to light by the Pecora hearings (Wang 2005). To reduce competition among commercial banks, they were prohibited from paying interest on demand deposits, and the Federal Reserve was authorized to set maximum rates for other kinds of deposits (the so-called Regulation Q) (Degen 1987: 75–6). Although the activities of commercial banks were curtailed in important ways, the New Deal reforms also offered them some significant advantages: The segmentation of the financial system reduced competition among financial intermediaries, and the interest rate ceilings ensured a steady supply of cheap funds (Mason 1997).

The Federal Deposit Insurance Corporation (FDIC) was established, which guaranteed the deposits held with Federal Reserve member banks (Golembe 1960). This guarantee did much to restore popular confidence in the banking system and to remove the rationale behind bank runs (Degen 1987: 74): After the introduction of deposit insurance, only a few banks every year would fail, compared to hundreds every year before (and thousands during the period 1929–33). In this way, deposit insurance also reduced banks' concern with liquidity and facilitated their pursuit of risky investment strategies. In particular, it removed commercial banks' residual concerns about the expansion of consumer lending (Calder 1999: 283). Federal deposit insurance, however, was a blessing not only for the banks and the public, but equally for the Federal Reserve. During the 1920s, the latter's ability to pursue a more active financial policy had been hampered by its constitution as a bankers' bank, functioning as a lender of last resort. The foundation of the FDIC had the effect of partly untying the Federal Reserve's hands, diminishing its responsibility for the lender-of-last-resort function and allowing it to focus more deliberately on the regulation of credit creation. To that end, the Federal Reserve was given new powers, including full discretionary control over reserve requirements, lending policies, and associated eligibility requirements. These powers were not, however, handed over to an unreformed Federal Reserve System: Policy control was largely taken away from the Reserve Banks and centralized in the Board (located in Washington) (Bach 1971; Woolley 1984; Greider 1987: 312).

But the New Deal reforms also promoted developments that over time would complicate the Federal Reserve's efforts to expand its authority over the financial system. Thrifts – institutions taking savings deposits and making mortgage loans – had been growing over the previous decades (Mason 2004), and the aftermath of the crisis provided populist forces with an opportunity to make them more competitive vis-à-vis the commercial banks and financial markets (Johnson 1998; Hoffmann 2001). A structure of federally chartered thrifts (the Federal Home Loan Bank System) was established (Jackson 1985), and this sector was given "a range of direct and indirect subsidies, including deposit insurance, guaranteed deductible mortgages, public housing programs, and urban renewal schemes" (Johnson 1998: 120). Several years later, the government founded the Federal National Mortgage Association (commonly known as Fannie Mae) and charged it with the task of creating a secondary market for home mortgages by employing securitization procedures, that is, by buying mortgages from banks and thrifts and pooling them to create tradable mortgage-backed securities (Vidger 1961; Stanton 2002). The New Deal period also laid the foundations for the growth of institutional investors such as insurance companies and pension funds. The growth of federal employment in the wake of the New Deal meant a huge boost for pension funds (Clark, Craig, and Wilson 2003), and private pension schemes and health insurance companies expanded as a result of labor legislation (Thomasson 2002). These developments created a basis for the growth of financial processes outside the purview of Federal Reserve authority (Johnson 1998: 120).

THE TRANSFORMATION OF FOREIGN FINANCIAL POLICY

The transformation of the policy templates of the U.S. state also had important implications for foreign policy. The System of 1896 had been characterized by strong mercantilist sentiments, which tended to view the international market economy as a zero-sum game where national interests were best defended by keeping other countries uncompetitive. The transition to a qualitatively new conception of the aims and purposes of economic policy meant that the expansion of the domestic and the international economy came to be seen as compatible and even mutually reinforcing. Connections between American capital and the international economy were no longer seen as primarily a threat to the sovereignty of the American state, and an awareness emerged that such linkages could in fact increase the leverage and capacities of American actors and policy makers. Thus, a very different approach to foreign economic policy emerged, based on multilateral free trade and reciprocal tariff reduction.

But of course this new approach to foreign policy emerged only gradually. The global situation of the 1930s was less than auspicious for the conscientious application of such liberal-internationalist principles, and domestic considerations took precedence. Initially, the Roosevelt administration was so consumed with the task of domestic crisis management that it eagerly exploited the easiest ways to quickly enhance its leeway to pursue inflationary policies at home. It refused to reschedule the debts, left the tariffs in place, and devalued the dollar. Although this is often seen as a continuation of America's interwar isolationism, "to Roosevelt it seemed simply to be an announcement of how America was going about its own economic recovery" (Hudson 2003: 109). In other words, it is important to appreciate the way in which Democratic policies differed from those of the Republican administrations of the 1920s. The early policies of the Roosevelt administration were not primarily motivated by a desire to squeeze the European economy and a conservative attitude toward America's involvement in the world but rather aimed to enlarge the scope for activist domestic policies designed to pull the

U.S. economy out of the Great Depression. The Roosevelt administration was not opposed to European recovery and realized that, in time, such might even assist the American recovery; the gravity of the situation of the moment nevertheless demanded an immediate domestic reflation and a degree of domestic policy autonomy that, given the circumstances, could not but come at the expense of European economies.

Thus, as Europe slowly descended into protectionism and nationalism, the United States, having provided itself with the necessary domestic policy leeway, took a rather different turn. It was on the basis of a devalued dollar that the United States could set about to fundamentally revise its orientation toward the use of tariffs (Mikesell 1954). The Trade Agreements Act of 1934 lowered U.S. tariffs and established a new set of principles for the multilateral lowering of trade barriers (Arrighi 1994: 71; Hudson 2003: 112). Due to the internal transformation of the American state, American policy makers broadened their perspective on the gains it could derive from the international economy. The novel principles of multilateral free trade and reciprocal tariff concessions would become central to U.S. foreign policy during the following decades.

CONCLUSION

The New Deal was an important turning point with regard to the composition and orientation of the American state. It laid the institutional basis for the growth of American finance through the integration of the American population into the financial system at the same time as it expressed a new awareness of the potential for institutional regulation. That is, the New Deal introduced an inchoate yet crucially important understanding that economic and financial processes had come to exhibit sufficient systemic properties as to render them amenable to new forms of institutional steering. In this sense, New Deal policy making reflected a further development of the Progressive awareness of the potentially symbiotic relationship between capitalist expansion and regulatory capacity. It expressed a vision of integral statehood through the creation of organic linkages between formal state institutions and the socioeconomic institutions governing everyday economic dynamics. Such reconfiguration ensured that the expansion of American finance would proceed in a much more stable fashion during the next decades. Yet a fuller materialization of the vision of the American state's infrastructural capacity would take considerable time: Much of post–World War II development needs to be understood precisely in terms of the tensions between an expanding domestic financial system and the New Deal regulatory framework. In other words, the same constellation of institutions that was responsible for the continued expansion of structural power in American finance did a great deal to complicate the state's infrastructural capacity to steer and regulate those financial relations. Similar tensions would beset the state's foreign policy orientation. Although the new conception of foreign policy saw connections between American capital and the international economy as potentially advancing the structural capacity and autonomy of the American state, the pressures on the U.S.'s balance of payments produced by the globalization of American capital would still do much to trouble the minds of policy makers.

8

Contradictions of the Dollar

INTRODUCTION

IPE scholars have often regarded the post–World War II Bretton Woods system as the height of American power in international finance (Block 1977; Ruggie 1982; Gilpin 1987; Cerny 1993a, 1993b). According to this perspective, after the disastrous events of the interwar period the United States adopted a more enlightened understanding of its national interest and emerged as a hegemonic power – not only able but also willing to provide the international markets with stabilizing institutional foundations. American policies, it is argued, ensured the reproduction of a liberal international economy by embedding it in regulatory institutions: The "embedded liberal" structures of the Bretton Woods system allowed liberal economic relations to develop while at the same time shielding countries from the vagaries of unregulated international capital movements. Similarly, the decline of Bretton Woods and the accelerating expansion of international financial markets have often been seen as marking the end of American financial hegemony. More recent strands in IPE have begun to reconsider this picture of post–World War II order by relativizing the coherence of Bretton Woods and presenting a more nuanced analysis of hegemonic decline (Strange 1986; Walter 1993; Helleiner 1994; Germain 1997). But they have not broken with the idea that the transition from embedded liberalism to disembedded markets holds the key to understanding financial developments from World War II to the present day.

This chapter begins the task of advancing an interpretation of the post–World War II development of American finance that does not rely on these Polanyian categories. The concept of "embedded liberalism" has little purchase on some key developments during the early post–World War II period: Liberalism was not so much embedded as nonexistent, and the key problem was not how to constrain but how to revive international finance. As during the interwar period, America's international financial power remained highly dependent on direct political authority, supported by traditional channels of foreign policy and diplomacy: It was buttressed by an infrastructure of private credit relations only to a very limited extent. The weakness of European economies greatly limited the extent of financial liberalization during the late 1940s and 1950s and in this context it was almost by default that New York became the main international financial center and the dollar the new reserve currency. The United States made full use of the dollar's special status, spending freely on national security and foreign aid, and by the late 1950s this had resulted in the growth of an offshore pool of American dollars that put pressure on the international position of the dollar. When an international payments system based on currency convertibility was finally restored in 1958, this only added to such pressure. Because America's seigniorage privileges were not organically embedded in mechanisms of private international finance, the "dollar overhang" created considerable problems for the American state. The Democratic administrations of the 1960s tried to manage the problem by limiting capital outflows but were largely unsuccessful in doing so.

But at the end of the decade, the Nixon administration took a rather different approach to the dollar overhang and allowed the balance of payments deficit to grow unchecked. This policy turn and the subsequent abandonment of Bretton Woods have often been interpreted as an admission of defeat, signaling the decline of America's financial hegemony. More recent work has pointed out that although these developments sealed the fate of Bretton Woods, they also laid the basis for the growth of more indirect forms of U.S. financial power. However, such approaches typically do not specify exactly what had changed in the institutional parameters of financial expansion that now permitted the Nixon administration to stop worrying so much about the growth of American indebtedness. Most IPE approaches, by reasoning in terms of the interacting but nonetheless distinct forces of global markets and American state power, fail to do justice to the ways in which during the 1960s the expansionary dynamics of American finance had begun to externalize and to shape global finance to its core. As the institutional forms of American finance became networked to the strategies of a wide range of global actors, the state's international capacity acquired substantial structural dimensions. Only an approach that emphasizes this "inside-out" dynamic (Panitch 1994, 1996) enables us to construe the organic linkages between the American state and global finance that permitted Nixon's policy turn. This chapter outlines the contradictions that emerged during the 1960s; the next chapters trace the processes whereby the homegrown expansion of American finance began to take on external dimensions, resulting in the construction of a transnational infrastructure of dollar-centered credit relations.

BRETTON WOODS

From the start of World War II, the European Allies were dependent on U.S. funds and resources (Woods 1990). The Roosevelt administration was not interested in saddling Europe with debts that far exceeded its capacity to pay and were bound to cripple Europe's postwar reconstruction efforts and instead used the war debts as a point of leverage, demanding European commitments to American plans for a postwar system of multilateral trade and payments (Kolko 1968: 249–50; Hudson 2003: 121–2). American pressure for moves toward multilateralism was targeted at the British system of Imperial Preference, formally established at the Ottawa Conference in 1932 and based on sterling credits. During the late 1930s, the sterling bloc had done much to sustain Britain's position in the world economy, putting a major constraint on the growth of American exports (Kolko 1968: 246). Britain's own plan for the postwar international financial system envisaged a clearing union operating on the basis of a new international currency (the "bancor") that would take the place of gold (Penrose 1953: 42; Black 1991). In this way, Britain hoped to transform its existing debts into much more general debts to the international community that no country would have a clear incentive to demand repayment on (Hudson 2003: 146), so permitting it to avoid pressures to abolish its exchange and import controls. The international financial fund as pictured by the Americans would not be able to create a new source of international liquidity and would make loans only to countries taking measures to ensure that they would be able to earn sufficient foreign exchange to repay the loans. This entailed an in built pressure for the liberalization of national policies preventing countries from returning to the protectionist policies of the 1930s.

To be sure, the United States recognized that there existed a potential conflict between, on the one hand, the ability of European countries to reconstruct their economies and to participate in a system of international trade and, on the other hand, the convertibility of European currencies that American financiers regarded as the precondition for a strong position of the dollar and the growth of New York as an international financial centre. American policy makers envisaged postwar institutions not as instruments to cajole European countries into a premature process of liberalization but as offering considerable protection from the discipline and volatility of international finance. Early plans considered the extensive use of controls to limit destabilizing flows of speculative capital. But although this found considerable support among corporate elites (Helleiner 1994: 43–4), New York bankers saw little in a world of inconvertible currencies and administratively controlled financial flows, and they argued that capital controls should be strictly temporary measures (Helleiner 1994: 39). The final Bretton Woods agreement envisaged a significant but limited and temporary role for controls.

The outcome of the Bretton Woods negotiations of 1944 thus reflected both the highly uneven power relations that marked the international system and the specific way in which the reconstituted American state had come to define the national interest. The Bretton Woods institutions – the International Monetary Fund (IMF) and the International Bank for Reconstruction and Development (later the World Bank) – were dedicated to the promotion of a multilateral system of convertible currencies, elimination of exchange controls, reduction of tariffs, and growth of world trade and private foreign investment (Kolko 1968: 257). The international monetary system functioned on the basis of fixed exchange rates (currencies were pegged to the dollar, which was the only currency convertible into gold), both because of a general concern about the instability associated with floating exchange rates but also to prevent the competitive currency devaluations that European countries would be tempted to use to compensate for their lack of competitiveness vis-à-vis the American economy. The IMF was responsible for coming to the aid of countries experiencing temporary balance of payments difficulties and foreign currency shortages. Essentially, these facilities for the provision of international liquidity somewhat loosened the discipline of gold and, by thus counteracting some of the effects of the concentration of gold in American hands, ensured its preservation as the international standard of value (Hudson 2003: 150).

FROM MARSHALL AID TO CONVERTIBILITY

Investment bankers, with their political influence restored under the Truman administration, seized on Europe's need for dollars to advance their interests, offering Britain a large loan in exchange for an accelerated return to convertibility (Helleiner 1994: 52; Burnham 2003: 7). However, by the time Britain made sterling convertible in 1947, much of the proceeds of the loan had already returned to the United States. Little had changed in the structural position of European countries, and they still experienced an acute shortage of dollars (Bloch 1953). Quickly becoming subject to a drain on its reserves and speculative attacks on sterling, Britain was forced to restore import and exchange controls after only a few weeks. European financial relations reverted to bilateral currency arrangements and discriminatory trading practices, and Britain moved to tighten its relation with the sterling bloc (Mikesell 1954; Strange 1971). American financial elites had overplayed their hand, and the attempt to force Britain to resume convertibility was called off for the time being (Langley 2002: 72).

The 1947 crisis drove home the point that convertibility only stood a chance if European payments balances were in fundamentally better shape. The crisis had thrown into sharp relief Europe's economic fragility and the fact that the dollar shortage was a structural constraint on the ability of Europe to buy American goods. The multinational interests in American industry focused attention on putting in place the conditions for Europe's recovery and began to advocate a comprehensive program of American aid for Europe. Such more active American engagement in the rebuilding of Europe was a matter of considerable contention, as isolationist sentiments still held strong sway. But the idea of America's security and way of life being threatened by the evil of Soviet Communism won them over to the necessity of European reconstruction (Williams 1959; Cox and Skidmore-Hess 1999): Financial aid for Europe came to be viewed not only as a means of encouraging European economic recovery and promoting its ability to buy American exports, but also as instrumental in containing the spread of Soviet Communism and preventing the radicalization of Western European labor movements (Hogan 1987). It was under these conditions that the Marshall Aid program was conceived and implemented.

However, now that the United States had relented with regard to the question of multilateral convertibility, there was a clear danger that American aid would end up facilitating Europe's efforts to rebuild its economy on the basis of bilateral trade and restrictive payments arrangements. It was in light of this concern that the U.S. government made its financial assistance conditional on increased European cooperation (Germain 1997: 83–4), which it hoped would lay a basis for a partial (intra-European) kind of multilateralism that could later on, once Europe was back on its feet, be smoothly integrated into a wider, global multilateral payments system controlled by the United States (Burnham 1990: 10). The European Payments Union (EPU) created an intra-European clearing system operated by European central banks (Kaplan and Schleiminger 1989). But it ended up functioning as essentially a soft currency bloc that gave European governments considerable leeway from the disciplinary effects of international financial flows (Battilossi 2002a: 9), while Britain remained aloof altogether and reinforced its relations with the sterling area (Burnham 1990: 12). New York financiers continued to press for the resumption of convertibility, but they made little headway as economic reconstruction and the ability of European governments to pursue expansionary policies had risen to the top of the agenda. For the next years, the Americans would not put any significant pressure on European countries to resume convertibility.

Thus, during most of the period 1944–58, Bretton Woods was effectively suspended (Forbord 1980). Bilateral trade and currency arrangements proliferated during the late 1940s and 1950s, becoming even more dominant than during the interwar period (Nordyke 1976; Kaplan and Schleiminger 1989: 7; Walter 1993: 161). Throughout the 1950s "international financial relations remained largely inter-governmental and politically motivated" (Battilossi 2002a: 8), and it was highly discretionary U.S. government policies that functioned to assuage the key contradiction of international finance during the 1940s and 1950s – the dollar shortage – that the Bretton Woods institutions were unable to solve (Walter 1993: 157). Private international finance was not embedded but really did not exist in the way we know it today. This meant that America's international financial power during the 1940s and 1950s did not operate through a liberal system of multilateral payments but was intensely reliant on more direct modalities of state power. The period was marked by a discrepancy between America's overwhelming political power on the one hand and the limits on the growth of U.S.-centered private credit relations on the other (Ingham 1994). American finance did not go abroad or otherwise assume crucial international functions. World War II had virtually destroyed the foreign branch networks of American banks and even by the late 1950s the number of foreign American branches remained very limited. Financial relations with European countries were limited to correspondent banking based on conservative, pre–World War I methods of bill financing (Zweig 1995: 86). Despite the changes in international trade and finance wrought by the war, the United States was nothing like an international entrepot or a clearing center; by 1950, for instance, the United States suffered a

Contradictions of the Dollar

sizeable deficit on financial and commercial services (Ingham 1994: 41). The discount market for bills of exchange (the size of which gives a good indication of the role banks play in the financing of foreign trade) failed to recover to any significant extent (Stern 1951: 51).

These observations should not, however, lead us to downplay the importance of the early post–World War II period for the construction of U.S. financial power. It was crucial in two ways. First, the organizational frameworks of European states became significantly imbricated with the reproduction of U.S. power (Panitch 2000; Gowan 2002). This political insertion of European states into an international order dominated by the United States, while not providing the American state with the leverage and capacities it might have derived from a central position in a liberal infrastructure of multilateral payments and transnationalized intermediation, meant that it was nonetheless capable of setting many of the institutional parameters that would shape post–World War II financial expansion. Second, although the global role of American banks remained limited and "from the late 1940s through the 1960s ... the United States exercised no *entrepôt* functions of global significance," it was nonetheless "the 'container' of a self-centered, largely self-sufficient, continent-sized economy" (Silver and Arrighi 2003: 339). American finance at home was far from repressed and was in fact experiencing a period of sustained expansion, characterized by the innovation of financial techniques, growing depth and liquidity of financial markets, and penetration of financial forms and relations into new layers of social life. When, during the 1960s, these expansionary dynamics could no longer be contained within the domestic institutional framework, they began to assume external dimensions and so drove the expansion of global finance. We will examine the first development and the contradictions for the American state that it gave rise to in the rest of this chapter; the domestic expansion of American finance will be the focus of the next chapter. In Chapter 10, the two stories will be joined to present an account of the contradictory construction of American financial power during the post–World War II period.

CONTRADICTIONS OF THE DOLLAR

Even in 1958, Nordyke could write that "[t]he centralization at New York has progressed most in terms of the international monetary reserves held there by foreign entities; it has progressed least in terms of the financing by institutions there of trade which is neither United States exports nor imports" (1976 [1958]: 247). During the early 1950s, the continued significance of sterling in the financing of international trade (Dam 1982: 182; Burnham 2003: 2), in combination with restrictions on speculative transactions, put limits on the dollar's role as a private transactions currency (Nadler, Heller, and Shipman 1955: 302). But New York nevertheless became the main international financial center almost by default (Battilossi 2002a: 10): Because European governments imposed a range of constraints on the issue of foreign securities and the export of capital, New York was the only place where foreigners could issue bonds.

The dollar quickly became the main reserve currency. Foreign, especially European central banks accumulated large amounts of dollar assets (Mikesell and Furth 1974; Dam 1982: 182). The system of fixed exchange rates made it more necessary than ever for countries to hold reserves because they needed to be able to intervene in foreign exchange markets to maintain the par value of their currency. Gold had traditionally been the most obvious reserve asset, but European central banks held large amounts of dollar assets – not only because of American suasion but also because U.S. Treasury bills, the short-term dollar assets in which the bulk of dollar reserves was held, had become highly liquid assets.[1] In part, this was a consequence of the Federal Reserve's support of the Treasury's debt funding policies: To keep the rate on Treasury bills low, the Federal Reserve pegged the market for government securities by declaring its willingness to buy any quantity of bills at a fixed price, rendering them almost perfectly liquid (but, unlike gold, they still yielded interest) (Klopstock 1965; Knipe 1965). Thus, what was crucial to the rise of the dollar as a reserve currency was the development of an open market in short-term U.S. government debt large enough to absorb the demand from a number of foreign central banks (Scott 1965). In addition, for a currency to develop into an international reserve currency it requires a stable rate of exchange (Gilbert 1985). In this regard, the dollar possessed a major advantage over sterling during the early postwar period, which was continuously surrounded by expectations of devaluation due to Britain's payment deficits.

The dollar's special status bestowed seigniorage privileges on the United States, allowing it to spend on such things as national security and foreign aid without any immediate constraints (Pauls 1990: 891;

[1] "From 1949 to 1958, world reserves grew from US$45.6 bn. to US$57.3 bn. Gold's share declined from 73.5% to 65.3%; the foreign exchange component (virtually only US dollar) went up from 22.8% to 30%. In 1958 the USA had 39.2% of total world reserves, vis-à-vis 60.8% of the rest of the world; shares were 56.5% and 43.5%, respectively in 1949" (Battilossi 2002a: 31 n44, drawing on Argy 1981: 33–4).

Barkin 2003: 139). But America's ability to shift the burden of adjustment onto other countries was far from perfect: The exploitation of the dollar's privileged position came to undermine its ability to function as the source of international liquidity. From the late 1950s, capital outflows began to outstrip the trade surplus (causing the American balance of payments to turn negative), and by the early 1960s the dollar shortage had been transformed into a dollar glut, fueling the growth of an offshore pool of American dollars (the Eurodollar market) outside the institutional structures of Bretton Woods. The pressure on the dollar thus created was magnified by the return to currency convertibility in 1958. The amount of dollars in circulation in relation to America's gold reserves caused foreigners to question the credibility of America's commitment to convertibility. Thus, the birth of the "real" Bretton Woods system and the reemergence of private international finance had the effect of undermining the position of the dollar (Odell 1982; Helleiner 1994: 84–5).

Concerns regarding the stability of the dollar and its ability to function as the fulcrum of the international monetary system were widespread by the early 1960s, and other countries began to campaign for reform of the international monetary system (Solomon 1982; Rae 2003: 52–3). Robert Triffin (1961) famously pointed out that there was an inherent conflict between the dollar's role as a national currency and its role as the primary source of international liquidity: The more international liquidity was created, the higher the liabilities of the United States and the lower the confidence in the latter's ability to guarantee the convertibility of dollars into gold. This became the central issue of international finance during the 1960s, and the IMF and World Bank, which had not been able to play much of a role in addressing the dollar shortage of the pre-convertibility era, now found that the new problems entirely overwhelmed their capacities. It was the Treasury, the agency principally responsible for the external position of the United States and for the status of the dollar, that now emerged as a central player in international finance (Sarai 2008). Triffin's own plan required the United States to relinquish its role as the world's banker and envisaged the creation of an international fund responsible for the management of world liquidity. But the U.S. Treasury was adamantly opposed to the creation of a new source of international liquidity or any other measure that might fundamentally jeopardize the position of the dollar (Odell 1982: 104–5).

Treasury officials favored domestic adjustment through deflationary policies (Odell 1982: 104–6), but this was not an option for the Democratic administrations of the 1960s (Calleo 1982). Thus, American policy makers tried to forestall the necessity of such fundamental changes through a range of measures. The introduction in 1961 by the Kennedy administration of Operation Twist sought to "twist" the structure of interest rates so that long-term rates would remain low and stimulate the domestic economy while short-term rates would rise and make Treasury bills more attractive to foreigners. Other solutions involved looking for "ways in which the strength of other currencies could be mobilized to give peripheral support to the dollar" and "ways of enlisting some of the other leading currencies in various short-term arrangements" (Robert Roosa, quoted in Odell 1982: 102).[2] As the decade progressed, it became clear that the U.S. payments position failed to improve. Gold outflows accelerated, in part because the French, who took great offense at America's "exorbitant privilege," converted ever larger amounts of dollars into gold. More generally, European countries expressed growing reluctance to finance America's ever-growing balance of payments deficit (Conybeare 1988). The United States now turned to capital controls. The first measure was a tax on purchases of foreign securities designed to iron out interest differentials and so to discourage foreigners from borrowing in the United States and prevent gold outflows. The success of this program was limited, as the tax could easily be evaded through overseas affiliates. Other capital control programs sought to impose further restrictions on U.S. lending to foreigners as well as to overseas branches of American corporations.

The capital controls practically closed off the American credit market for foreign borrowers (Solomon 1982). This meant a setback for New York's growth as a financial center: Since the return to convertibility, American bankers had become more engaged in foreign lending and third-party trade financing, but the growth of New York-centered private credit relations now slowed (Langley 2002: 70). The controls did little, however, to reduce the outflows of capital associated with foreign direct investment by American companies. Of crucial importance in this regard was the Eurodollar market (Levich 1988), which was beyond the

---

[2] In response to speculative pressure on the dollar, in 1960 the Treasury initiated the creation of the so-called London Gold Pool: Several countries cooperated to supply gold to the London market and so keep its price down vis-à-vis the dollar. The next year, the German mark was revalued, adding further pressure on the dollar, and the United States responded by resuming "operations in foreign-exchange markets, selling marks forward in New York to try to hold the price down until the storm passed" (Odell 1982: 103). The Treasury even created what would come to be known as Roosa bonds, U.S. government bonds denominated in currencies other than the dollar.

immediate control of American monetary authorities and provided both foreign and American borrowers with easy access to dollar funds. Indeed, the availability of the Eurodollar market constituted a huge incentive for American multinational corporations to establish overseas branches. Thus, capital controls were relatively ineffective in addressing the ever-growing balance of payments deficit. Although they would be definitively eliminated only in 1974, policy makers had become aware of their futility by the late 1960s.

In this context, the Nixon administration shifted toward a policy of "benign neglect," which presaged its decision to abandon the Bretton Woods system altogether several years later. Traditionally the policy turn of the Nixon administration has been seen as an admission of weakness in the face of a growing dollar overhang and the growth of financial activity outside the structures of Bretton Woods. More recent accounts have emphasized that the reemergence of private international finance and the rise of the Eurodollar markets not only had the effect of undermining the U.S.-dominated institutions of the Bretton Woods order but also served to loosen some of the external financial constraints on the American state (Gowan 1999; Seabrooke 2001; Panitch and Gindin 2005). From such a perspective, the Nixon administration's policy turn appears less as an admission of weakness than as an attempt to exploit the opportunities presented by a particular pattern of power relations in global finance.

Nixon was no less bent on retaining domestic policy autonomy and the option of pursuing inflationary policies than the Democratic administrations of the 1960s had been (Beck 1984). But his administration had a greater sense of some of the power resources at America's disposal than its predecessors. That is, even if policy makers had only a dim awareness of the mechanisms at work, the Nixon administration realized that America's position in international finance was such that its growing balance of payments deficit (i.e., its debts to the rest of the world) was not exclusively America's own problem. The market for Eurodollars was no longer seen primarily as a threat to U.S. power but now appeared as a source of great seigniorage opportunities. The Nixon administration abandoned any pretensions that it might be interested in a cooperative repair of the Bretton Woods system on the basis of a more balanced organization of international liquidity and reserve functions, and its benign neglect policies allowed the balance of payments deficit and the dollar overhang to grow unchecked (Gavin 2004). From the late 1960s, the Treasury worried considerably less about capital outflows, and the capital control programs became increasingly irrelevant.

The following chapters will be devoted to tracing the social and institutional sources of the capacities that the American state found it could command. They will do so by examining the domestic development of American finance since the New Deal, zooming in on the financial innovations that emerged in the United States after World War II, were later exported to the Euromarkets, and became the basis for the subsequent expansion of private finance. In this way, we will trace the interaction between the growing depth of America's domestic financial markets and the outward proliferation of American financial techniques and credit relations.

CONCLUSION

This chapter has shown why the Bretton Woods period is more fruitfully understood as the construction phase than the pinnacle of American power in international finance (Panitch and Gindin 2005: 48). Until well after the war, the power of the American state, while overwhelming in terms of military might and diplomacy, was not harnessed by a system of private international finance. The networks of financial relations that made up the domestic financial system were growing apace and the post–New Deal state enjoyed considerable infrastructural capacity. But in international affairs the structural, organically embedded dimensions of American power remained limited. Moreover, the reprivatization of international finance that occurred after the return to convertibility contributed to the problems of managing the Bretton Woods system and was perceived as posing a threat to the role of the dollar and the position of the United States in the international financial system.

However, as the American state was consumed by attempts to preserve existing arrangements, processes were already in motion that gradually transformed the infrastructure of global finance. As we will see in the next chapters, the external proliferation of distinctly American financial relations and techniques served to enhance the status of the dollar and so steadily reduced its dependence on gold. In other words, the same developments that weakened the U.S. position when evaluated in traditional economic terms (such as the balance of payments deficit) also served to project U.S. structural power abroad and so laid the foundations for the growth of the American state's infrastructural capacities. American policy makers began to clue into aspects of their increased policy leverage by the end of the 1960s: They worried less about external constraints and began to discern possibilities for the abandonment of Bretton Woods. This growth of structural power was the result of how American finance had externalized and shaped the system of global private finance in its own image, and so we cannot hope to understand these processes by confining our focus to the international sphere. Instead, we need to return to the domestic development of American finance, taking up the story where we left it after the New Deal and tracing how processes of outward expansion emerged out of domestic dynamics.

9

The Domestic Expansion of American Finance

INTRODUCTION

If the idea of "embedded liberalism" fails to capture the nature of international finance during the early post–World War II period, it might be even less suitable as a means to conceptualize the domestic development of American finance. Far from being subordinated to the constraining capacities of regulatory institutions, American finance underwent a dynamic of dramatic expansion after the New Deal.[1] Although the segmentation of the financial system meant that investment bankers were unable to leverage their strategies by using "other people's money" (Brandeis 1967 [1914]) the industry's self-regulation under the auspices of the SEC ushered in a golden age of relationship banking. But an even more vigorous dynamic of expansion was to be found in the development of the commercial banking sector – propelled by industrial recovery, heavy government lending, and the progressive integration of ever more layers of the American population into the financial system. A world of opportunities was created by the ways New Deal policy makers had facilitated the expansion of mortgage and consumer lending to promote the growth of a well-disciplined public of citizen-consumers. Over the course of the post–World War II period, the American working classes would become ever more fully incorporated into the financial system, not only as investors and savers but also as borrowers and consumers.

But the growing network power of American finance would generate new contradictions: By the mid-1950s, after years of steady expansion

[1] During the five-year period between 1949 and 1954, total private debt increased almost three times faster than during the five years leading up to the Crash of 1929 (Grant 1992: 265).

Domestic Expansion

of the lending business, banks' ability to make loans was running up against some of the features of the New Deal's institutional matrix. Attempting to circumvent these regulatory restrictions, banks pursued a range of new strategies that had the effect of further transforming the basis of financial intermediation. The dynamics this set in motion and their interaction with the responses from monetary authorities will be examined in greater detail in Chapter 10, as they are crucial to our understanding of the subsequent development of American finance and must be the starting point for an analysis of the processes through which it globalized.

THE FEDERAL RESERVE SYSTEM AFTER THE NEW DEAL

The New Deal reorganization of the financial system had set the Federal Reserve System on a new path: It could no longer think of itself as a bankers' bank but was expected to use its powers to prevent economic downturns. In the context of recovery from the Depression, this meant facilitating expansionary fiscal policies (Wood 2005: 219), and for some time the Federal Reserve essentially came to function as an assistant to the Treasury. This was in part due to political pressure, but the Federal Reserve's activities became functional to the Treasury's objectives in a more organic way as well. The Crash had dealt a huge blow to the money market (it had practically destroyed the markets for call loans, bills of exchange, and commercial paper [Simmons 1951]) and as a result banks, unable to acquire assets, ended up with large amounts of cash liquidity (Lewis 1948; Ahearn 1961; Lipsey 1988). Consequently, the discount window fell into disuse (Anderson 1965), and emphasis shifted to open market operations, which were conducted in the market for government securities (Chandler 1971). As the Federal Reserve accumulated government securities, it acquired a stake in safeguarding the stability of this market and supporting the value of government debt (Anderson 1965: 84; Greider 1987: 314).

As the United States prepared for World War II, the Federal Reserve came to function fully as a facilitator of the Treasury's debt funding efforts (Bach 1971). Mindful of the role investment bankers had played during the interwar period, the Roosevelt administration was reluctant to rely exclusively on their services. As a result, the burden of financing the war fell to a large extent on the commercial banking system. The Federal Reserve used open market operations to keep the price of government securities at a minimum level and the rates low (Degen 1987: 103). Its orientation to supporting the Treasury's debt funding policies meant that it had little control over liquidity creation. For, to maintain the bonds' support price, the Federal Reserve had to be prepared to buy any amount of government securities offered at that price (Degen 1987: 104). The fact that banks could sell any amount of government securities at favorable rates meant that they became highly liquid assets. Because the Treasury was flooding the financial markets with government debt, the ability of banks to create credit was practically without limitation (Gaines 1962: 59).[2]

For commercial banks, the Federal Reserve System's enlistment in the Treasury's funding efforts was somewhat of a blessing, as loan demand had taken a huge hit during the Depression and recovered only partly during the late 1930s. Because the American state opted to finance the industrial production associated with war mobilization through a branch of the Reconstruction Finance Corporation, commercial and industrial lending remained very weak until after the war and would not make up a significant portion of banks' asset portfolios until the end of the 1940s. Consumer lending did considerably better: It was precisely the decline in national income during the Depression that had opened up opportunities in consumer credit. But even these developments were most significant in terms of how they reconfigured the institutional environment in which the extraordinary post–World War II expansion of consumer finance would take place. It was after the war that banks would put their extraordinarily high degree of liquidity to good use.

THE SECURITIES INDUSTRY AFTER THE NEW DEAL

While commercial banks functioned as administrators of low-yield but abundant government paper, the situation for investment banks was more complicated. Glass-Steagall had barred the former from acquiring certain kinds of assets but had cut the latter off from a key source of funds. Moreover, during the rest of the 1930s the amount of new corporate issues remained low: In the post-Crash climate, issuing stock just did not seem a very appealing proposition (Myers 1951b). During the war, corporate issues would decline even more dramatically due to the government's direct involvement in the financing of the bulk of wartime investment. The supply of state and municipal bonds would fall off drastically too, and the bulk of federal debt would be placed through the commercial banking system. To be sure, investment bankers had certainly not

---

[2] The credit of the Federal Reserve Banks increased almost tenfold during the period 1939–45 (Degen 1987: 105–6).

failed to notice that the New Deal system had barred commercial banks from competing for securities business (Knee 2007: 42; Morrison and Wilhelm 2007: 210). Although this restriction of competition brought little comfort as long as overall levels of business were low, it did hold out considerable promise (Mahoney 2001).

Meanwhile, investment bankers sought to make the most of the new situation and, returning to time-honored practices, applied themselves to the reorganization of their industry on a more cooperative basis. Of key importance in this process was the role of the SEC. The emergent awareness of the integral dimensions of the state was highly pronounced in the way the SEC extended its authority through the vesting of regulatory authority in the self-governing associations of the securities sector. From the start, the SEC declined to pursue a very activist role. Many policy makers felt that New Deal legislation had already effected such a sweeping transformation of the financial landscape that there was no need for the SEC to invoke the full range of its powers. A moderate course was in addition motivated by an awareness that Wall Street's cooperation was still vital to the government's ability to pursue the kind of expansionary fiscal policies deemed necessary to economic recovery and that attempts to further squeeze the securities industry might well prove counterproductive (Seligman 2003: 103). Thus, the SEC quickly came to conceive of its own role as one of "policing" the securities industry, and it focused its efforts on the enforcement of disclosure requirements (Wang 2005). Pragmatic cooperation with Wall Street soon acquired an additional rationale: It came to be seen as "a means to enhance the agency's regulatory reach ... By giving the industry a role in oversight and enforcement, the SEC could oversee a much broader regulatory effort" (Khademian 1992: 39–40). On that basis, the SEC managed to considerably expand its reach. Often the threat of SEC regulation was sufficient to prompt self-regulation by an industry organization (e.g., an exchange or an association of brokers) (Seligman 2003).

Real challenges to the securities industry came from other directions. In 1937, Congress had established a committee to investigate the securities industry. Of particular concern was the question of competitive bidding. The war prevented any immediate action, so it was took until 1947 for the Justice Department to announce a suit against seventeen of the largest investment banks, charging them with having "entered into a combination, conspiracy and agreement to restrain and monopolize the securities business of the United States" (quoted in Carosso 1970: 463). The trial, lasting from 1950 to 1953, took place in a substantially altered political climate (radical New Deal sentiments had waned and anticommunism was on the rise) and came to revolve around the evidence for a conspiracy – a much stricter criterion than had been used by the Pujo and Pecora investigations, which were concerned not so much with bankers' intentions as with actual practices and structures. Acquittal represented a major victory for the investment banks, giving public license to a highly concentrated industry structure[3] that would remain in place until the 1960s[4] (Carosso 1970: 451; Hayes, Spence, and Marks 1983).

Although investment bankers were now less central figures than they had been in the late nineteenth and early twentieth centuries, they did well for themselves. The decade of the 1950s was marked by the steady (if uneventful) growth of corporate issues but especially of municipal and state bonds. As the only open financial center, New York attracted most of the foreign securities business, but this nonetheless was small in comparison to the volume of domestic American issues (i.e., $4 billion vs. $126.5 billion [Battilossi 2002a: 12–3]). Furthermore, the rise of institutional investors also gave a boost to the securities sector (Schmidt and Stockwell 1952). Total trading volume increased steadily throughout the 1950s and 1960s (Geisst 1990: 27; Khademian 1992: 60). Banks with a strong retail orientation, like Merrill Lynch, took advantage of this growth by expanding their sales and trading operations (Morrison and Wilhelm 2007: 233). This became the golden age of relationship banking (Knee 2007), when private banks were engaged in the preparation of initial public offerings and the brokering of securities deals, which required considerable business acumen and networking ability but demanded little in the way of technical skills. Investment firms could develop these capacities while being shielded from the competition from commercial banks and while being actively involved in the authoring of their industry's regulatory regimes.

THE EXPANSION OF COMMERCIAL BANKING AFTER WORLD WAR II

The dynamic of expansion that holds most significance for our understanding of the subsequent course of American and international finance

---

[3] "In 1939, ... the top fifteen investment houses managed 90 percent of all registered, publicly offered issues; in 1948 their share of the business had been cut to 81 percent. This decline, however, did not apply to the top three firms in the group. They actually increased the amount of their managements, from 41 percent in 1939 to 56 percent in 1948. Nor did the membership of the group change significantly" (Carosso 1970: 451).
[4] "In an extensive study of the investment banking business published in 1963, the SEC estimated that about 5 percent of the industry's firms grossed 60 percent of the income generated by the securities business as a whole" (Geisst 1990: 35).

Domestic Expansion

was to be found in the commercial banking sector. Until the late 1940s, commercial banks had

> operated according to what was only half-jokingly referred to as the "three-six-three rule: borrow at three, lend to the Federal Reserve at six, and get to the golf course at three." The National City Bank of the mid-1940s was less a bank than a bond portfolio. Of its total $5.59 billion in assets, National City held $2.93 billion in U.S. government obligations and just $1.24 billion in loans. (Zweig 1995: 46)

When this comfortable sleepiness came to an end by the late 1940s, the banks found themselves in an excellent position to expand their business and so compensate for the opportunities from which the New Deal legislation had cut them off. Banks were extremely liquid due to the large amounts of government securities in their portfolios. Moreover, they could take greater risks now that federal deposit insurance was in place as it had dramatically diminished the threat of bank runs. Their top priority was therefore to acquire high-yield assets. The world of commercial lending offered ample opportunities, and banks' asset portfolios shifted away from government bonds toward loans (Cleveland and Huertas 1985: 228–9).

Corporate lending occurred increasingly through the "term loan" (Sylla 2002: 57). It had its origins in the 1930s, when it was introduced by commercial banks in the hope of capturing the custom of large corporations that were reluctant to issue stock but had nonetheless grown used to capital being available on a long-term basis, and in the context of post–World War II it was used widely. For corporations, such loans offered some advantages over issuing stock or bonds: They were more flexible and did not have to be registered with the SEC (Cleveland and Huertas 1985: 231). The growing use of the term loan was accompanied by an evolution of banks' risk-assessment activities, focused on acquiring a detailed knowledge of the firm and its industry. The term loan was associated with a specific risk logic – whereby "projections of cash flow and profitability over a number of years are more important than analysis of a current balance sheet or valuation of collateral" (Cleveland and Huertas 1985: 232). In the context of rapid economic growth this principle found growing application, as traditional financing methods based strictly on the value of an asset "often bore little relationship to the cash such an asset could generate and consequently constrained a borrower's ability to grow" (Zweig 1995: 65).

Consumer and mortgage lending also grew. After the 1920s had seen the growing acceptance of consumer finance, the Depression years further strengthened its reputation as it did better than many other sectors (Calder 1999: 267–8). The reason was that repaying installment debt rose to the top of many people's list of priorities: With much of their money locked in already, they went to considerable lengths to avoid defaulting.[5] Long-term popular credit now came to appear as an excellent disciplinarian of the working classes, giving them a stake in the system and locking them into a life devoted to repaying the debt they had incurred in acquiring that stake – a logic that applied equally to mortgage credit. This trend was greatly reinforced by New Deal policies oriented to increasing popular access to mortgage and consumer credit (Hyman 2007). During the post–World War II years, the growth of consumer credit and mortgages accelerated dramatically (Enthoven 1957; Croteau 1960: 533; Robbins and Terleckyj 1960: 54; Klaman 1961; Chevan 1989; Calder 1999: 292–3). Banks offered credit cards, car loans, and second mortgages, all the while relaxing the terms of credit, lengthening the repayment period, and requiring lower downpayments (Grant 1992: 264). In this way, the American public became an integral part of the financial system, sustaining it through investing and saving but above all through borrowing and consuming.[6]

By the mid-1950s, after almost a decade of lending, loans had come to outstrip government securities in banks' asset portfolios. In fact, their ability to make profitable loans was running up against the limits of their supply of funds (Sylla 2002: 58). But banks' ability to do something about their need for additional funds was heavily constrained by Regulation Q and branch banking regulations. Such constraints became even more serious when, by the late 1950s, banks had to face not just a stagnation but an actual decline in their deposit liabilities. For one thing, the thrift industry, gradually coming into its own, managed to lure significant amounts of savings away from the commercial banking system (Zweig 1995: 83). Similarly, funds that previously would have ended up

---

[5] In 1939, consumer loans as a proportion of total bank assets was twice what it had been in 1929 (Calder 1999: 285).
[6] This integration of the working classes into American society's basic economic and financial mechanisms sets the New Deal institutions apart from the welfare states erected in Western Europe after World War II. Whereas the latter effected a significant degree of decommodification (Esping-Andersen 1990), the New Deal programs did not so much reduce as increase the working classes' dependence on markets. The ideological resiliency of popular aspirations for republican independence, having morphed into the notion of a "consuming public" (Jacobs 1999) after the defeat of yeoman producerism, permitted the ever fuller integration of the lower classes into a world of privatized consumption and the financial system that regulated it (McGovern 2006).

Domestic Expansion

as deposits in commercial banks were now channeled into pension funds and insurance schemes. Such disintermediation trends were reinforced by the rising interest rates that resulted from the Federal Reserve's abandonment of its support of the market in government securities: It gave large depositors incentives to shift their funds from banks into financial instruments such as commercial paper and Treasury bills (rates on which banks could not match because of Regulation Q) (Sylla 2002: 58). Nonbank financial institutions found themselves in a much better position to attract funds than banks (Johnson 1998: 123). There was an international aspect to this: From the late 1950s, corporations had the option of shifting their funds into the budding Euromarkets, which offered considerably higher rates as they were not under the same regulatory constraints as American banks and financial markets (Battilossi 2002b).

The upshot of these developments was that banks, to fund their lending activities, had to sell government securities, thereby undermining the liquidity they had taken for granted for so long. Banks' reduced liquidity made them more sensitive to the effects of Federal Reserve policy, and during periods of contractionary policies they found themselves forced to cut down on their corporate lending (Cleveland and Huertas 1985: 243–5). Corporations that had already been concerned about banks' financing capacity due to the strict limits on the size of loans now saw their access to bank loans restricted further and turned to the money market for funds, giving yet another boost to the commercial paper market (Sylla 2002: 58). Thus, like the 1920s, the 1950s saw an expansion of lending business that was cut short by disintermediation tendencies. Indeed, banks were now being bypassed in two ways, on both the liability side and the asset side. Due to higher interest rates, corporations were placing their surplus funds in the money market, and individuals withdrew their deposits to place them with savings and loan associations and financial markets (Mason 1997: 37); this restricted the pool of funds available to banks for lending out, and as a result borrowers had recourse to the money market for their borrowing requirements as well.

Reversing this vicious cycle of disintermediation was of vital importance to the banks (White 1992a: 8–9). Their access to the stock market and related speculative markets had been cut off, but the New Deal transformation of the financial system had opened up new types of securitization options. Banks could use these to replace longer-term balance sheet items with liquid assets, but the post–World War II period would also see the rise of financial innovations that were focused not on a bank's uses of funds but rather on its sources of funds. In the past, banks had had a fairly passive approach to the acquisition of liabilities, but they now became interested in more active methods of "liability management." Because banks' ability to attract deposits was seriously constrained, they pursued strategies aimed at raising funds in financial markets through liability-side securitization. Much of the development of American (and international) finance from the 1950s onward would be shaped by banks' strategies to circumvent regulatory obstacles and their interaction with the responses from monetary authorities.

CONCLUSION

This chapter has outlined the domestic dynamics of American finance from the New Deal to the early post–World War II period. After the New Deal, American finance could expand on a more stable footing. If investment bankers were no longer able to leverage their strategies by using other people's money and their control over the financial system was no longer so great as before, the segmentation of the financial system through Glass-Steagall also meant that they did not have to worry about competition from commercial banks with large balance sheets. Assisted by the SEC's eagerness to expand its regulatory scope through cooperation with private actors, before too long the securities industry began to reorganize itself through self-regulatory bodies, which allowed for the steady buildup of capacities for capital markets intermediation. But the growing network power embedded in American finance was especially pronounced in the commercial banking sector. The state's ability to enlist the Federal Reserve System as a whole in the war funding effort and to largely dispense with the services of investment bankers was reflective of the growth of infrastructural capacities since World War I. The Federal Reserve's policies left banks highly liquid for a long time after the war and put them in an excellent position to respond to the growing demand for credit generated by post–World War II patterns of growth and consumption. But as the network power of American finance widened and deepened, it also generated new contradictions that would serve as the catalyst for the post–World War II transformation of American and global finance.

10

Contradictions of Late Twentieth-Century Financial Expansion

INTRODUCTION

The idea that the end of "embedded liberalism" ushered in the decline of American finance has been challenged by IPE authors who have pointed out that the expansion of global markets was responsible for the creation of a new, more indirect and structural pattern of financial power relations in which the United States still occupied a central position (e.g., Strange 1986, 1988; Helleiner 1994; Germain 1997). In this and the following chapters, I seek to expand on this insight. It should be noted here that although these authors have offered trenchant critiques of orthodox IPE's focus on the formal state and its abstract separation from the economy, they have generally not gone far enough in remedying the problem. They take the system of global financial markets as their starting point and then locate U.S. power in relation to this system. But such an approach does not do sufficient justice to the decades-long buildup of the network connections of American financial power and the ways in which the systemic dynamics of modern global finance are functionally imbricated with them. In many ways, financial globalization is not best understood as the reemergence of "global" finance but as the processes whereby the expansionary dynamics of American finance began to take on international dimensions.

In IPE scholarship, the concepts of structural power and state power are still distinct, with several constitutive connections remaining underdeveloped: Despite the acknowledgment of the salience of the structural dimensions and socioeconomic sources of political authority, the categories of market and state have not been opened up in a way that allows for a construal of the multilayered networks through which they are constitutively interconnected. The continued reliance on an external conception of the relation between state and economy is especially apparent in the tendency to theorize the expansion of global finance since the early 1970s through the Polanyian metaphor of "market disembedding," which depicts financial expansion as a process through which financial markets autonomize themselves from the institutional frameworks that organize the economy's more basic productive functions. This tendency to see the growth of structural power as primarily a function of the tendency of financial markets to *escape* their institutional environment means that relatively little attention has been paid to the characteristics of the new institutional framework that during the 1960s emerged through the externalization of American finance. This relative neglect of the specific institutional foundations of financial globalization in turn means that it becomes difficult to see the nature of the linkages between international finance, the U.S. financial system, and the American state.

This book pays more explicit attention to the institutional basis, of distinctly American provenance, on which the expansion of international finance occurred. This will provide a clearer picture of the institutional threads connecting the American state to globalizing financial markets, including the contradictions that marked those. IPE authors tend to conceive of the limits to American structural power during the 1970s as a set of more or less external challenges, but such a focus tends to neglect the contradiction that was most deeply embedded in the practices and strategies responsible for the growth of structural power relations, one that only becomes apparent when we conceptualize financial globalization as driven first and foremost by the outward expansion of American practices and institutions. That is to say, the very same financial techniques and relations whose international extension was responsible for the growth of U.S. power were also the cause of the Federal Reserve's decreasing ability to control the domestic dynamics of money and credit creation; the strategies and innovations that extended the power of the American state in one respect made it more problematic in another.

These strategies emerged out of the contradictions in the pattern of post–New Deal domestic financial expansion that had emerged by the 1950s and were highlighted at the end of the previous chapter. To circumvent regulatory restrictions, banks employed a range of innovative financial devices, but the Federal Reserve sought to shut these down as it grew concerned about their inflationary effects. When banks began to search for strategies to escape Federal Reserve control, their eye fell on the Eurodollar markets. Although the opportunity to raise dollar funds to finance their domestic lending activities formed the main impulse behind the growth of American banks' international activities, banks quickly began to apply the full range of their financial techniques in the Eurodollar market.

The external expansion of American finance had contradictory effects. On the one hand, it propelled the creation of an international infrastructure of financial intermediation that was shaped and governed by American rules for the trading of dollar debt. Although it would take American policy makers a long time to develop a fuller understanding of the leverage afforded by these developments, the Nixon administration already realized that America's debt to the world had become as much the world's problem as America's own. On the other hand, the same strategies that did so much to entrench the dollar as the international currency also undermined the Federal Reserve's ability to control the creation of liquidity. The internal and external dimensions of American finance were locked into a mutually reinforcing relationship of accelerating expansion, and the contradictions of domestic monetary management came to a head by the end of the decade.

FINANCIAL POLICY DURING THE EARLY POST–WORLD WAR II PERIOD

The Federal Reserve's support for the government's debt funding operations had meant a significant buildup of inflationary pressures. Once wartime wage and price controls were abolished, inflation shot up. This strengthened the Federal Reserve's determination to end the easy money policies of the wartime period, but the Treasury demanded a continuation of pegging policies so as to minimize interest payments and facilitate the continuous refinancing of the debt. It ushered in a conflict between the Federal Reserve and the Treasury that would take several years to resolve. When the start of the Korean War triggered a new bout of inflation, the conflict came to a head. In 1951 an agreement was reached that allowed the Federal Reserve somewhat more freedom to pursue restrictive policies (Degen 1987: 117; Epstein and Schor 1995). During the early 1950s, under the chairmanship of William McChesney Martin, the Federal Reserve gradually reduced its support for the market in government securities and the policy emphasis shifted toward ways of controlling the creation of credit and money.

But while the Federal Reserve was extricating itself from its responsibility for propping up the market for government debt, government securities would continue to play a crucial role in its policies: The open market operations that had by now come to function as the key element in the Federal Reserve's policies were almost exclusively conducted through the market for Treasury bills (Roosa 1951). This was subsequently elevated to principle and came to be known as the "bills-only" policy – which would remain in place until 1961 (Whitesell 1964). The idea behind the bills-only policy was to create a market in short-term financial obligations that would function as a transmission channel for monetary policy (Alhadeff 1952; Degen 1987: 121). However, one of the key problems the Federal Reserve would be coping with for several decades was that large areas of financial activity were outside its control. Market arbitrage, both within and between different segments of the market, was in fact far from perfect and the Federal Reserve's control over capital market interest rates remained limited (Ahearn 1963: 62–5).

The Federal Reserve's lack of control over these wider dimensions of the financial system had to do with the persistence of operating procedures that still reflected the Federal Reserve's origins as a bankers' bank. The post–New Deal Federal Reserve was actively concerned with its role in macroeconomic stabilization: Its declared objective was to conduct a countercyclical policy (Greider 1987: 328). But for most practical policy purposes, the Federal Reserve's focus was still on banks' credit operations in the money market. The relationship of money market variables to the nation's money supply was a highly mediated one, and this complexity was not reflected in the Federal Reserve's policies (Anderson 1965; Bach 1971; Degen 1987; Greider 1987). Thus, while the Federal Reserve had come to think of itself as a modern central bank concerned with the health of the financial and economic system at large, it did not know how exactly to play this role.

In practical terms, this meant that the Federal Reserve's countercyclical policies became infused with an inflationary bias. Due to the imperfect transmission between different segments of the market in government securities, during recessions the Federal Reserve was forced to pump excessive amounts of liquidity into the Treasury bills market to influence long-term interest rates. This created problems during the upturn, as the system first needed to be drained of a mass of excess liquidity before the Federal Reserve could engage in restrictive policies (Ahearn 1963: 120). The fact that the Federal Reserve needed to flood the money market with liquidity to effect relatively small changes in long-term interest rates also meant that during a recession short-term interest rates declined proportionately much more than long-term rates. From the second half of the 1950s, this created problems for America's international financial position. Growing balance of payments deficits were financed through an accumulation of U.S. Treasury bills in foreign hands (as discussed in Chapter 8), and low short-term interest rates negatively affected foreigners' willingness to hold U.S. Treasury bills, which put pressure on the dollar (Gemmill 1961). When the Federal Reserve, in response to pressure from the Kennedy administration, engaged in open market operations in longer-term government debt to keep lower long-term rates at the same time as it raised the rate on short-term government debt (Operation Twist), it effectively abandoned the bills-only doctrine (Degen 1987: 123). But the Federal Reserve's involvement with the Treasury bills market would remain very close throughout the post–World War II era.

TRANSFORMATIONS OF THE BANKING SYSTEM

Despite the problems of policy making, the financial system of the early and mid-1950s possessed at least a semblance of stability. But from the late 1950s onward, the American financial system would be reshaped profoundly by banks' attempts to circumvent the New Deal's legal restrictions. Through the use of holding companies banks were able to expand the range of their activities (Fischer 1961; Zweig 1995: 216). During the early 1960s, the Comptroller of the Currency challenged the regulatory ambitions of the Federal Reserve and the SEC and so facilitated the banks' objectives (De Cecco 1976: 390; Zweig 1995: 147) – but the securities industry sued successfully and most of the Comptroller's bank-friendly policies were subsequently thrown out in court (Zweig 1995: 215).

Of far greater importance was another set of strategies that banks developed, building on their long-standing familiarity with securitization techniques. The most obvious way to increase a bank's ability to make new loans was to free up resources by replacing longer-term items on the balance sheet with more liquid items. Banks no longer had access to the stock market and the call loan market, but the New Deal reorganization of the financial system had opened up new types of securitization options, primarily in the form of a steady supply of mortgage-backed securities that were created through the intermediary activities of Fannie Mae and therefore enjoyed a governmental stamp of approval. Banks could use these to replace longer-term balance sheet items with liquid assets, but over the course of the post–World War II period they would also make increasing use of a different type of asset securitization – that is, off-balance sheet securitization. Banks began to devise ways to remove items from their books altogether by placing them with investment vehicles created for that purpose.

However, crucial to our understanding of the dynamics of financial expansion was the development by banks of new kinds of securitization techniques that allowed them not only to make better use of the funds they had but precisely to expand their sources of funds – that is, liability-side securitization. Traditionally, the profession of banking was primarily about managing assets on the basis of a given structure of deposit liabilities (Degen 1987: 130). The new approach of active "liability management" essentially turned the old one upside down. Instead of managing assets on the basis of a given liability structure, the burden of securing the bank's liquidity and profitability shifted toward the management of the bank's liabilities (Chernow 1990: 54). This meant that the bank would first set a target for the growth of its assets (based on the opportunities for profitable lending it could identify) and then go after the funds needed to match this. Unable to attract deposits by paying for them (due to Regulation Q), banks turned to the money market. Whereas in the traditional approach to banking the money market was a place where banks *bought* financial assets, in the new approach it started to function as a market where banks *sold* obligations and "bought money" (Selden 1963: 2–3).

One way of acquiring funds was provided by the federal funds market – the market where banks trade their excess reserves.[1] Hitherto the federal funds market had typically been used by banks only when they suffered temporary shortfalls in their reserve position. But in the new situation it became highly tempting to enlist the federal funds market in strategies of liability management and as a source of funds for financing banks' normal operations (Degen 1987: 131; Klebaner 1990: 221). The boost that this market received during and after the 1960s[2] also meant that the Federal Reserve increasingly used the federal funds rate as the key money market indicator (Meulendyke 1988: 9): During the next decades, the federal funds market would become a fulcrum in Federal Reserve control over the banking and financial system. However, as a systematic strategy for obtaining funds, the federal funds market had clear limits: There was nothing the banks could do to change the overall level of excess reserves available for trading.

---

[1] The market had come into existence during the 1920s, shrivelled into insignificance during the 1930s when banks were rolling in cash, and was resuscitated after World War II as the Federal Reserve abandoned its pegging policies and banks could no longer take their liquidity for granted (Boughton 1972; Stigum 1990; Sylla 2002: 59–60).
[2] During the 1960s, the amount of federal funds traded grew from $1.5 billion to $9 billion – and it would increase further to reach $25 billion in 1973 (Mayer 1974: 210).

The most important instrument for liability management was the negotiable certificate of deposit (CD) (Sylla 2002: 60).[3] CDs were not exempt from the interest rate ceilings, but because they were issued for a minimum period banks were allowed to offer a higher rate. At the same time, the banks engaged in a sustained and more or less concerted effort of "market making," creating a secondary market in CDs that allowed any holder of this paper to dispose of it at a moment's notice (Degen 1987: 131). The liquidity of CDs rested not on any characteristics of the asset itself, but derived entirely from its marketability and tradability (i.e., the wider networks of financial relations in which it was embedded) (Hester 1981: 150; Cleveland and Huertas 1985: 255). Consequently, CDs functioned as demand deposits with interest rates that were comparable to those on time deposits and could compete with the rates on money market instruments. In this way, banks were able to attract funds that they had lost when depositors started shifting funds into the money market (Mayer 1974; Wojnilower 1987; Landi and Lusignani 1997).

Had the Federal Reserve been minded to do so, it could have choked off the nascent market by lowering the interest rate ceilings on time deposits. It did the opposite, however, raising the ceiling step by step during the first half of the 1960s. There were two key reasons for the Federal Reserve's accommodating attitude. First, the Federal Reserve was engaged in Operation Twist, which required it to raise short-term interest rates. Second, the banks had managed to place the Federal Reserve before a fait accompli: The market in CDs had grown so much in such a short period that by the time the Federal Reserve had fully clued in to the implications of this development, it could not have killed off the market without causing a serious financial crisis. Nevertheless, the Federal Reserve became increasingly concerned about the inflationary effects of banks' liability management strategies. For their access to reserves meant, of course, a dramatic loosening of the constraints on their capacity to create credit. Moreover, the continuous raising of the rates on time deposits had an unanticipated side effect. By 1965, the rate on time deposits had surpassed the interest ceilings on savings deposits (i.e., the maximum rate that the public was able to obtain at savings banks) and, as a consequence, depositors began to shift their funds from thrifts to commercial banks (Mayer 1974: 195). This precipitated a major crisis in the thrift sector, which dragged the housing sector down with it (Mayer 1974: 195–6).

---

[3] The CD had been around for some time, but it was only in 1961 that its use as a money market instrument was pioneered by Citibank (Zweig 1995: 141).

The Federal Reserve's own concern with inflation converged with political pressure to prompt it to more actively resist banks' liability management strategies. In 1966, it engineered a contraction of credit that produced higher money market rates (Dickens 1995), and this time the Federal Reserve refused to raise the interest rate ceiling on term deposits. As a consequence, banks suddenly found themselves strapped for funds. This experience motivated banks to step up their efforts in financial innovation and "to invent a veritable funhouse of tricks that could be used next time to get around Reg Q and any public policy to restrain the growth of banking assets" (Mayer 1974: 197). But escaping Federal Reserve control was easier said than done. For instance, banks began to issue commercial paper through their holding companies (Sylla 2002: 66), but the Federal Reserve quickly redefined such funds as deposits, rendering them subject to the interest rate ceilings (Mayer 1974: 226). The same happened with repurchase agreements (the sale of an asset accompanied by an agreement to buy it back against a higher price, with the difference representing an interest payment in disguise) (Mayer 1974: 227). The Federal Reserve was continually adjusting its regulations and definitions to rapidly changing circumstances.[4] Rather than one side dealing a clear and decisive blow to the other, the Federal Reserve and the banks were involved in what seemed like an endless tug of war. It was the international arena that offered American banks an additional escape from Federal Reserve control (Cassis 2006: 226).

INTERNATIONAL BANKING AND FEDERAL RESERVE CONTROL

The Depression and World War II had obliterated the network of American bank branches in Europe. Banks' room for maneuver was circumscribed by the capital and exchange controls (Huertas 1990), and, in any case, domestic business was booming. By the end of the decade, only seven U.S. banks had branches overseas (Jones 1998: 137). What international banking was going on during the late 1940s and the early

---

[4] The Federal Reserve's definition at this time of what constituted a bank deposit would not have been recognized by a nineteenth-century banker: "a member bank's liability on any promissory note, acknowledgment of advance, due bill, or similar obligation (written or oral) that is issued or undertaken by a member bank principally as a means of obtaining funds to be used in its banking business" (quoted in Mayer 1974: 227). As Mayer comments, the formulation "has about it a quality of quiet desperation" (1974: 227).

1950s was predominantly old-style international banking, based on bill financing and correspondent banking (Jones 1998). City Bank's overseas division in the mid-1950s

> could only be described as antediluvian. Things had gotten so bad that [chairman] Sheperd and [president] Rockefeller seriously contemplated folding the division altogether. With plenty to do in the United States, and with the economies of western Europe still recovering from World War II, the overseas division had been virtually ignored by the bank's management and remained a sleepy backwater of American capitalism. (Zweig 1995: 86–7)

Europe became more interesting with the return to convertibility (Battilossi 2002a: 10), but American corporations were often self-financing and the number of American banks in Europe remained relatively small. New York assumed financial-center functions like third-party dollar financing, but this development was cut short by the imposition of capital controls in 1963 (Langley 2002: 70). To fully understand the growth of international banking, we need to examine developments closely related to the domestic dynamics of American finance.

As we saw in Chapter 8, since the war large amounts of American dollars had been exported to Europe in the form of aid, military expenditures, and foreign direct investment. Over time, the dollar shortage had been transformed into a dollar glut and come to constitute a pool of nonresident dollars. When, during the 1957 sterling crisis, the Bank of England raised interest rates and imposed limits on the use of sterling for financing international transactions, many banks began to offer dollar credits on the basis of their dollar deposits (Helleiner 1994: 84). The demand for dollars multiplied, effectively leading to the formation of an offshore market in dollars in London (Shaw 1978; Schenk 1998; Burn 1999; Battilossi 2002a). The unregulated Euromarkets offered higher rates than American markets, and American multinational corporations shifted their deposits to British banks (Burn 1999: 230; Battilossi 2000). At this point, therefore, the Eurodollar market was nothing but yet another source of disintermediation for American banks. But the response of U.S. banks was not long in coming. Seeking to recapture lost business, American banks began to enter the Euromarket in growing numbers. The growth of this market received a major impetus from the American attempts, from 1963 onward, to prevent outflows of capital (Sylla 2002: 63). It meant that the American financial system became practically closed to foreigners in need of dollar credit and useless to American corporations going abroad, and the solution was for these actors to turn to the Eurodollar market. The Eurobranches of American banks were well positioned to respond to this demand.

The ability of American banks to engage in Euromarket operations was contingent on the quiet cooperation of American authorities, which granted banks' foreign branches exemptions from some of the capital controls (Helleiner 1994: 89). The assumption that underlay this regulatory leniency was essentially that the burgeoning Eurodollar market functioned to "cream off" the financial business that could not be accommodated at home and so to take some pressure off the domestic U.S. financial system. Moreover, the Treasury felt that the Eurodollar market served to encourage Europeans to hold their deposits in dollars and reduce their inclination to convert them into gold, thus easing pressure on the dollar generated by the dollar overhang. However, as the decade progressed it became clear that the Euromarket was not quite as compatible with American financial policies as had initially been hoped. Whatever the Eurodollar market's influence on Europeans' willingness to hold dollars, gold outflows continued steadily. It became increasingly clear that the Eurodollar market did not just function to absorb the business that could not be accommodated by the American financial system but was the main reason capital controls were ineffective in restraining the activities of American banks and corporations (Odell 1982).

It was, however, not just the Treasury's but also the Federal Reserve's policy objectives that were foiled by the Eurodollar market. The 1966 crisis had the effect of promoting the use of the Eurodollar market as a source of bank funds (Battilossi 2002b): Liability management now went abroad (Hester 1981: 155). The first Eurodollar CDs were introduced in 1966 and gradually other financial instruments originally developed in the U.S. were introduced in the Euromarket as well, allowing banks to attract dollar funds and then send them home to the parent bank in the United States. The credit crunch of 1969 confirmed and extended the new use to which American banks could put the Eurodollar market and from then on it played a permanent role in their strategies (De Cecco 1987; Dickens 1990, 1995).[5] Thus, a major reason for U.S. banks to go abroad during the 1960s was to secure funding for domestic operations (Huertas 1990: 254). The exit options that the Eurodollar market provided to American capital are often understood

---

[5] The role that the Euromarket played in banks' liability management strategies grew exponentially. "At the end of 1969, total liabilities of US banks to foreign branches stood at about $13 billion. As late as 1967 they had been less than $2 billion" (De Cecco 1987: 190).

Late 20th Century Financial Expansion

primarily in terms of the opportunities for capital export that they offered; however, it is crucial to see that the Eurodollar market not only allowed American capital to find its way abroad and so to circumvent the Treasury's capital controls but also enabled American banks to import reserve funds and so to circumvent the Federal Reserve's domestic regulations (Mayer 1974: 457). While the Treasury's main objective was to contain the growth of the pool of nonresident dollars, the Federal Reserve was also deeply concerned with the ways banks managed to (re)patriate these funds, allowing them to circumvent its attempts to control the creation of credit.

U.S. banks' activities in the Euromarkets meant that the Federal Reserve was losing control over the dynamics of the American financial system. Although the Federal Reserve was well aware of its role in macroeconomic stabilization, its operational approach to the regulation of money and credit creation was still focused on money market indicators (Degen 1987: 139) – above all, the state of the federal funds market. The FOMC sought to raise or lower the federal funds rate by setting a target for the banks' free reserves (the reserves that banks have available over and above the reserves they are required to hold to satisfy the Federal Reserve's requirements), which the Open Market Desk then sought to hit by pumping liquidity into or taking it out of the system through open market operations (Meulendyke 1988, 1989). But the financial innovations of the 1960s rendered these policies increasingly ineffective (Degen 1987: 140): To target a desired free reserves position gave no guarantees concerning the total level of reserves in the banking system. In a situation in which banks are passive receivers of deposits, controlling free reserves and controlling total reserves (and hence bank liabilities and the money supply) amounts to the same thing; but in a situation in which banks actively acquire reserve funds, this relationship no longer holds.[6] In other

---

[6] It might be useful to illustrate this point with a simple numerical example. To simplify matters, let us ignore for the moment the multiplier effect of additions to banks' reserves. Suppose a bank has liabilities worth $100 and reserve assets in the amount of $15. The bank's reserve requirement is 10%, so its excess reserves are $5. In the old days, when banks were relatively passive receivers of deposits, keeping the bank's excess reserves at the existing level would provide a reliable means to control the overall level of reserves and the overall amount of credit extended and money created. However, now suppose that the bank uses a newly invented CD to raise funds, adding $10 to its reserves. On the basis of this amount, the bank can extend credit in the amount of $90 (rather than $100, as the issue of the CD has already increased its liabilities by $10). Its excess reserves are still the same as before, that is, $5. However, its total amount of reserves has increased from $15 to $25 while its liabilities have doubled. What this means is that, in the context of banks actively buying their own reserves, effective control over the amount of free reserves is no guarantee for control over the amount of total reserves in the system and the amount of credit created.

words, Federal Reserve control over the creation of credit and money rests on reserve requirements as a real constraint on bank behavior, and it is precisely the banks' liability management strategies that loosened this constraint. As the Federal Reserve entered the decade of the 1970s, a certain despair concerning its ability to control the creation of liquidity had set in (Maisel 1973).

BENIGN NEGLECT AND THE END OF BRETTON WOODS

Interestingly, while the Federal Reserve was growing ever more frustrated with its lack of control over the dynamics of the American financial system, the Treasury gradually let go of its attempts to control capital outflows. To the Treasury, the Eurodollar market represented a balance of payments problem; to the Federal Reserve, it was the source of domestic inflation. These problems were, of course, closely related, and the Treasury and the Federal Reserve were throughout in close consultation over these matters. But the difference of emphasis is important for understanding why, from the late 1960s, the Treasury felt comfortable sitting back and letting things happen while the Federal Reserve was frantically groping around for the levers of monetary control.

Although the internationalization of American financial capital had contributed to serious balance of payments problems, the export of distinctly American practices and techniques had also created a highly integrated transnational web of credit relations that was premised on the liquidity of dollar debt. The incorporation of large swathes of global economic activity into a system driven by the expansionary dynamics of American finance served to enhance the infrastructural leverage of the American state. The full extent of the possibilities opened up by this would only become clear over the course of the 1970s. But even though the Nixon administration's policy turns were still motivated by a degree of despair concerning the efficacy of capital controls, its officials were beginning to surmise that America's pivotal position in global finance and the dollar's role as the fulcrum of this system meant that America's debt to the world was in fact a significant power resource.

The futility of capital controls had become apparent by the late 1960s. The Nixon administration responded by shifting toward a strategy of benign neglect, allowing the balance of payments deficit to grow unchecked. The unilateral move of the Nixon administration had the effect of making clear to Europeans that dollars had already ceased to be backed by gold in any meaningful way and that an attempt by Europe to cash in its dollars would be self-defeating (Mikesell and Furth 1974: 56). That is, a run on the dollar would force the United States to close the gold window, at which point European countries could respond either by trying to get rid of their dollars – thereby pushing down the exchange rate of the dollar and giving a boost to U.S. competitiveness – or trying to maintain the value of the dollar by continuing to hold U.S. Treasury bills, thereby locking themselves ever further into a pure dollar standard (Hudson 1977). Given this configuration of financial forces, such a new monetary standard was evolving by default. In August 1971, the Nixon administration suspended the convertibility of the dollar into gold (Gowa 1983). This made "benign neglect explicit: foreign central banks were being told that they would hold dollars whether they liked it or not" (Conybeare 1988: 261). The dollar was devalued, capital controls lost much of their relevance, and what in the 1960s had appeared to be America's problem was now Europe's problem. The end of Bretton Woods meant that all checks on the growth of the stock of expatriate dollars were gone. "After 1971 the world was flooded with dollars" (Parboni 1981: 38). In other words, the suspension of convertibility had dramatically loosened the American balance of payments constraint.[7]

A number of authors have questioned the traditional interpretation of the breakdown of Bretton Woods as signaling the end of U.S. hegemony in international finance. They stress that that the growth of global private finance did not so much overwhelm American power but rather produced new, more structural and indirect patterns of power that still centered on the United States (e.g., Strange 1986, 1988; Walter 1993; Arrighi 1994; Germain 1997; Gowan 1999). Yet, in the work of many of those authors we still find an interpretation of post–Bretton Woods financial expansion as a process of "market disembedding": Because of the removal of institutional obstacles, it is argued, American and international finance were able to expand without their former constraints. And although this had the short-term effect of boosting America's centrality in international finance, its longer-term consequences are seen to have included precisely the erosion of the institutional supports of financial power. In this way, such perspectives return to a "markets vs. states" perspective that is allied to a revised thesis of American decline.

[7] In 1976, the U.S. government even "ceased calculating the statistics previously used to determine the overall state of the US balance of payments (the balance as calculated on the basis of official settlements, on the basis of the balance of payments model of the IMF, and on the basis of net liquidity), furnishing only partial balances of current items and some varieties of capital movements" (Parboni 1981: 89–90).

This chapter, by contrast, argues that the unprecedented expansion of private global finance could only take place in virtue of the presence of a new institutional matrix of credit relations and financial intermediation for which the basis had been laid during the 1960s. If the demise of the formal institutions of Bretton Woods certainly created a space for financial expansion that had hitherto not existed, it did so precisely by permitting the proliferation of new, more flexible financial rules and techniques that reflected the distinctive institutional makeup of American finance. Conceptualizing the growth of structural power in terms of its institutional basis and specificities allows us to grasp its linkages to state power. This is especially important because the American state's relation to the financial expansion that followed the end of Bretton Woods was highly contradictory: Because the driving force behind the growth of U.S. financial power in global finance was financial innovation, its flipside was the difficulty of controlling domestic inflation. Although America's balance of payments problem had become much less pressing, the lack of control over the domestic mechanisms of liquidity creation and the resulting inflation were seen as more of a problem than ever. Thus, whereas the transformation and subsequent internationalization of American finance gave a huge boost to some aspects of the infrastructural capacity of the American state, it also threw into jeopardy other aspects. The next section will address the position of the United States in international finance; the subsequent section will zoom in on the motor forces of financial expansion as well as the regulatory contradictions they generated.

THE UNITED STATES IN INTERNATIONAL FINANCE DURING THE 1970S

After the end of Bretton Woods, financial markets, interacting with the new international monetary system, expanded at an unprecedented rate. The financial techniques that American banks brought to the Euromarket inspired a pattern of competitive emulation (Forsyth 1987), which propelled the continual development of new techniques for liquidity and risk management and entailed an ever more integrated marketized approach to both sides of a bank's balance sheet (Battilossi 2002b: 127). All items in a bank's portfolio were now in principle seen as marketable securities that could be assigned a certain level of risk and liquidity (Harrington 1987; Battilossi 2000). Floating exchange rates greatly expanded the opportunities for the application of the new financial techniques through speculation (Berger et al. 1995; Sylla 2002: 67). Banks also began to make ample use of derivatives (such as futures and options), and the expansion of derivatives markets did much to increase the volatility of global financial markets (Harrington 1987; Tickell 2000: 88) – which in turn became one of the main sources of exploitable financial risk and produced a self-reinforcing dynamic of financial expansion (Dodd 2005). These trends were further reinforced by the massive flows of "petrodollars": The oil shocks led to an accumulation of funds in the hands of Middle Eastern states, who channeled most of their earnings into the Eurodollar markets.

The upshot of these developments was that the dollar's key currency status became more entrenched than could ever have been imagined under Bretton Woods. U.S. intermediaries had developed an extraordinary capacity to sell dollar-denominated debt and U.S. liabilities had become the fulcrum of the international monetary system. The dollar's special status became more organically embedded in the mechanisms of global finance, and consequently balance of payment constraints became less relevant (Gowan 1999). The Eurodollar markets, which earlier had been such a source of concern, now appeared as a market where the United States could exercise extraordinary seigniorage privileges. The combination of the new logic of financial securitization and risk, floating exchange rates, and petrodollars fueled instability in global financial markets, but the United States, growing more aware of the ways in which it benefited from these dynamics, resisted attempts to devise a new formal international regulatory system, thus allowing financial expansion to proceed at an undiminished rate (Langley 2002: 87).

All this is better understood as a process of the American state seeking to loosen some external constraints and in doing so growing aware of the leeway it enjoyed and the structural power it commanded than as the implementation of a grand imperial design. The 1970s are in fact best seen as a transitional decade, during which the reconstruction of the rules of international finance remained a contradictory and uncertain process. For one thing, the hegemony of the dollar was not entirely uncontested (Arrighi 2003): At various times private investors and central banks sought to diversify their portfolios. The reason this never developed into a fundamental redirection of capital movements was that other financial markets lacked the depth and liquidity that characterized dollar markets and were unable to absorb such inflows of financial capital without huge upward pressure on their exchange rates (Gordon 1995). But such challenges to the structural position of the dollar are best seen as consequences of more deep-seated tensions in the new financial regime. The contradiction at the very heart of (i.e., internal to the operation of) American financial power was that the very same financial practices responsible for the loosening of external constraints on the American state were also at the root of the loss of control by American authorities over the creation of money and credit at home. Although the American state had become much less jittery about the dangers posed by the dollar overhang and balance of payments deficits, what continued to pose a massive regulatory problem were the inflationary consequences of banks' operations in the Eurodollar market. Breaking the back of domestic inflation would be a major precondition for the more coherent growth of American financial power.

FINANCIAL EXPANSION AND MANAGEMENT DURING THE 1970S

Long after the Treasury had made its peace with its inability to control capital flows and come to realize that a passive approach served U.S. interests quite well, the Federal Reserve was doing everything in its power to gain a firmer grip on the creation of dollar liquidity. The accelerating pace of financial innovation and liquidity creation meant that the Federal Reserve's task of domestic monetary management became even more complicated than it had been during the 1960s.[8] Price and income controls were effective in bringing inflation down for some time (Wells 1994), but things again spiraled out of control from 1973, when the abolition of controls, the oil shock, militant labor unions, the falling dollar, and expansionary policies conspired to produce double-digit inflation. Stagflation, the puzzling combination of economic stagnation and inflation, was born.

During the 1970s, disintermediation trends were reinforced by the rapid "financialization" of the economy. Corporations were not just anymore shifting funds from banks to money market instruments but also diverting their cash flows away from productive investments and into financial markets (Arrighi 2003; Krippner 2003). As corporate profitability declined and opportunities for productive investment became scarce (Brenner 1998), corporations saw their holdings of cash increase. Tempted by rising market interest rates, corporations began channeling these

---

[8] Of course, the causes of inflation were manifold and involved such factors as oil prices, sticky wages, and fiscal policy. Because an analysis of the complex interaction of these factors lies well beyond the scope of this book, it is important to stress here that although pressure on the substantial validity of the American currency came from many directions, all such influences ultimately operated through the channels of money and credit creation.

funds into money market instruments like commercial paper (Cargill and Garcia 1985). The decade also saw the dramatic growth of institutional investors. Mutual funds pooled small savings to invest them in securities, so making it easier for ordinary people to invest in financial markets and take advantage of rising interest rates (Stigum 1990: 1176; Edwards 1996: 16).[9] Pension funds too grew at a rapid pace, as the post–World War II baby-boomer generation entered the labor market and started saving for their retirement incomes.

These growing flows of investment funds were absorbed by growing household debt. Consumer debt expanded rapidly, but it was especially the amount of mortgage-backed debt that received a huge boost (Grant 1992: 352; Fink 1996). The founding of Freddie Mac in 1970 was intended to introduce more competition into the sector and to secure the baby-boomer generation's access to suburban home ownership (Brendsel 1996). Freddie Mac and Fannie Mae "created uniform underwriting standards, monitored them, and offered investors quasi-government guarantees on securitized products at highly attractive yields" (Kendall 1996: 6; see also Wallison and Ely 2000). In addition, the Community Reinvestment Act of 1977 prohibited discrimination in lending and established procedures for monitoring lending practices (Dymski 2007: 8) and so access to mortgage credit became more widely available. Similar securitization techniques also found application in other sectors such as credit card debt and student loans.

Having become a central part of the financial scene (Harmes 2000), institutional investors came to constitute an important pressure group for the opening up of the securities industry.[10] Emphasizing the interests of ordinary investors, the liberalization lobby managed to capitalize on a series of scandals triggered by the rise in the number of cases of fraud and insider trading (Moran 1991, 1994). Of course, the self-regulatory structures of the securities industry were vigorously defended by vested interests, but the investors' cause found considerable support among retail- and transaction-oriented investment firms like Merrill Lynch, who viewed the oligopolistic structures of the securities industry as an

---

[9] The rate of growth of mutual funds was astounding: During the period 1975–79, the assets of mutual funds grew more than tenfold (Cargill and Garcia 1985: 49).
[10] Institutional investors, generally risk averse and continually engaged in the rebalancing of their portfolios, generate a high volume of transactions (Grahl and Lysandrou 2006). They felt that the advantages they could potentially derive from the sheer scale of their operations were negated by the existing structures of self-regulation that privileged a cartel-like network of brokers operating on the basis of fixed commissions.

obstacle to further growth (Geisst 2001). The SEC responded with a shift away from its support for the cartel-like structures of brokers, investment firms, and corporate managers that had dominated capital markets for several decades (Lütz 2002: 208), and Congress passed legislation giving the SEC more instruments to enforce competitive market structures (Seligman 2003).

In the wake of the opening up of the securities industry, capital markets activity underwent a major transformation. During the early post–World War II period, stocks were handpicked on the basis of a broker's judgment, deals were made on the basis of long-established relationships, and trading took place only when clear threats or opportunities presented themselves. In the emerging configuration of highly competitive and densely populated markets, more fine-tuned instruments were needed to carve out opportunities and to exploit smaller margins (Bernstein 2005: 8; Morrison and Wilhelm 2007: 6). In this context, investment banks, fund managers, and brokers saw considerable potential for the application of mathematical and statistical techniques (Whitley 1986a, 1986b; Bernstein 2005: 3; Mackenzie 2006). Risk assessment was no longer used primarily to decide what financial entanglements to avoid, but rather to determine how a given portfolio could be invested with an optimal risk and return profile. Anything could be "valued at risk." Relationship banking, meanwhile, did not so much decline as instead transform. White-shoe firms like Morgan Stanley explored ways to make more money off their corporate business (Chernow 1990: 595; Kaufman and Englander 1993: 79) and began to proactively propose mergers and takeovers to corporations (Augar 2005: 35) and to charge for advice that in the past they had given for free. Soon enough, all major banks had their own specialized M&A departments (Knee 2007: 78; Morrison and Wilhelm 2007: 258), and the American financial system came to feature a market in corporate control (Useem 1996; Höpner and Jackson 2001).

Investment banks' development of their competitive capacities made considerable claims on their resources (Geisst 2001), and they sought to access new funds by expanding the range of financial services for the general public (Zweig 1995: 540), thereby encroaching on areas that had been the preserve of commercial banks. The latter, under growing pressure from all sides, embarked on a campaign for greater entrepreneurial freedom (Sobel 1994), also claiming to speak on behalf of the small saver. They took aim at the interest rate ceilings, which by the late 1970s were lower than the rate of inflation, as well as Glass-Steagall, arguing that it merely shielded investment banks from competition. But it would take time for these efforts to bear fruit. As long as the New Deal institutional framework was still in place, banks continued to pursue strategies to circumvent its regulations (Litan 1987; Edwards 1996). They transformed illiquid loans into tradable asset-backed securities, which could then be sold to a third party or transferred to special investment vehicles, allowing banks both to earn fee income and to free up funds for other purposes (Berger and Udell 1993: 229; Wolfe 2000: 354; Grosse 2004). They continued to raise funds through CDs and related instruments, at home and abroad. And in the growing Euromarket, banks expanded their investment banking functions (Harrington 1987: 49; Battilossi 2000: 169–70, 2002b: 114–5) and exploited the dynamics of derivatives and foreign exchange markets (Berger et al. 1995; Edwards 1996; Ennis 2004). They also began lending large amounts to developing countries that often had poor credit ratings and did not enjoy ready access to international bond markets (Geisst 1990: 68; Klebaner 1990: 207–8).

During the early 1970s the Federal Reserve had still tried to contain inflation by working within and shoring up the existing system of regulation. However, its contractionary policies were caught in a pattern whereby they produced higher market interest rates, and so, given the interest rate ceilings, fueled disintermediation, which then encouraged banks to intensify their liability management strategies – leaving existing levels of inflation intact. And although banks were still capable of responding to disintermediation trends in this way, things were somewhat different for the thrifts: Liability management strategies were not nearly as feasible for the thrifts as for the banks, as it would have them bidding for funds by offering higher rates while their asset portfolio contained more long-term and often fixed-rate assets. On several occasions the Federal Reserve selectively imposed reserve requirements on specific types of instruments held by banks, but this motivated many banks to exit the Federal Reserve System and continue operations under a state charter. Thus, what became ever more obvious during the 1970s was that ever larger swathes of financial activity were outside the effective control of the Federal Reserve: Its policies had lots of undesirable side effects but little impact on the core problem of inflation. The Federal Reserve's responsibilities as a modern central bank were increasingly seen to be in conflict with its institutional constitution as a bankers' bank employing a money market strategy to pursue its policy objectives (Poole 1979; Mayer 1999).

As the 1970s progressed, it became clear that containing inflation was not just a matter of stepping on the brakes more forcefully, but that monetary policy needed to be adapted in essential respects. This need for adjustment motivated a more critical attitude toward the operating procedures of the 1950s and 1960s, which were now seen to have paid excessive attention to credit conditions in the money market to the exclusion of a broader concern with the aggregate money supply and price inflation. FOMC directives were now formulated in terms of total reserves and monetary aggregates instead of free reserves and the federal funds rate (Meulendyke 1988).

However, targeting total reserves and monetary aggregates was easier said than done. When it came to the execution of directives, the Open Market Desk had no choice but to operate through the money market. Since the rise of monetarist theory, the "money supply" is often presented as a directly operational target, understood in abstraction from all the messy intermediations of the money market, as if every day new additions to the money supply are dropped from an airplane and naturally find their way into the economy. However, in the real world of monetary policy making, central banks have some leverage over the mechanisms through which liquidity is created but no direct control over the money supply as such. Thus, although the FOMC directives were now concerned with monetary aggregates, their instructions to the manager of the Open Market Desk were still framed in terms of money market indicators, that is, the federal funds rate and free reserves. The target had changed, but the operating procedure remained the same (Degen 1987: 157).

However, whereas the practical significance of the focus on monetary aggregates remained limited, what had happened in terms of the growth of financial consciousness and the possibilities for financial policy opened up by this is not to be underestimated. Modern minds tend to conceive of the economy as a more or less homogeneous system that can be described by using such highly abstract concepts as money supply and monetary aggregate. But there is nothing natural about such an approach to economic phenomena. It was only in 1948 that the aggregate concept of "money stock" first appeared in a Federal Reserve publication (Degen 1987: 157). During the 1950s and 1960s, the concept would pop up every now and then, but it never informed policy decisions to any meaningful degree and Federal Reserve policy remained concentrated on the price and availability of credit as expressed by the conditions in the federal funds market. And it was only from the early 1970s that the Federal Reserve began tracking the growth of the money supply systematically and in quantitative terms (Degen 1987).

During the 1960s, Congress had at times exerted some mild pressure on the Federal Reserve to adopt more explicit targets for the permissible growth of the money supply. From the mid-1970s, when inflation was spiraling out of control, Congress took a firmer approach. In 1978, it passed the Federal Reserve Reform Act, instructing the Federal Reserve "to maintain long-run monetary and credit aggregates commensurate with the economy's long-run potential to increase production so as to promote effectively goals of maximum employment, stable prices, and moderate long-term interest rates" (Degen 1987: 159). Thus were codified in law the obligations of the Federal Reserve System to the economy at large. Although the Federal Reserve had been more than just a bankers' bank for some time – at least as far as its aims were concerned – it was only now that it was explicitly charged with responsibility for the American economy as a whole.

CONCLUSION

This chapter has examined the institutional foundations of the processes that simultaneously propelled the outward expansion and inward deepening of American financial power. Under great pressure to access new sources of funds, banks tried to circumvent the constraints imposed by the New Deal system through the development of a range of financial techniques. When the Federal Reserve tried to close off these avenues for innovation, the banks took their new strategies abroad, exporting American institutions and techniques and so reshaping the structures of global finance. In other words, the growing integration and density of the domestic financial system had created pressures on and opportunities for American financial intermediaries that they responded to by developing strategies that ultimately took them abroad. This process of externalization reshaped the institutional framework of private international finance in such a way as to dramatically boost the structural power of American finance. The capacity of American intermediaries to sell dollar debt ultimately also had the effect of loosening the American economy's external constraints. Thus, the internationalization of American financial practices and institutions served to extend American integral statehood beyond the territorial definition of the formal state.

This was not, however, a process without contradictions: The very same processes that were extending America's structural leverage in international finance rendered problematic the control of American monetary authorities over the domestic dynamics of money and credit creation. It is important to realize that this tension cannot be grasped in terms of the contrasting logics of market and states: Financial innovation extended the power of the American state in some respects yet made it more problematic in others. The same socioeconomic institutions whose spread meant a growth of the American integral state's external capacities also complicated the domestic linkages between formal authority and the framework organizing the dynamics of American finance. As the tentacles of the American integral state were being lodged at the heart of the institutional framework of global finance, domestically the exercise of financial authority became more precarious. This tension defined much of the 1970s, when the United States exploited its structural power in international finance but suffered rampant inflation at home. The challenge was to develop new forms of control over the dynamics of liquidity creation.

11

The Neoliberal Consolidation of American Financial Power

INTRODUCTION

This chapter examines how American monetary authorities managed to establish a new kind of control over the dynamics of financial expansion. The attention paid in this book to the evolving institutional ties between financial intermediation, social life, and the state's regulatory authority allows for a more precise interpretation of the turn to neoliberalism and monetarism at the end of the 1970s. It is important to situate the insights generated through this particular lens with respect to other views on the role of institutions in the neoliberal age. For by itself an emphasis on the continued salience of institutions in the era of financial globalization and neoliberalism is hardly new. One of the central theoretical points of recent work in IPE has been the role of the state in fostering the globalization of financial markets. Moreover, it is widely recognized that neoliberal policies do not involve a literal retreat of the state from society and that deregulation is always reregulation – that "freer markets" mean "more rules" (Vogel 1996). However, such interpretations tend to generate conceptual problems characteristic of a Polanyian understanding of markets, which stresses, on the one hand, their many institutional preconditions and, on the other, their periodically surfacing tendency to escape from that environment. That is to say, even if it is acknowledged that markets are always dependent on institutional supports, neoliberalism still tends to be considered in terms of the declining capacities of states vis-à-vis financial markets. Helleiner, for instance, describes the monetarist turn as the implementation of an austerity program that indicated America's willingness to accept external discipline and limit its own policy autonomy – that is, "to submit to the discipline of international financial pressures" (Helleiner 1994: 133). The point that tends to get lost is that monetarism involved a process of institutional reconfiguration that adjusted some of the key parameters of the relations between U.S. monetary authorities, American finance, and global finance in a way that enhanced rather than diminished the infrastructural capacities and policy autonomy of the American state.

Interpretations of America's turn to neoliberalism in terms of its submission to the imperatives of global markets and the acceptance of external discipline encounter an important problem: Monetarism never functioned in textbook fashion and in fact gave a huge boost to the processes that were at the root of the Federal Reserve's inability to control credit creation and inflationary pressures. When the Federal Reserve adopted a strategy based on the targeting of the money supply and left it to the market to set interest rates, the result was not financial discipline but rather an acceleration of innovation and the undiminished growth of liquidity creation. But compared to the previous decade, these processes of financial expansion no longer created similarly intense contradictions: After neoliberalism, liquidity generation was no longer a double-edged sword that propelled the deepening and proliferation of financial relations but at the same time undermined the regulatory capacities and objectives of the American state. The creation of credit was not brought to a halt but rather consolidated and embedded into a new institutional regime that served to enhance rather than jeopardize the capacities of the American state.

Thus, neoliberalism did not represent the return to a purer form of capitalism more in line with the prescriptions of classical liberalism, that is, "an attempt once again to disembed the market from society" and as such "merely the latest iteration of Polanyi's double movement" (Blyth 2002: 4). Instead, it connected the formal institutions of government in more functional ways to the networks of control and governance that had evolved at the levels of financial intermediation and everyday life, thereby improving the state's ability to govern those dynamics. The neoliberal era produced a further approximation of the vision of infrastructural capacity grounded in integral statehood that had emerged during the New Deal, which itself reflected a view of social dynamics and the possibility of manipulating their systemic properties that could only have arisen on the basis of the institutional innovations that American finance had undergone since the late nineteenth century.

The usefulness of interpreting neoliberalism through such lines of historical continuity rather than the logic of Polanyian reversals is also apparent when it comes to the politics of neoliberalism: If the transition to the neoliberal era certainly represented a break with the spirit of Progressive reform and gentle discipline, it was built on and took to a new level the ability of America's elites to manipulate the populist sentiments of the American public, exploiting widespread discontent to effect its further integration into the institutional forms of the financial system. The "Reagan Revolution" was carried by a capitalist elite whose composition and orientation had undergone significant transformation over the course of the post–World War II period (Ferguson and Rogers 1986; Burch 1997; Cox and Skidmore-Hess 1999). From the 1960s, low unemployment contributed to labor militancy and reduced capitalists' bargaining leverage, the expansion of welfare programs meant that the American system began to take on a few too many features of European welfare states, and all this occurred at a time when American industry was losing the competitive edge it had enjoyed since World War II (Brenner 1998). Many American businesses branched out to Southern states to take advantage of the availability of cheap, nonunionized labor, stimulating the growth of elites "steeped in a broth of Birchite conspiracism, traditionalist Protestant morality, and cultural nationalism" (Lyons 1998: 86). Aided by a battery of lobby groups and think tanks, they proved very capable of exploiting the American public's republican sentiments and enlisting them in a political project that served to greatly exacerbate socioeconomic inequalities.

The broad support for the neoliberal agenda of the early 1980s mirrored the ability of financial elites to enlist the middle class in their challenge to the securities industry's self-regulatory structures by playing up the scandals that those structures had given rise to. But the organization of the securities industry had represented only one part of the New Deal economic and financial system, and the struggle over its organization had remained fairly localized. To be sure, large New York commercial banks had joined the fray very early on, spearheading a campaign for the abolition of the interest rate ceilings, the branching restrictions, and Glass-Steagall. But it took the much broader economic and financial misery of the 1970s (epitomized by rampant inflation) to effect a more significant institutional reconfiguration. In the name of the American worker and the American dream, the Reagan administration not only reformed financial institutions in such a way as to multiply the options available to financial capital, but also implemented massive (corporate and income) tax cuts, boosted military expenditure, dismantled social programs, privatized government corporations, and initiated an assault on labor unions. Wage stagnation, growing inequality, and the dismantling of public arrangements for income provision entailed a growing reliance on financial markets for income provision – through both borrowing and investment. This further penetration of relations of credit and debt into the mechanisms of everyday life locked the American middle and working class into a regime of intensifying financial pressure. The disciplinary effects of neoliberalism are thus not best understood as a constraint imposed by international financial markets on the American state, but rather as the deeper penetration of financial norms into social life in a way that further concentrated capacities for agency and control in the hands of financial elites and enhanced the infrastructural leverage available to the American state. The proliferation of power relations in society did not diminish state power but precisely served to enhance it.

MONETARISM

By the end of the 1970s a new oil shock, labor militancy, and pressure on the dollar had pushed inflation up to new heights (Greider 1987; Axilrod 2009: 92). The Carter administration's attempts to push inflation down to acceptable levels through price and wage controls all failed, and the appointment of Paul Volcker to the Federal Reserve chairmanship in 1979 was meant to signal a strong commitment to inflation fighting. After some ineffective initial attempts to combat inflation by means of conventional policies, Volcker came to feel that inflation could only be conquered through a drastic revision of the modalities of monetary management, and to this end he looked to monetarist theory. In October 1979, in an attempt to cut through the problems and policy dilemmas generated by its existing policy orientation, the Federal Reserve announced a major policy change: It would no longer target free reserves in the federal funds market but total reserves (Axilrod 2009: 95). Whereas the relation between interest rates and the money supply was only indirect (and increasingly tenuous), the relation between total reserve and the money supply was much more direct (Volcker 2002) – after all, a given amount of reserves can back a given amount of deposit liabilities, and no more (Timberlake 1993: 350). To be sure, Volcker did not have strong feelings about the theoretical merits of monetarism. In an important sense, the adoption of monetarism was a public relations strategy (Johnson 1998: 179). The Federal Reserve declared that it would be targeting total reserves and no longer concern itself with conditions in the federal funds market – and when, as could be expected, banks would bid up the federal funds rate

Neoliberal Consolidation

to unprecedented levels in a scramble for reserve liquidities, the Federal Reserve could wash its hands of it. It now was market actors, not the Federal Reserve, setting interest rates (Krippner 2003: 131–2).

However, during the 1970s, restrictive Federal Reserve policies had resulted in the drainage of funds from depository institutions, problems in the housing sector, the acceleration of liability management and financial innovation, flight to the Euromarkets, and exit from the Federal Reserve System. The Federal Reserve was well aware of the potential consequences of its new policy; and that was exactly why it was so concerned to disavow responsibility for it. By creating a situation in which the status quo would become completely untenable, it was as if Volcker sought to force the issue. This was of course not merely wishful thinking but fully in tune with political realities. The problems of the 1970s had created a certain degree of general awareness that key aspects of the banking sector's regulatory framework were in need of revision (Cargill and Garcia 1985). A program of liberalizing reforms was in the works that the Federal Reserve expected would undercut many of the unpleasant side effects of its monetarist policies. Crucially, however, neither the Federal Reserve nor Congress looked at these measures as an abandonment of regulatory ambitions: Instead, what had emerged was a political willingness to remove regulations that had ceased to have productive effects and so to create more coherent modalities of financial governance. Indeed, the Federal Reserve's argument for an expansion of its authority over the financial system met with wide congressional agreement.

This program was implemented through two pieces of legislation – the 1980 Depository Institutions Deregulation and Monetary Control Act and the 1982 Garn-St. Germain Depository Institutions Act. They relaxed the interest rate ceilings associated with Regulation Q, made available to depository institutions a much wider range of sources of funds, and increased the uses to which they could put these funds (Cargill and Garcia 1985: 57–60, 67–70; Hester 2008: 154). At the same time, they extended the coverage of deposit insurance and enhanced the powers of the Federal Reserve. The latter was authorized to set reserve requirements for all depository institutions, which put a de facto end to the dual (federal/state) banking system and meant that the Federal Reserve no longer needed to worry about the threat of exit from the system (Cargill and Garcia 1985: 60–2). Thus, banks and thrifts were now better able to compete with the money and capital markets so that the danger of disintermediation became less relevant. It was in this context that the Volcker shock worked its effects.

In an important sense, the Federal Reserve's turn to monetarism was highly successful: Interest rate levels skyrocketed to historic levels and over the next few years inflation came down. But monetarist policies worked in very different ways than monetarist theory would have it. Soon after the initial shock, bank credit began to expand again and the rate at which it did so even accelerated (Wojnilower 1980: 305–6; Greider 1987: 140). The reason was that banks were able to find the reserves they needed elsewhere: The monetarist targeting of total reserves and the money supply had not rendered financial innovation impotent and, indeed, deregulation had only fortified banks' ability to engage in innovation. Liability management, in other words, was given free rein and banks were able to raise ample funds both at home and in the Eurodollar markets (Greider 1987: 142).[1] The Federal Reserve was taken aback by this explosion of credit: Although Volcker and Federal Reserve officials obviously did not share monetarist theory's premise that authorities have a direct grip on the supply of money, they nonetheless did not fully realize the extent to which such abstractions invalidated monetarism's core propositions. The Federal Reserve had shifted its focus from conditions in the federal funds market to total reserves, but this did not mean that it was actually able to effectively control the latter. In a definitional sense it was of course true that there existed a direct relation between reserves and the money supply, but the point was precisely that, owing to the mechanisms of credit creation that had evolved over the previous decades, the Federal Reserve was unable to control the quantity of reserves.

Initially the Federal Reserve responded with attempts to regulate the Euromarkets (Hawley 1984). These met with considerable domestic and foreign opposition (Helleiner 1994: 137) and in any case quickly proved ineffective. But there was another aspect to the Federal Reserve's abandonment of attempts to regulate the Euromarket: It found, somewhat to its surprise, that the dramatic expansion of credit and liquidity no longer fanned the flames of price inflation. Something fundamental had changed in the institutional parameters of the processes driving the expansion of American finance: Banks' access to the Euromarket funds no longer had the same effects as in the 1970s.[2] While the Federal Reserve's policies

---

[1] Whereas in 1978, 34.5 percent of commercial bank liabilities had come from sources other than traditional deposits, by 1982 this had risen to 59.9 percent (Seabrooke 2001: 114) – an enormous shift in the sources of bank funding.
[2] In 1981 the Federal Reserve even allowed the introduction of so-called International Banking Facilities (i.e., the establishment by American banks of "overseas" branches on American soil), which greatly enhanced banks' ability to acquire Euromarket funds.

were still unable to restrict credit creation, the difference was that now most of that liquidity stayed within the financial sphere. The high interest rates had caused a major recession in the manufacturing sector and served to suck funds into the financial sector: They did not make money more scarce or limit the creation of credit, but kept consumer price inflation down by transforming it into asset price inflation. Monetarism therefore did not stamp out inflationary pressures but rather redirected them: Inflation was concentrated in a particular sector and so transformed from a generalized problem into a source of strength for financial capital.

The acceleration of financial innovation rendered the focus on reserves and monetary aggregates increasingly problematic. Innovation served to erode the supposedly fixed relation between reserves and monetary aggregates from both ends: It facilitated banks' ability to acquire funds, but also did much to improve the liquidity of financial instruments so that it was increasingly less clear what was money and what was not. The Federal Reserve did what it could to keep up with changing circumstances by redefining monetary aggregates,[3] but continuous financial innovation rendered such efforts futile (Degen 1987: 191–2). In 1982, therefore, only three years after the adoption of monetarist philosophy, the Federal Reserve abandoned its focus on monetary aggregates and once again targeted the federal funds rate (Meulendyke 1988: 15; Krippner 2003: 133–5; Bell-Kelton 2006: 6). Policy makers began to realize that the real significance of the Volcker shock lay not so much in the targeting of monetary aggregates but rather in enhanced control over market interest rates (Rude 2004). Nevertheless, the Federal Reserve did not want to be seen as completely abandoning the idea of monetarist targeting – which it felt could be useful for whenever inflation would reemerge (Krippner 2003: 138) – and so monetary policy shifted "away from monetarism toward eclecticism" (Degen 1987: 191).

THE CONSEQUENCES OF THE MONETARIST SHOCK

The Federal Reserve's turn to monetarism can thus be seen as a shock therapy that reconfigured some key parameters of financial growth (Rude 2004: 40; Panitch and Gindin 2005). When the American economy emerged

---

[3] The process had already started in the 1970s: Whereas in 1970 the Federal Reserve used only one definition of money, by 1975 it used five. By the early 1980s the Federal Reserve even adopted a measure of L, denoting all liquid assets – essentially admitting that any attempt to separate money from other liquid assets had become more or less arbitrary (Degen 1987: 191–2).

from the doldrums after 1982, some basic conditions had changed. The manufacturing sector had been dealt a huge blow, and the financial sphere had become a much better place to put one's money than the real economy (Krippner 2003). The high interest rate regime gave a boost to processes of financialization that had started during the 1970s (Duménil and Lévy 2004), drawing in funds from corporations, savers as well as foreign investors. The large flows of capital pushed up the exchange rate of the dollar and so reinforced the economic recession, thus giving a further impetus to financialization (Wigmore 1997; Arrighi 2003). The growth of financial markets provided intermediaries with ample opportunity to apply the liquidity-producing financial techniques and strategies – asset securitization, liability management, off-balance activities, and operations in derivatives markets – that they had developed over the past two decades (Simpson 1992: 119). These flows of liquidity served to finance growing public and private indebtedness (Guttmann 1994; Duménil and Lévy 2004: 78–85). America was borrowing like never before: Total American debt in 1984 was twice as high as in 1977 (Greider 1987: 658).

In the capital markets, demand for credit surged owing to the vastly expanded range of opportunities for speculation (Greider 1987: 658). Mergers and acquisitions activity also grew: The active market in corporate control not only promised fees from advising and arranging corporate mergers, but also allowed for unsolicited hostile takeovers and leveraged buy-outs. The latter involved using borrowed money (often raised through high-risk and high-yield "junk bonds") to buy control over a company, reorganize it, and then resell it against much higher prices (Knee 2007: 78–9; Morrison and Wilhelm 2007: 260).[4] Furthermore, the recession, in combination with the Reagan administration's social policies, had a devastating impact on the income of the lower strata of the American population, leaving them with little choice other than to borrow against unfavorable rates and often to borrow more to be able to repay their loans and interest charges when they came due. Many got caught in a vicious cycle of consumer debt. The growing leverage of financial intermediaries thus evolved hand in hand with tightening pecuniary constraints on the American working class.

---

[4] The high returns on such investments gave a boost to the number of private equity firms, with firms like Blackstone emulating the example set by Kohlberg Kravis and Roberts, which had pioneered modern private equity practices during the 1970s (Baker and Smith 1998). Contemporary private equity practices bear some resemblance to the strategies employed by J. P. Morgan in the railroad industry a century earlier, as they seek to use debt to leverage the return on equity (Smith 2000).

The American state too found its strategic room for maneuver greatly enlarged. Tax cuts in combination with increases in military spending meant huge budget deficits for the Reagan administration, and the Treasury experienced little difficulty funding historically unprecedented levels of public debt. The bulk of the growing supply of Treasury debt was bought by foreigners, but as the growth and increasing volatility of bond markets created the prospect of large capital gains, it attracted significant funds from Americans as well (Canterbery 2000). But if the Treasury's ability to sell massive amounts of debt was perhaps the most striking manifestation of the fact that the financial regime had been reconfigured in such a way as to eliminate some of its most serious contradictions, things were very different for the Federal Reserve as well: The financial innovation that it had always had such a hard time controlling no longer produced double-digit levels of inflation. Although this did not solve all its problems, it did mean that the Federal Reserve no longer resembled an old man chasing around a mole that was popping up somewhere else every time, creating a space in which it could work toward new operating procedures.

Thus, the massive upward pressure on asset prices was a process that differed fundamentally from the price inflation of the previous decade (Canterbery 2000). Financial innovation was no longer responsible for a dysfunctional dynamic incompatible with other structures in place to organize economic activity, but had become organically connected to wider networks of institutions and policies and so had come to possess much greater systemic coherence and viability. Indeed, as much as the high level of asset inflation stood in stark contrast with the low level of consumer price inflation, they should be seen as different sides of the same coin. The Volcker shock did not eradicate inflationary pressures but made them more functional to U.S. financial power (Arrighi 2003). Liquidity creation was embedded in a reconfigured institutional regime that served to redirect credit flows in a way that ensured a more coherent expansion of the network power of American finance.

THE VORTEX OF NEOLIBERALISM

During the 1970s domestic inflation had posed the major obstacle to the coherent crystallization of the power of American finance, preventing the United States from being able to fully leverage off the institutional infrastructure for dollar debt in international finance. The monetarist turn eliminated the contradiction embedded in the financial regime that had emerged since the 1960s (Panitch and Gindin 2005): Financial innovation and liquidity creation were no longer Janus-faced phenomena, enhancing U.S. power in international finance but undermining the domestic capacity of the American state. Internal state capacity had become aligned with external state capacity. In this context, the massive capital inflows during the early 1980s and America's growing indebtedness[5] served to lubricate the mechanisms of the mutually reinforcing interaction of the internal deepening and external power of American finance. The growing depth of U.S. financial markets promoted Wall Street's dynamism and facilitated innovation, so making it still more attractive to invest in U.S. financial assets and further strengthening the dollar's international position (Gowan 1999). The United States dealt with its increasing indebtedness during this period not through strategies to settle these debts or to cut down on the amount of new debt it was taking on (e.g., by taking measures to improve the trade balance), but precisely through the continuous development of new techniques enhancing its ability to sell dollar debt (Seabrooke 2001).

The dynamics of the neoliberal era tend to confuse most of the spatial metaphors used by political economists. The idea of "externalization," which usefully serves to draw our attention to the American origins of financial globalization, fails to capture some of the dynamics that emerged following the monetarist shock. Those trends often resembled a process of "internalization," a vortexlike process whereby foreign systems and credit relations are pulled into the American financial system. The neoliberal turn and the subsequent accumulation of American debt in foreign hands turned the United States into a financial entrepot and boosted the size and status of New York as an international financial center (Sassen 1991; Silver and Arrighi 2003: 346). Externalization, in other words, can create conditions that allow for internalization: Globalization operates as the extension of the constitutive forms of a hegemonic political economy and so creates a network of linkages that serve to heighten its policy leverage, to increase its "pull."[6] The vortex metaphor can be used to highlight another aspect of the specific nature of American financial power as well: The global expansion of American finance has not only been shaped

---

[5] U.S. acquisition of foreign assets during the early 1980s declined dramatically (from $110.2 billion in 1982 to $15 billion in 1984), while the increase in foreign purchases of American securities (from $8.1 billion in 1980 to $71.4 in 1985) was no less spectacular (Frankel 1988: 586–7).

[6] This pull is illustrated by the effects of the deregulation of international banking: American banks' ability to run overseas branches from American soil through International Banking Facilities effectively served "to internalize aspects of [the Euromarkets] within the US domestic financial system" (Seabrooke 2001: 111) – or, as Kapstein (1994: 52) puts it, it had the effect of at least partly bringing the Euromarket back home.

by the nature of its domestic institutions, but it has continued to exist in a relationship of functional interdependence with its domestic dynamism.

Processes of internalization continued to be accompanied by the outward projection of American financial power. Having reconfigured its financial system in such a way as to make it the main beneficiary of global financial expansion, the United States became more active in forcing other countries to open up their financial systems (Simmons 2001; Soederberg 2004). The U.S. Treasury abandoned its benign neglect approach and became very active in the construction of a more liberal international financial regime, the opening up of foreign financial markets, and the management of international crises (Sarai 2008). Whereas most states found themselves more or less forced to adopt more austere policies and went to great lengths to preserve their policy autonomy in the face of the disciplinary effects of global finance, the United States was not observing any degree of austerity while actively promoting financial liberalization. America's interest in financial liberalization was further evident in its role in pushing the policies of the IMF and the World Bank in a new direction (Woods 2006). With their roots in the Bretton Woods order of fixed exchange roots, these organizations had never been able to play the role envisaged for them, having first been powerless in the face of the dollar shortage and then overwhelmed by the growth of global financial markets. During the 1970s both the IMF and the World Bank reconstituted themselves as key drivers behind liberalization, seizing on countries' need for credit to force them to adopt deregulation measures (Bradshaw and Huang 1991).

FINANCIAL INSTABILITY DURING THE 1980S

Although the expansion of American finance no longer generated the same contradictions as during the 1970s, it certainly produced new sources of instability. The first major event was the debt crisis, which hit in 1982. During the 1970s, American commercial banks had made large loans to developing countries (Cohen 1986: 207–8). The high interest rates that resulted from the Volcker shock put tremendous pressure on developing countries' ability to service their debts. When banks realized the gravity of the situation, they refused to roll over existing debts and demanded repayment (Dymski 2003). Mexico threatened to default on its debts in 1982 and several other countries were heading for the same solution to their problems. A series of defaults would have had a huge impact on America's largest banks, many of which were considered "too big to fail." The Treasury responded by stepping in to bail out the banks while the U.S.-dominated

IMF conducted negotiations with the debtor countries over a rescheduling of their debts in return for structural liberalizing reforms.

The next year the thrift sector went into crisis. The sector's difficulties had been relieved somewhat by the deregulation measures of the early 1980s, but while they were faced with rapidly rising costs for their deposits, a significant share of their assets still consisted of long-term credit locked in against low interest rates (Wells 2004: 163). They sought to compensate for this by investing large amounts of funds in junk bonds – the high-risk, high-reward obligations that drove a feverous market in mergers and acquisitions (Augar 2005: 10). Their willingness to make such risky investments was heightened by the fact that the legislation of the early 1980s had done much to improve government guarantees for savings deposits, leading thrifts to assume, correctly, that the government would step in to bail them out if things were to turn sour. Government guarantees, in other words, produced "moral hazard." From 1985 the number of failures in the thrift sector rose quickly, and it evolved into a full-blown crisis that ended up absorbing huge amounts of public funds (Mayer 1990; Bernstein 1994).

The savings and loan (S&L) crisis gave rise to widespread calls for financial reform, but the next crisis hit before these could have any practical effects. From 1980 onward, the large capital inflows had been pushing up the exchange rate of the dollar and America's trade deficit, spawning concerns that the dollar was overvalued (Seabrooke 2001: 131). A managed depreciation of the dollar was organized through the Plaza Accord of 1985 (Pauls 1990; Henning 1994), but the trade deficit continued to grow and foreign investors, concerned about America's "double deficit," began to sell U.S. assets. Through the Louvre Accord of 1987 the United States arranged for coordinated central bank interventions to support the dollar, but these proved insufficiently effective (Helleiner 1994: 184). Unwilling to use draconian domestic measures to reduce its trade deficit, the United States decided to let the dollar fall (Seabrooke 2001: 132). The dollar dragged financial markets down with it, and the NYSE and stock markets worldwide crashed in October 1987. A major factor in the crash was the activity of arbitragers who "[bet] with futures that the market would go down and then [sold] shares to ensure that it did" (Augar 2005: 126). Profits from capital markets intermediation remained down for the rest of the 1980s (Augar 2005: 127) and the leveraged buyout boom soon ran out of steam, culminating in the failure of several large corporate buyouts and highly publicized prosecutions of several fraud cases towards the end of the decade.

Within a period of five years, the American financial system had been rocked by several crises. The instability gave rise to a widespread concern that the capital inflows of the 1980s had been bought at the expense of the fundamental, longer-term health of the American economic and financial system. The high interest rates were seen as having demolished the U.S. manufacturing base and having boosted the American trade deficit. Economic fundamentals were thus seen to militate against America's ability to validate its unprecedented levels of public and private indebtedness. American banks were no longer to be found in the upper regions of the international ranking tables (Litan 1991) and their dominant position in international finance appeared to have permanently passed to Japanese banks. To many it seemed that an economic meltdown even worse than that of 1987 – one that would be characterized by a complete loss of confidence and the massive pull-out of foreign capital – was imminent. The financial malaise contributed to the sense that American international power was waning, and the 1980s saw the flourishing of theories of American hegemonic decline (e.g., Kennedy 1987).

FINANCIAL MANAGEMENT DURING THE 1980S

As we now know, such predictions concerning the decline of American financial power were rather premature: The edifice of American finance has proved considerably less fragile than many presumed during the 1980s. The narrative of this book has framed debt as a complex social relation whose meaning is crucially dependent on the practices through which it is produced and the institutional connections in which it is embedded. The financial infrastructure that had evolved over the previous decades and been reconfigured with the neoliberal turn would prove sufficiently resilient to weather the instability of the 1980s, to allow the United States to finance growing trade and budget deficits and to function as the basis for the regeneration of the competitive strength of American banks during the 1990s. And a crucial ingredient of that institutional configuration was the American state's growing ability to manage and stabilize financial expansion. This emphasis on the state's enhanced capacity is by no means to suggest that financial management had become smooth sailing – merely that the American state was no longer mired in or overwhelmed by the tensions generated by the financial system and had created sufficient leeway for itself that it could engage the extant contradictions of that system more constructively.

The growth of the American state's managerial capabilities took place in the context of the implementation of a formal framework for the regulation of international banking. The debt crisis had accelerated a change in regulatory thinking that had been in the making since the early 1970s. Whereas traditionally the soundness of a bank had been conceptualized in terms of its reserves position, the rampant financial innovation from the 1960s onward and, in particular, the advent of liability management techniques made this focus increasingly meaningless. Under these circumstances, policy makers began to shift their focus toward another aspect of a bank's balance sheet, the ratio of capital to assets.[7] In the wake of the debt crisis, Congress instructed American regulators to coordinate with foreign authorities to create an international regime of capital requirements (Kapstein 1991; Wagster 1996). The United States initially found little enthusiasm for such an international regime among other countries (whose financial systems were less heavily securitized), but when it began working toward a bilateral accord with Britain, new regulatory institutions emerged that other countries had little choice but to subsequently join (Seabrooke 2001: 137). The 1988 Basel Capital Accord provided a stabilizing international framework that was heavily weighted toward the institutional specificities of the American financial system and consecrated the obligations of the U.S. Treasury as virtually risk-free liquidity (Levich and Walter 1989; Porter 1993; Singer 2004).

It was in this context that the American state set out to expand its domestically situated capacities for financial management. Following the 1987 crisis, Reagan created the Working Group on Financial Markets to coordinate the activities of a wide range of public and private financial actors (Parenteau 2005: 136–7). Over the course of the neoliberal era, the "Plunge Protection Team" would evolve into one of the main, if largely unseen, bodies for coordination and cooperation among America's key financial practitioners and policy makers and play a central role in the development of the American state's capacities for dealing with financial instability. As such, it reflected and advanced a broader process of reconfiguration of regulatory authority.

---

[7] Of course, banks had always been under capital requirements, and in the early nineteenth century, when American commercial banks experienced difficulty attracting deposits and emulating British commercial banking practices, bank capital had formed the key component of banks' liabilities. But over time capitalization had lost much of its significance as a measure of a bank's soundness. Now that the Federal Reserve was confronted with a system where banks were able to access reserve funds to incur a wide range of risks, it seemed that the best way to create a buffer was to force banks to raise their ratio of capital to assets.

The expansion of financial activity during the neoliberal era meant that the formal definition of particular agencies' jurisdictional reach became even less meaningful and more precarious than during previous decades, and proactive cooperation became a more attractive option than defensive attempts to preserve exclusive say over a particular piece of financial life. Regulatory capacities were consolidated into a more coherent regime marked by greater mutual accountability and a clearer hierarchy of authority with the Federal Reserve and the Treasury at the top.

Central to this emerging regime was the construction of an informal "too big to fail" policy (De Cecco n.d.). The Treasury's interventions during the debt crisis and the S&L crisis created expectations for the way in which monetary authorities would deal with the imminent failure of financial intermediaries in the future. Public responsibility for the fundamental soundness of the American financial system was thus gradually extended to include an implicit guarantee that the government would bail out institutions whose bankruptcy could destabilize the financial system. This socialization of risk introduced a major element of moral hazard into the American financial system: A financial institution large enough to have a potentially destabilizing effect on the system as a whole or with connections to politically sensitive economic sectors could take all manner of irresponsible risks, secure in the knowledge that authorities would come to its aid with public funds if it got into trouble. This element of moral hazard has become especially pronounced because of the progressive concentration of the U.S. banking industry since the early 1980s (Dymski 1999; Ferguson 2003: 397). But it is crucial to appreciate that, however troubling too-big-to-fail may be from an ethical point of view, moral hazard has never just been a problem: It has been a central driving force behind American intermediaries' unrivalled propensity for innovation and the creation of an infrastructure of incentives that continually generates new products and services. This makes it comprehensible that policy makers and legislators have been less concerned with finding ways to reduce moral hazard than with expanding the sources of funds available for the socialization of risk (Lewis and Pescetto 1996; Seabrooke 2001: 144; Hester 2008: 161).

FINANCIAL EXPANSION DURING THE 1990S

American finance now expanded in a more stable way. During the "roaring nineties" (Stiglitz 2004), institutional investors grew exponentially (Useem

1996),[8] mobilizing massive amounts of savings and so ensuring a steadily growing flow of funds into financial markets. Innovation became increasingly organized around their investment needs (Clark 2000; Clowes 2000; Morrison and Wilhelm 2007). The decade witnessed first a significant recovery and then a veritable explosion of initial public offerings, underwriting, and trading activity. Commercial banks were eager to participate in the burgeoning fund management industry and to this end they originated devices and instruments allowing them to work around Glass-Steagall. In doing so they were taking advantage of the opportunities that had already been created by deregulation (Degen 1987: 189–90; Deeg and Lütz 2000: 395–6) as well as the many exemptions granted and loopholes opened up by regulators who saw little point in trying to maintain barriers that banks would find ways to circumvent in any case. Banks were now allowed to engage in virtually any kind of business through their holding companies, and as the ability to offer a full range of financial services afforded competitive advantages they made full use of the opportunities opened up. Such advantages of scale were also a driving force behind mergers and growing concentration in the banking sector (Berger et al. 1995: 61; Dymski 1999; Ennis 2001, 2004; Wells 2004: 169). Glass-Steagall would be formally repealed in 1999 (Spong 2003: 87).

If the growth of the stock market was the most visible element of the financial growth of the 1990s, the massive growth of derivatives and bond markets was no less crucial in absorbing investment flows. Derivatives markets had grown substantially since the breakdown of Bretton Woods, and in the bull market of the 1990s such instruments increasingly served to leverage investment positions, allowing for more effective market manipulation and providing more tailored financial solutions (Morrison and Wilhem 2007: 10). Similarly, fixed-income markets became key pillars of financial growth (Canterbery 2000: 24–5): Even as the growth of government debt stagnated during the second half of the 1990s (Dupont and Sack 1999), the dramatic expansion of consumer and mortgage debt during the 1990s more than compensated for this. In the wake of the S&L crisis, the government-sponsored enterprises Fannie Mae and Freddie Mac went from being important to central actors in the market for mortgage credit (MacDonald 1996, 2005: 667), guaranteeing the steady growth of a core volume of securitized mortgages and conferring implicit governmental guarantees on it. The availability of securitization procedures in these

---

[8] Between 1990 and 2000, institutional investors grew by nearly a factor seven (Engen et al. 2000: 797).

markets allowed banks to replace long-term loans with liquid securities or even to move such asset-backed securities off their balance sheet altogether by placing them with special purpose vehicles (Coles and Hardt 2000: 776; Hester 2008: 165). The latter option was particularly attractive because it allowed banks to exclude such loans from the risk-bearing assets over which they needed to calculate their capital requirements as per the Basel capital standards regime (Berger et al. 1995; Baron 1996: 83; Landis and Lusignani 1997). The emergence of the "originate and distribute" model permitted intermediaries to earn fees by creating debts and then pass the debt on to others, so avoiding the associated risk (Dymski 2007: 6).

The use of securitization techniques interacted with neoliberal social trends and policies to produce a massive expansion of asset-backed debt (Wolfe 2000: 353–4; Montgomerie 2006). The Clinton administration did little to reverse the Republican cutbacks on public schemes for income provision and instead made access to financial services a key pillar of its social policies. The government-sponsored enterprises were instructed to increase their investments in mortgages for lower-income borrowers, and the revisions to and reanimation of the Community Reinvestment Act in 1995 gave lenders a range of incentives to increase the amount of mortgage loans to those same groups. Extant restrictions like maximum interest rates were abolished to undercut the activities of illegal lenders and loan sharks (Gramlich 2007: 106).[9] But even as in public discourse policies promoting the integration of lower-income groups into the formal financial system were portrayed as promoting financial inclusion and drew broad-based support (Braunstein and Welch 2002: 448; Newstadt 2008), financial institutions increasingly viewed low-income households as a "captured market" (Montgomerie 2007: 21). Households that had previously been deemed unworthy of credit were now offered loans "with excessive fees, high penalties, and high interest rates" (Dymski 2007: 10). The period from the mid-1990s saw the steady growth of mortgage lending to borrowers with "subprime" credit ratings (MacDonald 2005: 672). The 1990s, then, saw the maturation of risk-based pricing: Risk assessments were used ever less for deciding which borrowers to exclude from credit extension and increasingly to justify high-risk premiums (White 2004; Marron 2007).

[9] Growing inequality and the dismantling of public income provision under the Reagan administrations had made poor people dependent on money marts and pawnbrokers and easy targets for illegal lenders and loan sharks. This became a focal point for advocacy groups, who uncovered evidence of widespread exploitative credit practices and so became a driving force behind revisions to the Community Reinvestment Act (MacDonald 2005).

The external projection of American financial power by no means suffered under these processes of domestic expansion. The U.S.-dominated IMF and World Bank applied themselves to opening up and liberalizing the financial systems of other countries (Wood 2006; Felder 2008), thus ensuring that American financial innovations enjoyed maximum leverage (Grahl 2001). Policies deemed unfavorable to financial capital could spark a sudden exit of financial capital from a particular country, and it was the depth and liquidity of American financial markets that provided investors with a safe haven (Burke 2001). Of course, the operation of this mechanism was contingent on the crisis not engulfing Western markets themselves – as, for instance, the Asian crisis of 1997 momentarily threatened to do. It was precisely for this reason that the active management of international finance by the Treasury, in conjunction with the IMF and World Bank (the "Washington Consensus"), was so important. As financial markets became much more globally interconnected and instabilities were transmitted much more rapidly across the globe (Solomon 1999), the American state began to assume ever greater responsibility for the management of the financial dynamics unleashed.

NEW FORMS OF FEDERAL RESERVE CONTROL

Indeed, during the mid-1990s the too-big-to-fail principle found most application abroad. At home it functioned as a background regime that was crucially important, but, owing to the decade's relatively stable growth, did not have to be invoked all that frequently. Domestically, the infrastructural characteristics of the power of the American state were more readily apparent in the tremendous policy leverage that the Federal Reserve developed. While the post–World War II period had seen a gradual rise in the Federal Reserve's influence, and if its monetarist muscle-flexing had propelled it into a central position in the country's economic system, it was during the 1990s that the Federal Reserve's status and authority reached an apogee. Alan Greenspan's reputation reached comic heights and his every statement was subjected to endless analysis and interpretation.

This kind of policy leverage had begun to emerge in the wake of the 1987 crisis and further developed over the course of the 1990s. Although the experience of the early 1980s had made clear that rampant innovation and credit creation were not necessarily forces undermining the Federal Reserve's objectives, the fact that these new dynamics came with their own sources of instability meant that Federal Reserve policy makers were still actively searching for new mechanisms of control. Aware that monetarism

Neoliberal Consolidation

had been a shock therapy that offered few guidelines for ongoing financial governance, they sought operating procedures that would permit a more consistent and predictable grip on the dynamics of the financial system. After 1982, the Federal Reserve's directives had been ambiguous and eclectic, but this approach to policy making became untenable in the wake of the stock market crash: Returning the markets to stability required that the Federal Reserve offer guidance by making clear its interest rate policy (Krippner 2003: 143–4). In a sense, this returned the Federal Reserve to its pre-Volcker shock policy modalities, focused on the manipulation of interest rates (Friedman 2000); but it gradually emerged that in the new, post-Volcker shock financial context this instrument occupied a very different structural position and acquired a very different significance.

The Federal Reserve now operated in a densely interconnected financial system, and its institutional linkages to markets were no longer plagued by the New Deal regulations and the perverse ways in which those refracted its policies. What had previously been a major problem for the Federal Reserve's ability to regulate the financial system – that is, banks' close institutional connections to financial markets – now emerged as a point of great policy leverage: The high degree of market depth and connectivity meant that changes in the federal funds rate were almost instantly transmitted to other markets (Phillips 1996). The federal funds rate emerged as the key point of reference for all financial actors, allowing the Federal Reserve to use it as a means to signal its objectives. The Federal Reserve still did not have control over the quantity of credit created but it developed an extraordinary capacity to steer, manage, and stabilize flows of credit. And it could use this capacity to solve market bottlenecks and promote ongoing financial expansion, thus ensuring that liquidity creation would not spill over into the real economy and cause inflation (Canterbery 2000: 28). Over time the Federal Reserve found that financial actors responded to its announcements by adjusting their behavior in the desired direction even prior to it having undertaken any open market operations (Krippner 2003: 151–4). Even the tone and wording of directives and chairman's statements became key policy instruments (Ehrmann and Fratzscher 2005; Bell-Kelton 2006: 6–8).

The Federal Reserve's regulatory authority was still profoundly dependent on its institutional linkages to financial life: Its capacity to steer the markets was strongly biased in favor of financial expansion (Parenteau 2005; Axilrod 2009). If the Federal Reserve had acquired the ability to talk markets up or down, the latter option was always much more conditional. On the occasions that the Federal Reserve tried to shift toward more restrictive policies (e.g., Greenspan's famous "irrational exuberance" lamentation), this created consternation and disarray but did little to slow down their dynamism on a structural basis. But as the Federal Reserve learned that instability remained manageable and inflationary pressures remained at bay even after several years of steady expansion, it abandoned most of its residual concerns about the pace of financial expansion. The Federal Reserve increasingly saw the creation of liquidity as existing in a mutually reinforcing relationship with its own authority, and in this context it became more and more willing to connect its governance modalities to the instruments that featured so prominently in banks' innovation strategies, approving a stream of bank applications to deal in a wider range of financial instruments and promoting banks' reliance on their own risk management techniques for the calculation of their capital requirements (Newstadt 2008).[10] The Federal Reserve became fully committed to verbally "guiding" the markets as they travelled the path of expansion (Parenteau 2005: 143).

INTO THE TWENTY-FIRST CENTURY

By the late 1990s, the dynamics of American finance had been consolidated into a regime that possessed more coherence than many had imagined possible during the previous decade. The most serious threats to the integrity of the system were more or less external (i.e., originating in developing countries) and the American state was fully capable of managing these crises to its advantage (Gowan 1999). But many commentators continued to view the financial gyrations of the 1990s as little more than a massive buildup of speculative debt and fictitious capital – that is, of finance spinning out of control. And so, when instability hit at home in the guise of the implosion of the dot-com driven stock market boom (it turned out that large amounts of venture capital had been poured into companies with poor business prospects), many interpreted this crisis as signaling the dissolution of American financial power (e.g., Brenner 2003; Pollin 2003; Duncan 2005). Subsequent years saw the policies of the Bush administration that resembled so much those of the Reagan administration (large tax cuts in combination with steep increases in military spending) and were viewed by many as expressing and precipitating the waning of hegemony (Block 2003; Seabrooke 2004).

---

[10] Indeed, the Federal Reserve's in-house research took its cue from and worked to advance the risk management tools, econometric models, and forecasting techniques used by Wall Street banks (Newstadt 2008: 108).

Such notions of collapse and decline during the first years of the twenty-first century now seem almost less well-founded than similar predictions during the 1970s and 1980s. The dynamics of the stock market boom and its unraveling remained well within the institutional parameters of the neoliberal financial order consolidated during the previous decades. Although the Federal Reserve's efforts could not prevent the bursting of the bubble itself, its reputation and ability to guide market expansion survived largely intact (ensuring Alan Greenspan's virtual apotheosis when he retired in 2006). Indeed, what really stands out about the dot-com meltdown as well as the financial shock after 9/11 were the relative ease and efficiency with which the Federal Reserve's policies were capable of containing the effects of events that might easily have proved fatal had they occurred in a less-well-institutionalized system. The resilience of neoliberal institutional structures was also evident when it came to the political capacities that the American government and financial elites displayed as they set about to reconstruct the modalities of financial governance: Intense popular anger, triggered by revelations of collusion and fraud, was defused through reforms that laid the foundations for further financial integration and renewed expansion. The Sarbanes–Oxley Act of 2002 made corporate governance practices more accountable and transparent to investors (Augar 2005: 19) and so did much to restore popular trust in the financial system while only scratching the surface of the leverage and control that American financial elites derive from their positions (Soederberg 2008). Financial markets soon resumed their pace of growth.

CONCLUSION

This chapter has shown how the transition to neoliberalism served to consolidate the expansion of American finance and the regulatory capacities of the American state. The monetarist reconfiguration of the institutional parameters of financial growth resolved many of the contradictions of the 1970s, ensuring that the financial strategies responsible for the extension of dollar credit no longer generated intractable problems for the ability of financial authorities to manage the system. In this way it laid the foundations for a mutually reinforcing interaction between the expansion of American structural power at home and abroad – that is, between the internal deepening of the networks of American finance through the integration of the American public and their external widening through the extension of financial relations based on dollar liquidity.

Thus, the turn to monetarism and neoliberalism did not serve to subject public purpose and power to the external discipline of disembedded global markets. Such Polanyian interpretations of the neoliberal era set too much store by the ideological representations of that era and lose sight of the fact that official professions of institutional retreat were always accompanied by the institutionalization of an intricate web of financial power. The power relations that were built in this way had little to do with the generalized subordination of private and public actors to market imperatives; rather, they involved an intensification of disciplinary pressure on the bulk of the population that found its counterpart in the growth of the state's capacities and the increased leverage commanded by financial elites. In other words, neoliberalism has involved the construction of mechanisms of control that serve as sources of power for the state and those who enjoy privileged access or connections to its organizational mechanisms.

As this book has emphasized, the prevalence of liberalism as an ideology should be understood not as corresponding to an actual attenuation of state authority but precisely as reflecting a consolidation of state-economy linkages ensuring that the power relations embedded in the financial sphere serve as an effective vehicle of dominant interests and that the deployment of political authority can consequently assume a more organic quality. The period following the monetarist shock saw the rise of precisely such a regime, based on a new degree of congruence between the regulatory authority of the American state, intermediaries' innovative propensities, and the financial practices of ordinary Americans. After monetarism, the American financial system had become much more sensitive to the manipulation of its basic institutional parameters, and financial authorities enjoyed a higher degree of infrastructural capacity than ever before.

12

Contradictions of the Present

INTRODUCTION

Neoliberal financial growth did not just produce the kind of instability that could be effectively addressed within the institutional parameters of the neoliberal regime. The expanding networks of American financial power also produced interdependencies that the governance capacities consolidated during the neoliberal era were only poorly equipped to deal with. In a context of growing economic inequality, the penetration of financial forms and pressures into the fabric of everyday social life produced tremendous strains on the capacities of ordinary Americans to participate in this financial system and service their debts. In 2007, the American financial system was hit by a major crisis that started with the discovery of large amounts of "bad debt" in the "subprime" segment of the mortgage market and would evolve into the most serious economic downturn since the Great Depression. The Federal Reserve's policy levers did not work the way they had during the past decades and market liquidity was not easily restored. Many commentators interpreted the situation as the inevitable outcome of America's unsustainable financial practices, of the way it had been relying on speculation and excessive borrowing to stave off fundamental economic constraints. This chapter presents an alternative account of the nature of the crisis, analyzing it not in terms of the sudden imposition of accumulated financial pressures on a system that had been living beyond its means for decades, but in terms of the emergence of new contradictions within a regime of financial power characterized by its own internal institutional logic. The infrastructure of American finance was not fully configured and equipped to deal with these tensions, but this did not render the American state powerless by any means. If authorities were forced to deploy the full range of their institutional capacities, the effect of this was to preserve the integrity of America's key financial institutions. Although this gives no guarantees for the future of American finance, it does mean that we should not examine present-day financial change through a focus on the alleged tendency of gyrating markets to overwhelm public capacities, but rather as ongoing, contradiction-ridden processes of institutional construction.

FROM NEOLIBERAL EXPANSION TO THE SUBPRIME CRISIS

Even during the first years after the dot-com crisis, before the stock market could recover, American finance was sustained by its other institutional pillars. The Federal Reserve's interest rate policies were effective in solving market bottlenecks, and American banks' securitization strategies served to counteract the most serious effects of the liquidity crunch (Hirtle and Stiroh 2007). The expansion of securitized asset-backed debt had been briefly interrupted by the bursting of the dot-com bubble but resumed pace well before any other sectors did. The liquidity of such debt was further enhanced by the Federal Reserve's announcement right after the crisis that it would henceforth treat mortgage-backed securities as highly liquid assets, second only to Treasury bills (Newstadt 2008: 109). American banks also had undiminished access to new sources of funds, which allowed them to take full advantage of the growth of asset-backed debt: They were able to increase their domestic access to liabilities, but also imported large amounts from the Eurodollar markets (McGuire 2004). Indeed, the effects of the global liquidity crunch were felt most acutely outside the United States, and in this context the American market came to function as an even more attractive destination for global capital flows. As the Bush administration cut taxes and massively increased military spending, the national debt once again began to grow rapidly, much of which was bought by foreigners (in particular China). American finance thus picked up its pace of expansion relatively easily, and New York grew faster than any other financial center (Konings 2008).

After the abolition of Glass-Steagall, capital market actors could fully draw on commercial banks' flexible access to funds (Knee 2007: 91), and this was a major factor in the relatively quick revival of capital markets. Before long, the securities industry had embarked on a new set of profitable strategies, including the further sophistication of the models used in hedge fund activities, a revival of leveraged buyouts, and the proliferation of "alternative" investment products. But although the "high finance" world of speculation and take over activity tended to be the main focus of financial reporting, the sector for securitized asset-backed debt grew even faster (Nesvetailova and Palan 2008; Schwartz 2009). A large and continually growing share of this debt was assumed by working people who, simultaneously faced with stagnant wages and the ample availability of credit liquidity, increasingly treated access to credit as a source of income to cover basic cost-of-living expenditures (Dymski 2007; Montgomerie 2007). Risk assessments were increasingly used not to decide what kinds of risks exposures to avoid but to determine the required rates of return. The ever more complex techniques for securitizing asset-backed debt were crucial here, as it meant that risks could almost always be passed on to others while ensuring high origination and resale fees (Blackburn 2008: 74). Mortgage bankers found their way into poor neighborhoods that even during the 1990s had been of little interest, and lending practices took on increasingly predatory qualities. If such trends did not go unnoticed by financial authorities, they generally saw it as an acceptable growth of risk (Greenspan 2007: 233). The Federal Reserve did not challenge the idea that banks' own models, in combination with the judgments of the credit-rating agencies, were the most appropriate means of assessing their risk exposure, and it also declined to regulate banks' ability to circumvent capital requirements by moving assets off their balance sheets and parking them with special purpose vehicles. Meanwhile, a new law, adopted in 2005, made it harder to file for bankruptcy. The financial difficulties of America's lower strata became a source of tremendous profits for Wall Street (Gowan 2009).

This deepening of American finance entailed an imposition of discipline that went well beyond the enlistment of subordinate actors into hegemonic patterns of control: By tightening the financial screws to the point of overstrain, American intermediaries undermined ordinary people's ability to function as competent social actors with access to the requisite set of debt-servicing capacities. In the summer of 2007, it became clear that many Americans had for some time been unable to cope with their debt burden. Many people who had had mortgages foisted on them against subprime rates turned out to be considerably less creditworthy than lenders and credit-rating agencies had assumed (Carlson and Weinbach 2007: A 57), and large amounts of subprime mortgage-backed securities turned out to be "bad debt." Because much of this bad debt was hidden in much larger pools of asset-backed securities, uncertainty spread rapidly. As any purchase could turn out be a lemon, markets quickly froze and those who happened to hold mortgage-backed securities at that point in time were stuck with them. The effects reverberated throughout the edifice of American finance and market liquidity froze up quickly (Nesvetailova 2010).

Just how serious the situation was became apparent over the course of the following year. The Federal Reserve's attempts to restore confidence by cutting rates did not have the hoped-for effects, nor did its efforts to devise creative solutions in cooperation with other American regulatory agencies through the President's Working Group make the difference that was required. When the crisis claimed its first major victim, the investment bank Bear Stearns, the Federal Reserve considered that it was too big to fail and responded by directing and guaranteeing its takeover by J. P. Morgan Chase. In the summer of 2008, it became clear that Fannie Mae and Freddie Mac, the pillars of the American mortgage securitization system, found themselves in considerable difficulties, due to the large amounts of bad debt on their books. In early September 2008, the U.S. government took control of these purveyors of the American dream. Even this was not sufficient to stabilize the system, and in the following weeks several other Wall Street giants got into major trouble. The government's one attempt to enforce financial discipline on a major financial institution (the firm Lehman Brothers was allowed to fail) backfired badly, and it quickly returned to the too-big-to-fail regime, arranging the take over of Merrill Lynch and bailing out AIG (which had insured many of the assets under pressure). Even after all this, there were plenty of firms that were still in the danger zone and it became clear that ad hoc bailouts were not going to save the edifice of American finance. The too-big-to-fail regime now became official policy and assumed new dimensions (Ferguson and Johnson 2009b). Beginning with the Troubled Asset Relief Program, during the past years the American state has extended unprecedented public guarantees to financial institutions, the exact extent of which is likely to remain unclear for some years to come.

INTERPRETING THE PRESENT

The dominant interpretations of the crisis have closely followed the kind of narrative that this book has criticized. Employing Polanyian metaphors, IPE authors were quick to argue that the roots of the crisis stemmed from the ways in which financial markets had disembedded themselves from their social and institutional context (Wade 2008; Ruggie 2008; Altvater 2009; Warwick Commission on International Financial Reform 2009;

Boyer 2010). From such perspectives, the financial expansion from which the United States had benefited so disproportionately was now revealed to have been a reckless gamble, a speculative mortgage on the future on which payment was now due: When it became apparent that America's mountains of public and private debt were not supported by solid institutional foundations, its financial house of cards crumbled in the most dramatic fashion possible (Baker 2009; Brenner 2009; Crotty 2009; Gamble 2009; Wray 2009). The economic constraints and market imperatives that the United States had defied for so long were now seen as asserting themselves with all the force they had gathered in the meantime, entirely overwhelming the powers of American regulators. The American state's response to the bursting of the bubble – interpreted as an irresponsible desperate and incoherent attempt to salvage its unsustainable ways by throwing trillions of dollars at the very actors who bore most responsibility for the drama – was seen as providing yet further relief to the contours of decline.

However, political economists' eagerness to cast the crisis as a confirmation of what they had long argued seems misplaced: After all, before 2007, few scholars or commentators had imagined that the inability of underprivileged people to keep up with the payments on their subprime mortgages could ever have thrown a wrench into the wheels of high finance and economic life at large. If the subprime crisis presented a much more significant threat to the integrity of the American financial system than any other crisis since the Great Depression, that had little to do with a disarticulation of the economic and social spheres but was precisely a product of the ways in which financial principles had penetrated ever more deeply into the fabric of social life. The neoliberal era and especially the first years of the twenty-first century had further eroded the boundaries between high finance and everyday life, and this was expressed in the specific character of the crisis, triggered by the inability of ordinary Americans to keep up with the repayments on the debt that they had incurred when they bought their stake in American society.

That the crisis cannot be understood in terms of the external imposition of market imperatives was apparent in the fact it did not assume the form of a massive flight out of dollar assets (Ferguson and Johnson 2009a). Far from the crisis leaving the fate of the United States at the mercy of European and Chinese investors, it did not take long for America's troubles to engulf the global economy and create a context in which precisely the market for Treasury bills began to function as a safe haven for global capital flows, sustaining the dollar's status as global currency (Chandler

2009). It quickly became clear that the agencies and institutional capacities that would decide how the situation would unfold were to be found within the United States itself. If the magnitude of their task was unlike anything they had faced in recent years, this was precisely because what they were facing was not an external challenge or constraint but a contradiction at the very heart of America's financial infrastructure. Thus, the subprime crisis is not best understood in terms of America's inability or reluctance to conform the operation of its financial system to an abstract model of liberal order; instead, it should be seen as born of contradictions internal to the specific logic of the intricately interwoven web of American financial relations.

This logic was not suddenly composed of nothing but contradictions: The American state's crisis management was characterized by considerably more coherence than most commentators gave it credit for. The American government's rescue efforts have been widely portrayed as a spectacular manifestation of the unsustainable nature of American financial practices. But there is something very one-sided and premature about such assessments. This book has argued that the state's willingness to assume responsibility for market risk has been an organic aspect of the infrastructure of American finance and in particular a consistent feature of its neoliberal era, characterized by frequent bailouts. The ability of financial elites to externalize the risks associated with their strategies gave a major impetus to financial innovation and so to the market expansion from which the American state benefited so much. This is of course not to deny that from a moral point of view the effects of such policies are highly problematic, but rather to insist that infrastructural public authority has never operated in the interest of an abstract common good: Infrastructural power is constructed on the basis of, and operates through, constellations of control mechanisms that are characterized by considerable inequality. Too-big-to-fail policies are inherently asymmetrical in nature, since access to their benefits is conditional on the degree of market power that actors already enjoy: The state's financial protections and guarantees have redounded to those actors that were pivotal in shaping and controlling the dynamics of financial life and so functioned as the key constituents of the state's infrastructural powers.

From a conceptual perspective that is not preoccupied with market disembedding and state attenuation, what is noteworthy is precisely the extraordinary degree of infrastructural capacity that the American state displayed in managing the crisis, that is, the fact that it could access hundreds of billions of dollars at a moment's notice and effectively target them

Contradictions of the Present

at those actors with whose interests its authority had become most deeply bound up. The policies undertaken over the past years should be understood in terms of the American state wielding capacities that it has built up over the course of the neoliberal era. And those public interventions were in fact successful in securing the integrity of the American financial system and preserving its key mechanisms. The tentacles of the integral state have been lodged at the heart of financial life, and it has been able to wield these to hold together the networks of American finance. Nor is the intense popular anger elicited by the crisis likely to be a fundamental threat to the continued growth of American finance: There has been little to suggest that Americans' discontent may not be addressed, in time-honored fashion, through reforms that seek to make financial institutions more inclusive and so lay the foundation for the further penetration of financial principles into the everyday life of American society.

Although these considerations should serve to caution against apocalyptic assessments of the short-term consequences of the crisis, this is not, however, to rule out the possibility that the future may see the emergence of serious challenges to American financial power. The crisis has made clear that the logic of financial integration and deepening has begun to generate contradictions that are particularly difficult to manage within the institutional parameters of the neoliberal regime. The crisis emanated from a dynamic of financial incorporation that this book has identified as central to the construction of American financial power, and the crisis may well represent the first in a series of threats to the ability of finance to serve as an instrument of social integration. Whether the American state will be able to access the institutional capacities required to address this problem must for the time being remain an open question. But how the American state manages the complex linkages through which is it is connected to the domestic and global networks of American finance will remain one of the central questions for those seeking to understand the dynamics of contemporary capitalism for some time to come.

CONCLUSION

This chapter has given an indication of the significance of the present moment in the development of American finance. But there can be little doubt that the current conjuncture has dimensions that will only become apparent in the years to come. We may well be staring at them on a daily basis yet be unable to discern them and grasp their significance. No matter how hard we may strive to adopt a stance that is critical of received wisdom, contemporary observers will always be too embroiled in the perspective of the moment to be able to approximate its full truth. But precisely because history is an open-ended process that will forever invent new ways to defy our conceptual grip, it is imperative that we break out of reified conceptualizations that hold us captive to hegemonic ways of thinking. This book has suggested that we may start doing so by adopting an analytical mindset that is not pre occupied by stylized concepts of state and market but instead is centrally concerned with the operation of power and its contradictions.

Bibliography

Abrams, P. (1977) "Notes on the difficulty of studying the state," *Journal of Historical Sociology*, 1(1).
Agger, E. A. (1914) "The commercial paper debate," *Journal of Political Economy*, 22(7).
Aglietta, M. (1979) *A theory of capitalist regulation*, London: NLB.
Ahearn, D. S. (1963) *Federal Reserve policy reappraised, 1951–1959*, New York/London: Columbia University Press.
Aitken, R. (2007) *Performing capital*, New York: Palgrave.
Albion, R. G. (1939) *The rise of New York port, 1815–1860*, New York: Charles Scribner's Sons.
Alhadeff, D. A. (1952) "Monetary policy and the Treasury bill market," *American Economic Review*, 42(3).
Altvater, E. (2009) "Postneoliberalism or postcapitalism? The failure of neoliberalism in the financial market crisis," *Development Dialogue*, 51 (January).
Anderson, C. J. (1965) *A half-century of Federal Reserve policymaking, 1914–1964*, Philadelphia: Federal Reserve Bank of Philadelphia.
Ansell, C. (2000) "The networked polity: regional development in Western Europe," *Governance*, 13(3).
Argy, V. (1981) *The postwar international money crisis: an analysis*, London: Allen & Unwin.
Arrighi, G. (1994) *The long twentieth century: money, power, and the origins of our times*, London/New York: Verso.
  (2003) "The social and political economy of global turbulence," *New Left Review*, 20 (March–April).
Ashworth, J. (1996) "Free labor, wage labor, and the slave power: republicanism and the Republican Party in the 1850s," in M. Stokes and S. Conway (eds.), *The market revolution in America*, Charlottesville/London: University Press of Virginia.
Augar, P. (2005) *The greed merchants*, London/New York: Penguin.

Avallone, P. (1997) "Public banks, trade and industry in southern Italy, seventeenth to eighteenth century," in A. Teichova, G. K.-v. Hentenryk, and D. Ziegler (eds.), *Banking, trade, and industry: Europe, America, and Asia from the thirteenth to the twentieth century*, Cambridge: Cambridge University Press.

Axilrod, S. H. (2009) *Inside the Fed. Monetary policy and its management, Martin through Greenspan to Bernanke*, Cambridge, MA: MIT Press.

Baack, B. (2008) "America's first monetary policy: inflation and seigniorage during the Revolutionary War," *Financial History Review*, 15(2).

Bach, G. L. (1971) *Making monetary and fiscal policy*, Washington, DC: Brookings Institution.

Baker, D. (2009) *Plunder and blunder. The rise and fall of the bubble economy*, Sausalito: Polipoint Press.

Baker, G. P. and G. D. Smith (1998) *The new financial capitalists. Kohlberg Kravis Roberts and the creation of corporate value*, Cambridge: Cambridge University Press.

Balabanis, H. P. (1980 [1935]) *The American discount market*, Chicago: University of Chicago Press.

Barber, W. J. (1993) "Neomercantilism in American official thinking in the 1920s and early 1930s," in L. Magnusson (ed.), *Mercantilist economics*, Boston: Kluwer Academic Publishers.

Barkin, J. S. (2003) *Social construction and the logic of money. Financial predominance and international economic leadership*, Albany: State University of New York Press.

Barnett, G. E. (1911) *State banks and trust companies since the passage of the National-bank Act*, Washington, DC: Government Printing Office.

Baron, N. D. (1996) "The role of rating agencies in the securitization process," in L. T. Kendall and M. J. Fishman (eds.), *A primer on securitization*, Cambridge, MA/London: MIT Press.

Baskin, J. B. (1988) "The development of corporate financial markets in Britain and the United States, 1600–1914: overcoming asymmetric information," *Business History Review*, 62 (Summer).

Baskin, J. B. and P. J. Miranti (1997) *A history of corporate finance*, Cambridge: Cambridge University Press.

Baster, A. S. J. (1937) "The international acceptance markets," *American Economic Review*, 27(2).

Battilossi, S. (2000) "Financial innovation and the golden ages of international banking: 1800–1931 and 1958–81," *Financial History Review*, 7(2).

(2002a) "Banking with multinationals: British clearing banks and the Euromarkets' challenge, 1958–1976," in S. Battilossi and Y. Cassis (eds.), *European banks and the American challenge. Competition and cooperation in international banking under Bretton Woods*, Oxford: Oxford University Press.

(2002b) "Introduction: international banking and the American challenge in historical perspective," in S. Battilossi and Y. Cassis (eds.), *European banks and the American challenge. Competition and cooperation in international banking under Bretton Woods*, Oxford: Oxford University Press.

Beck, N. (1984) "Domestic Political Sources of American Monetary Policy: 1955–82," *Journal of Politics*, 46(3).

Bibliography

Becker, W. H. (1982) *The dynamics of business-government relations. Industry and export 1893–1921*, Chicago/London: University of Chicago Press.
Beckert, J. (2002) *Beyond the market: the social foundations of economic efficiency*, Princeton: Princeton University Press.
  (2003) "Economic Action and embeddedness: how shall we conceptualize economic action?," *Journal of Economic Issues*, 37(3).
Beckert, S. (1993) *The monied metropolis. New York City and the consolidation of the American bourgeoisie, 1850–1896*, Cambridge: Cambridge University Press.
Beckhart, B. H. (1922) "Outline of banking history from the first bank of the United States through the panic of 1907," *Annals of the American Academy of Political and Social Science*, 99 (January).
Bell, S. and A. Hindmoor (2009) *Rethinking governance. The centrality of the state in modern society*, Cambridge: Cambridge University Press.
Bell-Kelton, S. (2006) "Behind closed doors. The political economy of central banking in the United States," *International Journal of Political Economy*, 35(1).
Bensel, R. F. (1990) *Yankee Leviathan. The origins of central state authority in America, 1859–1877*, Cambridge: Cambridge University Press.
  (2000) *The political economy of American industrialization, 1877–1900*, Cambridge: Cambridge University Press.
Benson, L. (1955) *Merchants, farmers, and railroads. Railroad regulation and New York politics 1850–1887*, Cambridge, MA: Harvard University Press.
Benston, G. J. (1989) *The separation of commercial and investment banking: the Glass-Steagall Act revisited and reconsidered*, Norwell: Kluwer Academic.
Berger, A. N., A. K. Kashyap, et al. (1995) "The transformation of the U.S. banking industry: what a long, strange trip it's been," *Brookings Papers on Economic Activity*, (2).
Berger, A. N. and G. F. Udell (1993) "Securitization, risk, and the liquidity problem in banking," in M. Klausner and L. J. White (eds.), *Structural change in banking*, Homewood: Business One Irwin.
Berger, P. L. and T. Luckmann (1966) *The social construction of reality*, New York: Anchor Books.
Berk, G. (1991) "Corporate liberalism reconsidered: a review essay," *Journal of Policy History*, 3(1).
  (1994) *Alternative tracks. The constitution of American industrial order, 1865–1917*, Baltimore/London: Johns Hopkins University Press.
Berk, G. and D. Galvan (2009) "How people experience and change institutions: a field guide to creative syncretism," *Theory & Society*, 38(6).
Bernstein, B. J. (1968) "The New Deal: the conservative achievements of liberal reform," in B. J. Bernstein (ed.), *Towards a new past. Dissenting essays in American history*, New York: Pantheon Books.
Bernstein, M. A. (1994) "The contemporary American banking crisis in historical perspective," *Journal of American History*, 80(4).
Bernstein, P. L. (2005) *Capital ideas. The improbably origins of modern Wall Street*, Hoboken, NJ: John Wiley and Sons.

Bierman, H. (1998) *The causes of the 1929 stock market crash*, Westport, CT: Greenwood Press.

Black, S. W. (1991) *A levite among the priests. Edward M. Bernstein and the origins of the Bretton Woods system*, Boulder, CO: Westview Press.

Blackburn, R. (2008) "The subprime crisis," *New Left Review*, 50 (March–April).

Bloch, E. (1953) "United States foreign investment and dollar shortage," *Review of Economics and Statistics*, 35(2).

Block, F. (1977) *The origins of international economic disorder*, Berkeley, CA: University of California Press.

(2003) "The global economy in the Bush era," *Socio-Economic Review*, 1(3).

Bloomfield, A. I. (1959) *Monetary policy under the international gold standard, 1880–1914*, New York: Federal Reserve Bank of New York.

Blyth, M. (2002) *Great transformations: Economic ideas and institutional change in the twentieth century*, Cambridge: Cambridge University Press.

Bodenhorn, H. (2000) *A history of banking in antebellum America: financial markets and economic development in an era of nation-building*. Cambridge: Cambridge University Press.

(2003) *State banking in early America. A new economic history*, Oxford: Oxford University Press.

Boorstin, D. J. (1953) *The genius of American politics*, Chicago: University of Chicago Press.

Boughton, J. M. (1972) *Monetary policy and the federal funds market*, Durham: Duke University Press.

Boyer, R. (2010) "How new will the next regulatory regime be?" *Socio-Economic Review*, 8(3).

Boyer-Xambeu, M.-T., G. Delaplace, and L. Gillard (1994) *Private money and public currencies. The 16th century challenge*, Armonk, NY: M.E. Sharpe.

Bradshaw, Y. W. and J. Huang (1991) "Intensifying global dependency: foreign debt, structural adjustment, and third world underdevelopment," *Sociological Quarterly*, 32(3).

Brandeis, L. D. (1967 [1914]) *Other people's money and how the bankers use it*, New York: Harper & Row.

Bratsis, P. (2006) *Everyday life and the state*, Boulder: Paradigm.

Braunstein, A. and C. Welch (2002) "Financial literacy: An overview of practice, research, and policy," *Federal Reserve Bulletin*, November.

Brendsel, L. C. (1996) "Securitization's role in housing finance: the special contributions of the government-sponsored enterprises," in L. T. Kendall and M. J. Fishman (eds.), *A primer on securitization*, Cambridge, MA/London: MIT Press.

Brenner, R. (1998) "Uneven development and the long downturn: the advanced capitalist economies from boom to stagnation," *New Left Review*, I/229.

(2003) "Towards the precipice," *London Review of Books*, February 6, 2003.

(2009) "What is good for Goldman Sachs is good for America. The origins of the present crisis," Center for Social Theory and Comparative History, UCLA, http://escholarship.org/uc/item/0sg0782h

Brinkley, A. (1995) *The end of reform. New Deal liberalism in recession and war*, New York: Alfred A. Knopf.
Brock, L. V. (1975) *The currency of the American colonies 1700–1764. A study in colonial finance and imperial relations*, New York: Arno Press.
Brown, W. A. (1940) *The international gold standard reinterpreted, 1914–34*, New York: National Bureau of Economic Research.
Broz, J. L. (1997) *The international origins of the Federal Reserve System*, Ithaca, NY: Cornell University Press.
Bruchey, S. (1990) *Enterprise: The dynamic economy of a free people*. Cambridge, MA: Harvard University Press.
Brunhoff, S. D. (1978) *The state, capital and economic policy*, London: Pluto Press.
Buder, S. (2009) *Capitalizing on change. A social history of American business*, Chapel Hill: University of North Carolina Press.
Bunting, D. and J. Barbour (1971) "Interlocking directorates in large American corporations, 1896–1964," *Business History Review*, 45(3).
Burch, P. H. (1981a) *Elites in American history. The federalist years to the Civil War*, New York/London: Holmes & Meier Publishers, Inc.
 (1981b) *Elites in American history. The Civil War to the New Deal*, New York/London: Holmes & Meier Publishers, Inc.
 (1997) "Reagan, Bush, and right-wing politics: elites, think tanks, power and policy," *Research in Political Economy*, 16, supplement
Burgess, W. R. (1936) *The reserve banks and the money market*, New York/London: Harper & Brothers.
Burk, K. (1992) "Money and power: the shift from Great Britain to the United States," in Y. Cassis (ed.), *Finance and financiers in European history, 1880–1960*, Cambridge/Paris: Cambridge University Press/Editions de la Maison des Sciences de l'Homme.
Burke, M. (2001) "The changing nature of imperialism: the US as author of the Asian crisis of 1997," *Historical Materialism*, 8(1).
Burn, G. (1999) "The state, the city and the Euromarkets," *Review of International Political Economy*, 6(2).
Burnham, P. (1990) *The political economy of postwar reconstruction*, New York: St. Martin's Press.
 (2003) *Remaking the postwar world economy: Robot and British policy in the 1950s*, New York: Palgrave.
Burnham, W. D. (1981) "The system of 1896: an analysis," in P. Kleppner (ed.), *The evolution of American electoral systems*, Westport, CT: Greenwood Press.
Burns, H. M. (1974) *The American banking community and New Deal banking reforms 1933–1935*, Westport/London: Greenwood Press.
Bushman, R. L. (1998) "Markets and composite farms in early America," *William and Mary Quarterly*, 3rd Ser., 55(3).
Calder, L. (1999) *Financing the American dream. A cultural history of consumer credit*, Princeton: Princeton University Press.
Calhoun, C. (1992) "The infrastructure of modernity: indirect relationships, information technology, and social integration," in H. Haferkamp and N. J. Smelser (eds.), *Social Change and Modernity*, Berkeley: University of California Press.

Calleo, D. P. (1982) *The imperious economy*, Cambridge, MA/London: Harvard University Press.
Calomiris, C. W. and Schweikart, L. (1991) "The panic of 1857: origins, transmission and containment," *Journal of Economic History*, 51(4).
Cannon, J. G. (1910) *Clearing houses*, Washington, DC: U.S. Government Printing Office.
Canterbery, E. R. (2000) *Wall Street capitalism. The theory of the bondholding class*, Singapore: World Scientific.
Cargill, T. F. and G. G. Garcia (1985) *Financial reform in the 1980s*, Stanford: Hoover Institutions Press.
Carlson, M. and G. C. Weinbach (2007) "Profits and balance sheet developments at U.S. commercial banks in 2006," *Federal Reserve Bulletin*, 93.
Carosso, V. P. (1970) *Investment banking in America*, Cambridge, MA: Harvard University Press.
Carosso, V. P. and R. Sylla (1991) "U.S. banks in international finance," in R. Cameron and V. I. Bovykin (eds.), *International banking 1870–1914*, New York/Oxford: Oxford University Press.
Carpenter, D. P. (2001) *The forging of bureaucratic autonomy: reputations, networks, and policy innovation in executive agencies, 1862–1928*, Princeton: Princeton University Press.
Carruthers, B. G. and S. Babb (1996) "The color of money and the nature of value: greenbacks and gold in postbellum America," *American Journal of Sociology*, 101(6).
Cassis, Y. (2006) *Capitals of capital. A history of international financial centres, 1780–2005*, Cambridge: Cambridge University Press.
Catterall, R. C. H. (1902) *The second bank of the United States*, Chicago: University of Chicago Press.
Cecco, M. De (1976) "International financial markets and US domestic policy since 1945," *International Affairs*, 52(3).
—— (1984a) *The international gold standard. Money and empire*, London: Frances Pinter.
—— (1984b) *Modes of financial development: American banking dynamics and world financial dynamics*, Working paper 84/122, European University Institute.
—— (1987) "Inflation and structural change in the Euro-dollar market," in M. De Cecco (ed.), *Monetary theory and economic institutions*, Houndmills, Basingstoke/London: Macmillan.
—— (n.d.) "The lender of last resort," Working paper 49, CIDEI.
Cerny, P. G. (1993a) "The deregulation and re-regulation of financial markets in a more open world," in P. G. Cerny (ed.), *Finance and world politics. Markets, regimes and states in the post-hegemonic era*, Aldershot: Edward Elgar.
—— (1993b) "American decline and the emergence of embedded financial orthodoxy," in P. G. Cerny (ed.), *Finance and world politics. Markets, regimes and states in the post-hegemonic era*, Aldershot: Edward Elgar.
Chandler, A. D. (1954) "Patterns of American railroad finance, 1830–50," *Business History Review*, 28(3).

Bibliography

Chandler, L. V. (1958) *Benjamin Strong, central banker*, Washington, DC: Brookings Institution.

—— (1971) *American monetary policy 1928–1941*, New York: Harper & Row.

Chandler, M. (2009) *Making sense of the dollar*, New York: Bloomberg Press.

Chernow, R. (1990) *The house of Morgan: an American banking dynasty and the rise of modern finance*, New York: Atlantic Monthly Press.

Chevan, A. (1989) "The growth of home ownership: 1940–1980," *Demography*, 26(2).

Clark, C. (1990) *The roots of rural capitalism: western Massachusetts, 1780–1860*, Ithaca: Cornell University Press.

—— (1997) "Rural America and the transition to capitalism," in P. A. Gilje (ed.), *Wages of independence. Capitalism in the early American republic*, Madison: Madison House.

—— (2002) "Reshaping society: American social history from revolution to reconstruction," in M. Stokes (ed.), *The state of U.S. history*, Oxford/New York: Berg.

Clark, G. L. (2000) *Pension fund capitalism*, Oxford: Oxford University Press.

Clark, R. L., L. A. Craig, et al. (2003) *A history of public sector pensions*, Philadelphia: University of Pennsylvania Press.

Clarke, S. V. O. (1967) *Central bank cooperation: 1924–31*, New York: Federal Reserve Bank of New York.

Cleveland, H. v. B. and T. F. Huertas (1985) *Citibank 1812–1970*, Cambridge, MA/London: Harvard University Press.

Clowes, M. (2000) *The money flood, how pension funds revolutionized investing*. New York: John Wiley & Sons.

Cohen, B. (1986) *In whose interest? International banking and American foreign policy*, New Haven: Yale University Press.

Cohen, H. (1971) *Business and politics in America from the age of Jackson to the Civil War. The career biography of W.W. Corcoran*, Westport: Greenwood Press.

Cohen, L. (2003) *A consumers' republic. The politics of mass consumption in postwar America*, New York: Alfred A. Knopf.

Conybeare, J. A. C. (1988) *United States foreign economic policy and the international capital markets. The case of capital export countries, 1963–1974*, New York/London: Garland Publishing.

Costigliola, F. (1984) *Awkward dominion. American political, economic, and cultural relations with Europe, 1919–1933*, Ithaca/London: Cornell University Press.

Costigliola, F. C. (1977) "Anglo-American financial rivalry in the 1920s," *Journal of Economic History*, 37(4).

Cottrell, P. L. (1991) "Great Britain," in R. Cameron and V. I. Bovykin (eds.), *International banking 1870–1914*, New York/Oxford: Oxford University Press.

Countryman, E. (1976) "'Out of the bounds of law': northern land rioters in the eighteenth century," in A. F. Young (ed.), *The American Revolution. Explorations in the history of American radicalism*, DeKalb: Northern Illinois University Press.

Cowen, D. J. (2000) *The origins and economic impact of the first bank of the United States, 1791–1797*, New York: Garland Publishing.
Cox, R. W. and D. Skidmore-Hess (1999) *U.S. politics and the global economy. Corporate power, conservative shift*, Boulder/London: Lynne Rienner.
Croteau, J. T. (1960) "Sources of consumer credit: instalment debt among institutional creditors," *Journal of Finance*, 15(4).
Crotty, J. (2009) "Structural causes of the global financial crisis: A critical assessment of the 'new financial architecture'," *Cambridge Journal of Economics*, 33(4).
Crowley, J. E. (1992) "Commerce and the Philadelphia Constitution: neo-mercantilism in federalist and anti-federalist political economy," *History of Political Thought*, 13(1).
— (1993) *The privileges of independence. Neomercantilism and the American Revolution*, Baltimore/London: Johns Hopkins University Press.
Dalton, B. (2004) "Creativity, habit, and the social products of creative action: revising Joas, incorporating Bourdieu," *Sociological Theory*, 22(4).
Dam, K. W. (1982) *The rules of the game. Reform and evolution in the international monetary system*, Chicago/London: University of Chicago Press.
Davies, G. (2002) *A history of money. From ancient times to the present*, Cardiff: University of Wales Press.
Davis, A. M. (1900) "Currency and banking in the province of the Massachusetts-Bay: Part I. currency," *Publications of the American Economic Association*, 1(4).
— (1901) "Currency and banking in the province of the Massachusetts-Bay: Part II. banking," *Publications of the American Economic Association*, 2(2).
Davis, R. (1973) *The rise of the Atlantic economies*, London: Weidenfeld and Nicolson.
Deeg, R. and S. Lütz (2000) "Internationalization and financial federalism. The United States and Germany at the crossroads?," *Comparative Political Studies*, 33(3).
Degen, R. A. (1987) *The American monetary system. A concise survey of its evolution since 1896*, Massachusetts/Toronto: D.C. Heath and Company/Lexington.
Dewey, D. R. (1968 [1934]) *Financial history of the United States*, New York: Augustus M. Kelley.
— (1972 [1910]) *State banking before the Civil War*, New York/London: Johnson Reprint Corporation.
Dickens, E. (1990) "Financial crises, innovations and Federal Reserve control of the stock of money," *Contributions to Political Economy*, 9.
— (1995) "The great inflation and U.S. monetary policy in the late 1960s: a political economic approach," *Social Concept*, 7(1).
Dobbin, F. (1994) *Forging industrial policy: the United States, Britain, and France in the railway age*, Cambridge: Cambridge University Press.
Dodd, N. (1994) *The sociology of money*, Cambridge: Polity.
Dodd, R. (2005) "Derivatives markets: sources of vulnerability in U.S. financial markets," in G. Epstein (ed.), *Financialization and the world economy*, Cheltenham: Edward Elgar.

Doerflinger, T. M. (1986) *A vigorous spirit of enterprise: merchants and economic development in revolutionary Philadelphia*, Chapel Hill: University of North Carolina Press.
Domhoff, G. W. (1967) *Who rules America?*, Englewood Cliffs, NJ: Prentice-Hall, Inc.
Donohue, K.G. (2005) *Freedom from want. American liberalism and the idea of the consumer*, Baltimore: Johns Hopkins University Press.
Duménil, G. and D. Lévy (2004) *Capital resurgent. Roots of the neoliberal revolution*, Cambridge, MA/London: Harvard University Press.
Duncan, R. (2005) *The dollar crisis*, New York: Wiley.
Dunlavy, C. A. (1991) "Mirror images: political structure and early railroad policy in the United States and Prussia," *Studies in American Political Development*, 5(1).
Dunn, R. G. (1997) "Self, identity, and difference. Mead and the poststructuralists," *Sociological Quarterly*, 38(4).
Dupont, D. and B. Sack (1999) "The Treasury securities market: overview and recent developments," *Federal Reserve Bulletin* (December).
Dymski, G. A. (1999) *The bank merger wave. The economic causes and social consequences of financial consolidation*, Armonk, NY/London: M.E. Sharpe.
— (2003) "The international debt crisis," in J. Michie (ed.), *The handbook of globalisation*, Cheltenham: Edward Elgar.
— (2007) "From financial exploitation to global banking instability: two overlooked roots of the subprime crisis," http://www.soas.ac.uk/economics/events/crisis/43938.pdf.
Eagleton, T. (1991) *Ideology: an introduction*, London: Verso.
Edwards, F. R. (1996) *The new finance. Regulation and financial stability*, Washington, DC: AEI Press.
Egnal, M. (1988) *A mighty empire. The origins of the American revolution*, Ithaca/London: Cornell University Press.
Ehrmann, M. and M. Fratzscher (2005) *Transparency, disclosure and the Federal Reserve*, Working paper no. 457, European Central Bank.
Eichengreen, N. and M. Flandreau (2008) *The rise and fall of the dollar, or when did the dollar replace sterling as the leading international currency?*, Working paper 14154, National Bureau of Economic Research.
Eliason, A. O. (1970 [1901]) *The rise of commercial banking institutions in the United States*, New York: Burt Franklin.
Ellis, R. E. (1996) "The market revolution and the transformation of American politics, 1801–1837," in M. Stokes and S. Conway (eds.), *The market revolution in America. Social, political and religious expressions, 1800–1880*, Charlottesville/London: University Press of Virginia.
Engen, E., A. Lehnert, and R. Kehoe (2000) "Mutual funds and the U.S. equity market," *Federal Reserve Bulletin*, December.
Ennis, H. M. (2001) "On the size distribution of banks," *Federal Reserve Bank of Richmond Economic Quarterly*, 87(4).
— (2004) "Some recent trends in commercial banking," *Federal Reserve Bank of Richmond Economic Quarterly*, 90(2).

Enthoven, A. (1957) "The growth of instalment credit and the future of prosperity," *American Economic Review*, 47(6).
Epstein, G. A. and J. Schor (1995) "The Federal Reserve-Treasury Accord and the construction of the postwar monetary regime," *Social Concept*, 7(1).
Ernst, J. A. (1973) *Money and politics in America, 1755–1775*, Chapel Hill: University of North Carolina Press.
Esping-Andersen, G. (1990) *The three worlds of welfare capitalism*, Princeton, NJ: Princeton University Press.
Ewen, S. (1976) *Captains of consciousness: advertising and the social roots of the consumer culture*, New York: McGraw-Hill.
Fearon, P. (1987) *War, prosperity and depression. The U.S. economy 1917–45*, Lawrence: University of Kansas Press.
Feinman, J. N. (1993) "Reserve requirements: history, current practice, and potential reform," *Federal Reserve Bulletin*, 79(6).
Felder, R. (2008) "From Bretton Woods to neoliberal reforms: The international financial institutions and American power," in L. Panitch and M. Konings (eds.), *American empire and the political economy of global finance*, New York: Palgrave.
Fenstermaker, J. V. (1965) *The development of American commercial banking: 1782–1837*, Kent, Ohio: Bureau of Economic and Business Research.
Ferguson, E. J. (1961) *Power of the purse: a history of American public finance*, Chapel Hill: University of North Carolina Press.
Ferguson, J. E. (1953) "Currency finance: an interpretation of colonial monetary practices," *William and Mary Quarterly, 3rd Ser.*, 10(2).
Ferguson, R. W. (2003) "Capital standards for banks: the evolving Basel accord," *Federal Reserve Bulletin*, September.
Ferguson, T. (1981) Critical realignment: the fall of the House of Morgan and the origins of the New Deal, PhD thesis, Princeton University.
—— (1983) "Party realignment and American industrial structure," *Research in Political Economy*, 6.
—— (1984) "From normalcy to New Deal: industrial structure, party competition, and American public policy in the Great Depression," *International Organization*, 38(1).
Ferguson, T. and J. Chen (2005) "Investor blocs and party realignments in American history," *Journal of the Historical Society*, 5(4).
Ferguson, T. and R. Johnson (2009a) "Too big to bail: the "Paulson put," presidential politics, and the global financial meltdown: Part I: from shadow financial system to shadow bailout," *International Journal of Political Economy*, 38(1).
—— (2009b) "Too big to bail: the "Paulson put," presidential politics, and the global financial meltdown: Part II: fatal reversal – single payer and back," *International Journal of Political Economy*, 38(2).
Ferguson, T. and J. Rogers (1986) *Right turn. The decline of the Democrats and the future of American politics*, New York: Hill and Wang.
Finegold, K. and T. Skocpol (1995) *State and party in America's New Deal*, Madison: University of Wisconsin Press.

Fink, L. (1988) "The new labor history and the power of historical pessimism: consensus, hegemony, and the case of the Knights of Labor," *Journal of American History*, 75 (June).
Fink, L. D. (1996) "The role of pension funds and other investors in securitized debt markets," in L. T. Kendall and M. J. Fishman (eds.), *A primer on securitization*, Cambridge, MA/London: MIT Press.
Fischer, G. (1961) *Bank holding companies*, New York: Columbia University Press.
Fishlow, A. (1965) *American railroads and the transformation of the ante-bellum economy*, Cambridge, MA: Harvard University Press.
Fisk, H. (1924) *The inter-Ally debts*, New York: Bankers Trust Company.
Flam, H. (1985) "Democracy in debt: credit and politics in Paterson, N. J., 1890–1930," *Journal of Social History*, 18(3).
Fligstein, N. (1990) *The transformation of corporate control*, Cambridge, MA/London: Harvard University Press.
Flynn, D. T. (2001) Credit and the economy of colonial New England, PhD thesis, Indiana University.
Foner, E. (1970) *Free soil, free labor, free men. The ideology of the Republican Party before the Civil War*, Oxford: Oxford University Press.
Forbord, T. A. (1980) The abandonment of Bretton Woods: the political economy of U.S. international monetary policy, PhD thesis, Harvard University.
Forsyth, J. H. (1987) "Financial innovation in Britain," in M. D. Cecco (ed.), *Changing money. financial innovation in developed countries*, Oxford/New York: Basil Blackwell.
Foulke, R. A. (1980 [1931]) *The commercial paper market*, New York: Arno Press.
Fraas, A. (1974) "The Second Bank of the United States: an instrument for an interregional monetary union," *Journal of Economic History*, 34(2).
Frankel, J. A. (1988) "International capital flows and domestic economic policies," in M. Feldstein (ed.), *The United States in the world economy*, Chicago/London: Chicago University press.
Fraser, S. (2005) *Wall Street: a cultural history*, New York: Faber & Faber.
Frieden, J. (1988) "Sectoral conflict and U.S. foreign economic policy, 1914–1940," in G. J. Ikenberry, D. A. Lake, and M. Mastanduno (eds.), *The state and American foreign policy*, Ithaca/London: Cornell University Press.
Friedman, B. M. (2000) "The role of interest rates in Federal Reserve policymaking," in R. W. Kopcke and L. E. Browne (eds.), *The evolution of monetary policy and the Federal Reserve System over the past thirty years*, a conference in honor of Frank E. Morris, Federal Reserve Bank of Boston.
Friedman, M. and A. J. Schwartz (1963) *A monetary history of the United States*, Princeton, NJ: Princeton University Press.
Gaines, T. C. (1962) *Techniques of treasury debt management*, New York: Free Press of Glencoe.
Galambos, L. (1983) "Technology, political economy, and professionalization: central themes of the organizational synthesis," *Business History Review*, 53 (Winter).
Gamble, A. (2009) *The spectre at the feast. Capitalist crisis and the politics of recession*, New York: Palgrave.

Gavin, F. J. (2004) *Gold, dollars, and power: the politics of international monetary relations, 1958–1971*, Chapel Hill: University of North Carolina Press.
Geary, D. (1981) *European labour protest, 1848–1939*, New York: St. Martin's Press.
Geisst, C. R. (1990) *Visionary capitalism: financial markets and the American dream in the twentieth century*, New York: Praeger.
 (2001) *The last partnerships. Inside the great Wall Street money dynasties*, New York: McGraw-Hill.
Gemici, K. (2008) "Karl Polanyi and the antinomies of embeddedness," *Socio-Economic Review*, 6(1).
Gemmill, R. F. (1961) "Interest rates and foreign dollar balances," *Journal of Finance*, 16(3).
Germain, R. D. (1997) *The international organization of credit. States and global finance in the world-economy*, Cambridge: Cambridge University Press.
 (2007) "Global finance, risk and governance," *Global Society*, 21(1).
Gilbert, M. (1985) "The gold-dollar system: conditions of equilibrium and the price of gold," in B. Eichengreen (ed.), *The gold standard in theory and history*, New York/London: Methuen.
Gill, S. R. and D. Law (1989) "Global hegemony and the structural power of capital," *International Studies Quarterly*, 33(4).
Gilpin, R. (1987) *The political economy of international relations*, Princeton: Princeton University Press.
Gische, D. M. (1979) "The New York banks and the development of the national banking system, 1860–1870," *American Journal of Legal History*, 23(1).
Goebel, T. (1997) "The political economy of American populism from Jackson to the New Deal," *Studies in American Political Development*, 11 (Spring).
Goede, M. de (2005) *Virtue, fortune and faith: a genealogy of finance*, Minneapolis: University of Minnesota Press.
Golembe, C. H. (1952) State banks and the economic development of West, 1830–1844, PhD thesis, Columbia University.
 (1960) "The deposit insurance legislation of 1933: an examination of its antecedents and its purposes," *Political Science Quarterly*, 75(2).
Goodhart, C. A. E. (1969) *The New York money market and the finance of trade, 1900–1913*, Cambridge, MA: Harvard University Press.
Gordon, C. (1994) *New deals. Business, labor and politics in America, 1920–1935*, Cambridge: Cambridge University Press.
Gordon, S. L. (1995) *The United States and global capital shortages: the problem and possible solutions*, Westport, CT: Quorum Books.
Gorton, G. (1985) "Clearing houses and the origin of central banking in the United States," *Journal of Economic History*, 45(2).
Gorton, G. and G. Pennacchi (1993) "Money market funds and finance companies: are they the banks of the future?" in M. Klausner and L. J. White (eds.), *Structural change in banking*, Homewood: Business One Irwin.
Gourevitch, P. A. (1984) "Breaking with orthodoxy: the politics of economic policy responses to the Depression of the 1930s," *International Organization*, 38(1).
Gowa, J. S. (1983) *Closing the gold window: domestic politics and the end of Bretton Woods*, Ithaca: Cornell University Press.

Gowan, P. (1999) *The global gamble*, London: Verso.
— (2002) "The American campaign for global sovereignty," in L. Panitch and C. Leys (eds.), *Socialist Register 2002*, London: Merlin Press.
— (2009) "Crisis in the heartland," *New Left Review*, 55 (January–February).
Grahl, J. (2001) "Globalized finance," *New Left Review*, 8 (March–April).
Grahl, J. and Ph. Lysandrou (2006) "Capital market trading volume: an overview and some preliminary conclusions," *Cambridge Journal of Economics*, 30(6).
Gramlich, E. M. (2007) *Subprime mortgages. America's latest boom and bust*, Washington, DC: Urban Institute Press.
Gramsci, A. (1971) *Selections from the prison notebooks*, London: Lawrence and Wishart.
Grant, J. (1992) *Money of the mind. Borrowing and lending in America from the Civil War to Michael Milken*, New York: Noonday Press.
Greef, A. O. (1938) *The commercial paper house in the United States*, Cambridge: Cambridge University Press.
Green, G. D. (1972) *Finance and economic development in the old South: Louisiana banking, 1804–1861*, Stanford: Stanford University Press.
Greene, J. P. and R. M. Jellison (1961) "The Currency Act of 1764 in imperial-colonial relations, 1764–1776," *William and Mary Quarterly*, 3rd Ser., 18(4).
Greenspan, A. (2007) *The age of turbulence*, New York: Allen Lane.
Greider, W. (1987) *Secrets of the temple: how the Federal Reserve runs the country*, New York: Simon and Schuster.
Grosse, R. (2004) *The future of global financial services*, Malden/Oxford: Blackwell.
Gutman, H. G. (1976) *Work, culture, and society in industrializing America: essays in American working-class and social history*, New York: Knopf.
Guttmann, R. (1994) *How credit-money shapes the economy. The United States in a global system*, Armonk, NY/London: M.E. Sharpe.
Hacker, L. M. (1949) *The triumph of American capitalism: the development of forces in American history to the end of the nineteenth century*, New York: Columbia Press.
Haeger, J. D. (1981) *The investment frontier. New York businessmen and the economic development of the old northwest*, Albany: State University of New York Press.
Hall, P. A. and D. Soskice, Eds. (2001). *Varieties of capitalism: the institutional foundations of comparative advantage*. Oxford, Oxford University Press.
Hammond, B. (1934) "Long and short term credit in early American banking," *Quarterly Journal of Economics*, 49(1).
— (1957) *Banks and politics in America. From the Revolution to the Civil War*, Princeton: Princeton University Press.
Hardy, C. O. (1932) *Credit policies of the Federal Reserve System*, Washington, DC: Brookings Institution.
Harmes, A. (2000) Mass investment: mutual funds, pensions funds and the politics of economic restructuring, PhD thesis, York University.
Harrington, R. (1987) *Asset and liability management by banks*, Paris: OECD.

Hartz, L. (1955) *The liberal tradition in America: an interpretation of American political thought since the Revolution*, New York: Harcourt, Brace.

Hattam, V. (1993) *Labor visions and state power: the origins of business unionism in the United State*, Princeton: Princeton University Press.

Hawley, J. (1984) "Protecting capital from itself: U.S. attempts to regulate the Eurocurrency system," *International Organization*, 38(1).

Hayes, S. L., A. M. Spence, et al. (1983) *Competition in the investment banking industry*, Cambridge, MA: Harvard University Press.

Headlee, S. E. (1991) *The Political economy of the family farm: the agrarian roots of American capitalism*, New York: Praeger.

Hedges, J. E. (1938) *Commercial banking and the stock market before 1863*, Baltimore: Johns Hopkins University Press.

Helleiner, E. (1994) *States and the reemergence of global finance. From Bretton Woods to the 1990s*, Ithaca, NY: Cornell University Press.

Henning, C. R. (1994) *Currencies and politics in the United States, Germany and Japan*, Washington, DC: Institute for International Economics.

Henretta, J. A. (1974) "Families and farms: mentalite in pre-industrial America," *William & Mary Quarterly*, 35(1).

(1979) "Social history as lived and written," *American Historical Review*, 84(5).

(2002) "The birth of American liberalism: New York, 1820–1860," in J. Heideking and J. A. Henretta (eds.), *Republicanism and liberalism in America and the German states, 1750–1850*, Cambridge: German Historical Institute/ Cambridge University Press.

Herrigel, G. (2010) *Manufacturing possibilities. Creative action and industrial recomposition in the United States, Germany and Japan*, Oxford: Oxford University Press.

Hester, D. D. (1981) "Innovations and monetary control," *Brookings Papers on Economic Activity*, 1.

(2008) *The evolution of monetary policy and banking in the US*, Berlin/ Heidelberg: Springer-Verlag.

Hidy, M. (1951) "The capital markets, 1789–1865," in H. F. Williamson (ed.), *The growth of the American economy*, Englewood Cliffs, NJ: Prentice-Hall.

Hidy, R. W. (1941) "The organization and functions of Anglo-American merchant bankers, 1815–1860," *Journal of Economic History*, 1 (December).

Hirtle, B. J. and K. J. Stiroh (2007) "The return to retail and the performance of US banks," *Journal of Banking and Finance*, 31(4).

Hobson, J. M. (2000) *The state and international relations*, Cambridge: Cambridge University Press.

Hoffmann, S. (2001) *Politics and banking. Ideas, public policy, and the creation of financial institutions*, Baltimore/London: Johns Hopkins University Press.

Hogan, M. J. (1987) *The Marshall plan: America, Britain, and the reconstruction of Western Europe, 1947–1952*. Cambridge: Cambridge University Press.

Holt, M. F. (1996) "From center to periphery: the market revolution and major-party conflict, 1835–1880," in M. Stokes and S. Conway (eds.), *The market revolution in America. Social, political and religious expressions, 1800–1880*, Charlottesville/London: University Press of Virginia.

(1999) *The rise and fall of the American Whig Party: Jacksonian politics and the onset of the Civil War*, New York: Oxford University Press.
Holzman, L. H. (1996) "Pragmatism and dialectical materialism in language development," in H. Daniels (ed.), *An Introduction to Vygotsky*. London/New York: Routledge.
Höpner, M. and G. Jackson (2001) *An emerging market for corporate control? The Mannesmann takeover and German corporate governance*, Discussion paper 01/4, Max-Planck-Institut für Gesellschaftsforschung.
Hudson, M. (1977) *Global fracture. The new international economic order*, New York: Harper & Row.
(2003) *Super imperialism*, London/Sterling, Virginia: Pluto Press.
Huertas, T. F. (1990) "US multinational banking: history and prospects," in G. Jones (ed.), *Banks as multinationals*, London/New York: Routledge.
Huston, J. L. (1987) *The panic of 1857 and the coming of the Civil War*, Baton Rouge/London: Louisiana State University Press.
Hybel, A. R. (2001) *Made by the USA. The international system*, New York: Palgrave.
Hyman, L. R. (2007) Debtor nation. How consumer credit built postwar America, PhD dissertation, Harvard University.
Ingham, G. (1994) "States and markets in the production of world money: sterling and the dollar," in S. Corbridge, R. Martin, and N. Thrift (eds.), *Money power and space*, Oxford/Cambridge, MA: Blackwell.
(1999) "Capitalism, money and banking: a critique of recent historical sociology," *British Journal of Sociology*, 50(1).
(2004) *The nature of money*, Cambridge/Malden: Polity.
Jackson, K. T. (1985) *Crabgrass frontier. The suburbanization of the United States*, Oxford: Oxford University Press.
Jacobs, L. M. (1910) "English methods of lending as contrasted with American," *Annals of the American Academy of Political and Social Science*, 36(3).
Jacobs, M. (1999) "'Democracy's Third Estate': new deal politics and the construction of a 'Consuming Public,'" *International Labor and Working-Class History*, 55 (April).
James, D. (1978) "The beginning of investment banking in the United States," *Pennsylvania History*, 45(2).
James, J. A. (1978) *Money and capital markets in postbellum America*, Princeton, NJ: Princeton University Press.
(1995) "The rise and fall of the commercial paper market, 1900–1929," in M. D. Bordo and R. Sylla (eds.), *Anglo-American financial systems. Institutions and markets in the twentieth century*, Burr Ridge/New York: Irwin Professional Publishing.
John, R. R. (1997) "Governmental institutions as agents of change: rethinking American political development in the early republic, 1787–1835," *Studies in American Political Development*, 11(2).
Johnson, P. A. (1998) *The government of money. Monetarism in Germany and the United States*, Ithaca/London: Cornell University Press.
Johnston, R. D. (2003) *The radical middle class. Populist democracy and the question of capitalism in Progressive Era Portland, Oregon*, Princeton/Oxford: Princeton University Press.

Jones, A. (2008) "Beyond embeddedness: economic practices and the invisible dimensions of transnational business activity," *Progress in Human Geography*, 32(1).

Jones, G. (1998) "Concentration and internationalization in banks after the Second World War," in S. Kinsey and L. Newton (eds.), *International banking in an age of transition. Globalisation, automation, banks and their archives*, Aldershot: Ashgate.

Kahn, T. K. (1993) "Commercial paper," *Federal Reserve Bank of Richmond Economic Quarterly*, 79(2).

Kantor, P. (1990) "The political economy of business politics in U.S. cities: a developmental perspective," *Studies in American Political Development*, 4.

Kaplan, J. J. and G. Schleiminger (1989) *The European Payments Union. Financial diplomacy in the 1950s*, Oxford: Clarendon Press.

Kapstein, E. B. (1991) Supervising international banks: origins and implications of the Basle Accord, *Princeton Essays in International Finance* 185.

(1994) *Governing the global economy: international finance and the state*, Cambridge, MA: Harvard University Press.

Katz, I. (1968) *August Belmont: a political biography*, New York: Columbia University Press.

Kaufman, A. and E. J. Englander (1993) "Kohlberg Kravis Roberts & Co. and the Restructuring of American Capitalism," *Business History Review*, 67(1).

Kazin, M. (1998) *The populist persuasion: an American history*, Ithaca, NY: Cornell University Press.

Keller, M. (1977) *Affairs of state. Public life in nineteenth century America*, Cambridge, MA/London: Belknap Press.

Kendall, L. T. (1996) "Securitization: a new era in American finance," in L. T. Kendall and M. J. Fishman (eds.), *A primer on securitization*, Cambridge, MA/London: MIT Press.

Kennedy, P. M. (1987) *The rise and fall of the great powers: economic change and military conflict from 1500 to 2000*, New York: Random House.

Kennedy, S. E. (1973) *The banking crisis of 1933*, Lexington: University of Kentucky Press.

Kerridge, E. (1988) *Trade and banking in early modern England*, Manchester: Manchester University Press.

Keynes, J. M. (1936) *The general theory of employment interest and money*, London: Macmillan.

Khademian, A. M. (1992) *The SEC and capital market regulation: The politics of expertise*, Pittsburgh, PA: University of Pittsburgh Press.

Kindleberger, C. P. (1973) *The world in depression, 1929–1939*, Berkeley: University of California Press.

(1993) *A financial history of Western Europe*, New York/Oxford: Oxford University Press.

King, D. and R. C. Lieberman (2007) "Ironies of state building: a comparative perspective on the American state," *World Politics*, 61(3).

Kinley, D. (1910) *The independent treasury of the United States and its relations to the banks of the country*, Washington, DC: Government Printing Office.

Kirkland, E. C. (1961) *Industry comes of age. Business, labor, and public policy*, New York: Holt, Rinehart and Winston.
Klaman, S. B. (1961) *The postwar residential mortgage market*, Princeton: Princeton University Press.
Klebaner, B. K. (1990) *American commercial banking. A history*, Boston: Twayne Publishers.
Klein, J. J. (1911–12) "The development of mercantile instruments of credit in the United States," *Journal of Accountancy*, 12–13.
Klopstock, F. H. (1965) "The international money market: structure, scope and instruments," *Journal of Finance*, 20(2).
Klubes, B. (1990) "The First Federal Congress and the First National Bank: a case study in constitutional history," *Journal of the Early Republic*, 10(1).
Knafo, S. (2008) "The state and the rise of speculative finance in England," *Economy & Society*, 37(2).
  (2010) "Critical approaches and the legacy of the agent/structure debate in international relations," *Cambridge Review of International Affairs*, 23(3).
Knee, J. (2007) *The accidental investment banker*, Oxford: Oxford University Press.
Knipe, J. L. (1965) *The Federal Reserve and the American dollar*, Chapel Hill: University of North Carolina Press.
Knodell, J. (1998) "The demise of central banking and the domestic exchanges: evidence from antebellum Ohio," *Journal of Economic History*, 58(3).
  (2006) "Rethinking the Jacksonian economy: the impact of the 1832 bank veto on commercial banking," *Journal of Economic History*, 66(3).
Knorr, Cetina, Karin D. and Urs Bruegger (2002) "Global microstructures: the virtual societies of financial markets," *American Journal of Sociology*, 107(4).
Kohn, M. (1999a) *Medieval and early modern coinage and its problems*, Working paper 99–02, Department of Economics, Dartmouth College.
  (1999b) *Early deposit banking*, Working paper 99–03, Department of Economics, Dartmouth College.
  (1999c) *Bills of exchange and the money market to 1600*, Working paper 99–04, Department of Economics, Dartmouth College.
Kolko, G. (1963) *The triumph of conservatism. A reinterpretation of American history, 1900–1916*, Chicago: Quadrangle Books.
  (1965) *Railroads and regulation, 1877–1916*, Princeton: Princeton University Press.
  (1968) *The politics of war: the world and United States foreign policy, 1943–1945*, New York: Random House.
  (1976) *Main currents in modern American history*, New York: Pantheon Books.
Konings, M. (2008) "European finance in the American mirror: financial change and the reconfiguration of competitiveness," *Contemporary Politics*, 14(3).
  (2010) "The pragmatic sources of modern power," *European Journal of Sociology*, 51(1).
Krippner, G. R. (2002) "The elusive market: embeddedness and the paradigm of economic sociology," *Theory and Society*, 30(6).

(2003) The fictitious economy: financialization, the state, and contemporary capitalism, PhD thesis, University of Wisconsin-Madison.
Krooss, H. (1967) "Financial institutions," in D. T. Gilchrist (ed.), *The growth of the seaport cities 1790–1825*, Charlottesville: University Press of Virginia.
Krooss, H. E. and M. R. Blyn (1971) *A history of financial intermediaries*, New York: Random House.
Kulikoff, A. (1989) "The transition to capitalism in rural America," *William & Mary Quarterly*, 3rd Ser., 46(1).
(2000) *From British peasants to colonial American farmers*, Chapel Hill/London: University of North Carolina Press.
Lacher, H. (1999) "Embedded liberalism, disembedded markets: reconceptualising the pax Americana," *New Political Economy*, 4(3).
Lamoreaux, N. R. (1985) *The great merger movement in American business, 1895–1904*, Cambridge: Cambridge University Press.
(1986) "Banks, kinship, and economic development: the New England case," *Journal of Economic History*, 46(3).
Landi, A. and G. Lusignani (1997) "Bank lending and the securitisation process: a comparative analysis," in J. Revell (ed.), *The recent evolution of financial systems*, Houndmills, Basingstoke/New York: Macmillan.
Langley, P. (2002) *World financial orders. An historical international political economy*, London/New York: Routledge.
(2008) *The everyday life of global finance. Saving and borrowing in Anglo-America*, Oxford: Oxford University Press.
LaRoche, R. K. (1993) "Bankers acceptances," *Federal Reserve Bank of Richmond Economic Quarterly*, 79(1).
Larson, H. M. (1936) *Jay Cooke, private banker*, Cambridge: Harvard University Press.
Larson, J. L. (2001) *Internal improvements. National public works and the promise of popular government in the early United States*, Chapel Hill/London: University of North Carolina Press.
Lemon, J. T. (1980) "Early Americans and their social environment," *Journal of Historical Geography*, 6(2).
Levich, R. M. (1988) "Financial innovations in international financial markets," in M. Feldstein (ed.), *The United States in the world economy*, Chicago/London: University of Chicago Press.
Levich, R. M. and I. Walter (1989) "The regulation of global financial markets," in T. Noyelle (ed.), *New York's financial markets. The challenges of globalization*, Boulder/London: Westview Press.
Lewis, A. and G. Pescetto (1996) *EU and US banking in the 1990s*, London: Academic Press.
Lewis, C. (1948) *The United States and foreign investment problems*, Washington, DC: Brookings Institution.
Lindert, P. H. (1969) "Key currencies and gold 1900–1913," *Princeton Studies in International Finance*, 24.
Lipsey, R. E. (1988) "Changing patterns of international investment in and by the United States," in M. Feldstein (ed.), *The United States in the world economy*, London/Chicago: Chicago University Press.

Litan, R. E. (1987) "Reuniting investment and commercial banking," in C. England and T. Huertas (eds.), *The financial services revolution. Policy directions for the future*, Boston: Kluwer Academic Publishers.
— (1991) *The revolution in U.S. finance*, Washington, DC: The Brookings Institution.
Livingston, J. (1986) *Origins of the Federal Reserve System. Money, class and corporate capitalism, 1890–1913*, Ithaca/London: Cornell University Press.
— (1987) "The social analysis of economic history and theory: conjectures on late nineteenth-century American development," *American Historical Review*, 92(1).
Lukes, S. (1974) *Power: a radical view*, New York/London: Macmillan.
Lustig, R. J. (1982) *Corporate liberalism. The origins of modern American political theory, 1890–1920*, Berkeley: University of California Press.
Lütz, S. (2002) *Der Staat und die Globalisierung von Finanzmärkten: Regulative Politik in Deutschland, Grossbritannien und den USA*, Frankfurt/New York: Campus Verlag.
Lyons, M. N. (1998) "Business conflict and right-wing movements," in A. E. Ansell (ed.), *Unraveling the right. The new conservatism in American thought and politics*, Boulder/Oxford: Westview.
MacDonald, H. (1996) "Expanding access to the secondary mortgage markets: the role of central city lending goals," *Growth & Change*, 27 (3).
— (2005) "Reforming private housing finance: evaluating the achievements of the Clinton administration," *Housing Studies*, 20(4).
Macesich, G. (1960) "Sources of monetary disturbances in the United States, 1834–1845," *Journal of Economic History*, 20(3).
Mackenzie, D. (2006) *An engine, not a camera: how financial models shape markets*, Cambridge, MA: MIT Press.
Maisel, S. J. (1973) *Managing the dollar*, New York: W.W. Norton & Company.
Mahoney, P. G. (2001) "The political economy of the Securities Act of 1933," *The Journal of Legal Studies*, 30(1).
Mann, M. (1984) "The autonomous power of the state: its origins, mechanisms and results," *European Journal of Sociology*, 25(2).
— (1993) *The sources of social power vol. 2. The rise of classes and nation-states, 1760–1914*, Cambridge: Cambridge University Press.
Marron, D. (2007) "'Lending by numbers': credit scoring and the constitution of risk within American consumer credit," *Economy and Society*, 36(1).
Martin, A. (1974) "Railroads and the equity receivership: an essay on institutional change," *Journal of Economic History*, 34(3).
Mason, D. L. (2004) *From buildings and loans to bail-outs: a history of the American savings and loan industry, 1831–1995*, New York: Cambridge University Press.
Mason, J. E. (1997) *The transformation of commercial banking the United States, 1956–1991*, New York/London: Garland Publishing.
Matson, C. (1998) *Merchants and empire. Trading in colonial New York*, Baltimore/London: Johns Hopkins University Press.
Mayer, M. (1974) *The bankers*, New York: Weybright and Talley.

(1990) *The greatest-ever bank robbery: the collapse of the savings and loan industry*, New York: Collier.
Mayer, T. (1999) *Monetary policy and the great inflation in the United States*, Cheltenham: Edward Elgar.
Mayhew, A. (1972) "A reappraisal of the causes of farm protest in the United States, 1870–1900," *Journal of Economic History*, 32(2).
McCaffrey, W. T. (1938) *English and American banking systems compared*, Syracuse: Kingsport Press.
McCormick, R. L. (1981) *From realignment to reform. Political change in New York state, 1893–1910*, Ithaca/London: Cornell University Press.
—— (1986) *The party period and public policy. American politics from the age of Jackson to the progressive era*, New York/Oxford: Oxford University Press.
McCoy, D. R. (1980) *The elusive republic. Political economy in Jeffersonian America*, Chapel Hill: University of North Carolina Press.
McCusker, J. J. (1976) "Colonial paper money," in E. P. Newman and R. G. Doty (eds.), *Studies on money in early America*, New York: American Numismatic Society.
McCusker, J. J. and R. R. Menard (1985) *The economy of British America, 1607–1789*, Chapel Hill: University of North Carolina Press.
McFaul, J. M. (1972) *The politics of Jacksonian finance*, Ithaca/London: Cornell University Press.
McGerr, M. E. (1986) *The decline of popular politics: the American North, 1865–1928*, New York: Oxford University Press.
—— (2003) *A fierce discontent: the rise and fall of the Progressive movement in America, 1870–1920*, New York: Free Press.
McGovern, C. (2006) *Sold American: consumption and citizenship, 1890–1945*, Chapel Hill: University of North Carolina Press.
McGraw, T. K. (1984) *Prophets of regulation*. Cambridge, MA: Harvard University Press.
McGuire, P. (2004) "A shift in London's Eurodollar market," *BIS Quarterly Review*, September.
McGuire, R. A. (2003) *To form a more perfect union: a new economic interpretation of the United States Constitution*, Oxford: Oxford University Press.
McKercher, B. (1988) "Wealth, power, and the new international order: Britain and the American challenge in the 1920s," *Diplomatic History*, 12(4).
McNamara, K. R. (2002) "State building, the territorialization of money, and the creation of the American single currency," in D. M. Andrews, C. R. Henning, and L. W. Pauly (eds.), *Governing the world's money*, Ithaca/London: Cornell University Press.
Mehrling, P. (1997) *The money interest and the public interest: American monetary thought, 1920–1970*, Cambridge, MA: Harvard University Press.
Meltzer, A. H. (2003) *A history of the Federal Reserve, volume 1, 1913–1951*, Chicago: University of Chicago Press.
Meter, R. H. V. (1971) The United States and European recovery, 1918–1923: a study of public policy and private finance, PhD thesis, University of Wisconsin.

Meulendyke, A.-M. (1988) "A review of Federal Reserve policy targets and operating guides in recent decades," *Federal Reserve Bank of New York Quarterly Review*, 13(3).
  (1989) *U.S. monetary policy and financial markets*, New York: Federal Reserve Bank of New York.
Michener, R. (2003) "Money in the American colonies," in R. Whaples (ed.), *EH. Net Encyclopedia*, http://eh.net/encyclopedia/article/michener.american.colonies.money
Michie, R. C. (2003) "Banks and securities markets 1870–1914," in D. J. Forsyth and D. Verdier (eds.), *The origins of national financial systems. Alexander Gerschenkron reconsidered*, London/New York: Routledge.
  (1986) "The London and New York Stock Exchanges, 1850–1914," *Journal of Economic History*, 46(1).
  (1987) *The London and New York Stock Exchanges 1850–1914*, London: Allen & Unwin.
Mikesell, R. F. (1954) *Foreign exchange in the postwar world*, New York: Twentieth Century Fund.
Mikesell, R. F. and J. H. Furth (1974) *Foreign dollar balances and the international role of the dollar*, New York: National Bureau of Economic Research.
Miller, H. E. (1927) *Banking theories in the United States before 1860*, Cambridge: Harvard University Press.
Minsky, H. (1986) *Can "it" happen again? Essays on instability and finance*, New York: M.E. Sharpe.
Mints, L. W. (1965) *A history of banking theory in Great Britain and the United States*, Chicago: University of Chicago Press.
Miranti, P. J. (1986) "Associationalism, statism, and professional regulation: public accountants and the reform of the financial markets, 1896–1940," *Business History Review*, 60(3).
Mitchell, T. (2005) "Economists and the economy in the twentieth century," in George Steinmetz (ed.), *The politics of method in the human sciences: positivism and its epistemological others*, Durham: Duke University Press.
Mitchener, K. J. and M. Weidenmier (2005) "Empire, public goods and the Roosevelt Corollary," *Journal of Economic History*, 65(3).
Montgomerie, J. (2006) "Giving credit where it's due: public policy and household debt in the United States, the United Kingdom, and Canada," *Policy and Society*, 25(3).
  (2007) *Financialization and consumption: an alternative account of rising consumer debt levels in Anglo-America*, CRESC Working paper series no. 43, University of Manchester.
Moore, B. (1966) *Social origins of dictatorship and democracy: lord and peasant in the making of the modern world*, Boston: Beacon Press.
Moran, M. (1991) *The politics of the financial services revolution. The USA, UK and Japan*, London: MacMillan.
  (1994) "The state and the financial services revolution: a comparative analysis," *West European Politics*, 17(3).
Morgan, H. W. (1956) "The origins and establishment of the First Bank of the United States," *Business History Review*, 30(4).

Morrison, A. D. and W. J. Wilhelm (2007) *Investment banking: institutions, politics, and law*, Oxford: Oxford University Press.

Mowery, D. C. (1992) "Finance and corporate evolution in five industrial economies, 1900–1950," in V. Zamagni (ed.), *Finance and the enterprise*, London: Academic Press.

Munro, J. (2000) "English 'backwardness' and financial innovations in commerce with the low countries, 14th to 16th centuries," in P. Stabel, B. Blondé, and A. Greve (eds.), *International trade in the Low Countries (14th-16th centuries): merchants, organisation, infrastructure*, Leuven: Garant.

Myers, M. G. (1970) *A financial history of the United States*, New York: Columbia University Press.

(1951a) "The investment market after the Civil War," in H. F. Williamson (ed.), *The growth of the American economy*, Englewood Cliffs, NJ: Prentice-Hall.

(1951b) "The investment market after 1919," in H. F. Williamson (ed.), *The growth of the American economy*, Englewood Cliffs, NJ: Prentice-Hall.

(1931) *The New York money market*, New York: Columbia University Press.

Nadler, M., S. Heller, and S. S. Shipman, Eds. (1955) *The money market and its institutions*, New York: Ronald Press.

Nash, G. B. (1976) "Social change and the growth of prerevolutionary urban radicalism," in A. F. Young (ed.), *The American Revolution. Explorations in the history of American radicalism*, DeKalb: Northern Illinois University Press.

Navin, T. R. and M. V. Sears (1955) "The rise of a market for industrial securities, 1887–1902," *Business History Review*, 29(2).

Neal, L. (1971) "Trust companies and financial innovation, 1897–1914," *Business History Review*, 45(1).

Neal, L. and S. Quinn (2001) "Networks of information, markets and institutions in the rise of London as a financial center, 1660–1720," *Financial History Review*, 8(1).

Nesvetailova, A. (2010) *Financial alchemy in crisis*, London: Pluto.

Nesvetailova, A. and R. Palan (2008) "A very North Atlantic crunch: geopolitical implications of the global liquidity crisis," *Journal of International Affairs*, 62(1).

Nettels, C. P. (1952) "British mercantilism and the economic development of the thirteen colonies," *Journal of Economic History*, 12(2).

(1962) *The emergence of a national economy, 1775–1815*, New York: Harper & Row.

Newstadt, E. (2008) "Neoliberalism and the Federal Reserve," in L. Panitch and M. Konings (eds.), *American empire and the political economy of global finance*, New York: Palgrave.

Nishimura, S. (1971) *The decline of inland bills of exchange in the London money market, 1855–1913*, Cambridge: Cambridge University Press.

Nordyke, J. W. (1976 [1958]) *International finance and New York*, New York: Arno Press.

Novak, W. J. (1996) *The people's welfare. Law and regulation in nineteenth-century America*, Chapel Hill/London: University of North Carolina Press.

(2008) "The myth of the 'weak' American state," *American Historical Review*, (June).
Nugent, W. T. K. (1963) "Money, politics and society: the currency question," in H. W. Morgan (ed.), *The gilded age*, Syracuse: Syracuse University Press.
Nussbaum, A. (1957) *A history of the dollar*, New York/London: Columbia University Press.
Nye, J. (1990) *Bound to lead: The changing nature of American power*, New York: Basic Books.
O'Brien, P. (2003) "The myth of Anglophone succession," *New Left Review*, 24 (November–December).
Odell, J. S. (1982) *U.S. international monetary policy. Markets, power and ideas as sources of change*, Princeton: Princeton University Press.
Olney, M. L. (1991) *Buy now pay later. Advertising, credit, and consumer durables in the 1920s*, Chapel Hill/London: University of North Carolina Press.
Orren, K. and S. Skowronek (2004) *The search for American political development*, Cambridge: Cambridge University Press.
Osterweis, S. L. (1932) "Security affiliates and security operations of commercial banks," *Harvard Business Review*, 11 (October).
Ott, J. (2007) When Wall Street met Main Street: The emergence of the retail investors and the quest for an investors democracy, 1890–1929, PhD thesis, Yale University.
(2009) "'The free and open people's market': political ideology and retail brokerage at the New York Stock Exchange, 1913–1933," *Journal of American History*, 96(1).
Panitch, L. (1994) "Globalisation and the state," in R. Miliband and L. Panitch (eds.), *Socialist Register 1994*, London: Merlin.
(1996) "Rethinking the role of the state," in J. H. Mittelman (ed.), *Globalization: critical reflections*, Boulder/London: Lynne Rienner.
(2000) "The new imperial state," *New Left Review*, 2 (March–April).
Panitch, L. and S. Gindin (2005) "Finance and American empire," in L. Panitch and C. Leys (eds.), *Socialist Register 2005*, London: Merlin.
Parboni, R. (1981) *The dollar and its rivals. Recession, inflation, and international finance*, London: Verso.
Parenteau, R. (2005) "The late 1990s' US bubble: financialization in the extreme," in G. A. Epstein (ed.), *Financialization and the world economy*, Cheltenham: Edward Elgar.
Parrini, C. P. (1969) *Heir to empire. United States economic diplomacy, 1916–1923*, Pittsburgh: University of Pittsburgh Press.
Patterson, E. L. S. (1916) "London and New York as financial centers," *Annals of the American Academy of Political and Social Science*, 68 (November).
Patterson, R. T. (1952) "Government finance on the eve of the Civil War," *Journal of Economic History*, 12(1).
Pauls, B. D. (1990) "U.S. exchange rate policy: Bretton Woods to present," *Federal Reserve Bulletin*, 76(11).
Peach, W. H. (1941) *The security affiliates of national banks*, Baltimore: Johns Hopkins University Press.

Penrose, E. F. (1953) *Economic planning for the peace*, Princeton: Princeton University Press.
Perkins, E. J. (1994) *American public finance and financial services, 1700–1815*, Columbus: Ohio State University Press.
— (1999) *Wall Street to Main Street: Charles Merrill and middle class investors*, Cambridge: Cambridge University Pres.
Perrow, C. (2002) *Organizing America. Wealth, power and the origins of corporate capitalism*, Princeton/Oxford: Princeton University Press.
Pessen, E. (1973) *Riches, class, and power before the Civil War*, Lexington, MA: D.C. Heath.
Phelps, C. W. (1927) *The foreign expansion of American banks. American branch banking abroad*, New York: Ronald Press Company.
Phillips, C. A. (1921) *Bank credit. A study of the principles and factors underlying advances made by banks to borrowers*, New York: MacMillan Company.
Phillips, S. M. (1996) "The place of securitization in the financial system: implications for banking and monetary policy," in L. T. Kendall and M. J. Fishman (eds.), *A primer on securitization*, Cambridge, MA/London: MIT Press.
Piore, M. J. and C. F. Sabel (1984) *The second industrial divide: possibilities for prosperity*, New York: Basic Books.
Platt, D. C. M. (1968) *Finance, trade, and politics in British foreign policy 1815–1914*, Oxford: Clarendon Press.
Polanyi, K. (1957) *The great transformation*, Boston: Beacon Press.
Pollin, R. (2003) *Contours of descent. U.S. economic fractures and the landscape of global austerity*, London/New York: Verso.
Polski, M. M. (2003) *The invisible hands of U.S. commercial banking reform. Private action and public guarantees*, Boston: Kluwer Academic Publishers.
Poole, K. E. (1951a) "Money and banking, 1865–1919," in H. F. Williamson (ed.), *The growth of the American economy*, Englewood Cliffs, NJ: Prentice-Hall.
— (1951b) "Money and banking 1919–1950," in H. F. Williamson (ed.), *The growth of the American economy*, Englewood Cliffs, NJ: Prentice-Hall.
Porter, T. (1993) *States, markets and regimes in global finance*, Houndmills, Basingstoke/London: St. Martin's Press.
Prechel, H. (2000) *Big business and the state. Historical transitions and corporate transformation, 1880s–1990s*, New York: State University of New York Press.
Pred, A. R. (1966a) *The spatial dynamics of U.S. urban-industrial growth, 1800–1914: interpretive and theoretical essays*, Cambridge, MA: M.I.T. Press.
— (1966b) "Manufacturing in the American mercantile city: 1800–1840," *Annals of the Association of American Geographers*, 56(2).
Quinn, S. (2004) "Money, finance, and capital markets," in R. Floud and P. Johnson (eds.), *Cambridge economic history of modern Britain*, Cambridge: Cambridge University Press.
Rae, M. F. (2003) International monetary relations between the United States, France, and West Germany in the 1970s, PhD thesis, Texas A&M University.
Redenius, S. A. (2007) "Designing a national currency: antebellum payment networks and the structure of the national banking system," *Financial History Review*, 14(2).

Redlich, F. (1944) *Essays in American economic history. Eric Bollmann and studies in banking*, New York: G.E. Stechert & Co.
  (1968) *The molding of American banking. Men and ideas*, New York/London: Johnson Reprint Corporation.
  (1970) "The promissory note as a financial and business instrument in the Anglo-Saxon world: a historical sketch," *Revue International d'Histoire de la Banque*.
Riesman, J. A. (1983) The origins of American political economy, 1690–1781, PhD dissertation, Brown University.
  (1987) "Money, credit, and Federalist political economy," in R. Beeman, S. Botein, and E. C. Carter (eds.), *Beyond confederation. Origins of the Constitution and American national identity*, Chapel Hill/London: University of North Carolina Press.
Ritter, G. (1997) *Goldbugs and greenbacks. The antimonopoly tradition and the politics of finance in America, 1865–1896*, Cambridge: Cambridge University Press.
Robbins, S. M. and N. E. Terleckyj (1960) *Money metropolis. A locational study of financial activities in the New York region*, Cambridge, MA: Harvard University Press.
Roberts, P. (1997) "The Anglo-American theme: American visions of an Atlantic alliance, 1914–1933," *Diplomatic History*, 21(3).
  (1998) "'Quis custodiet ipsos custodes?' The Federal Reserve System's founding fathers and Allied finances in the first world war," *Business History Review*, 72 (Winter).
  (2000) "Benjamin Strong, the Federal Reserve, and the limits to interwar American nationalism part II: Strong and the Federal Reserve System in the 1920s," *Federal Reserve Bank of Richmond Economic Quarterly*, 86(2).
Robertson, D. B. (1989) "The bias of American Federalism: the limits of welfare-state development in the progressive era," *Journal of Policy History*, 1(3).
Rochester, A. (1936) *Rulers of America: a study of finance capital*, New York: International Publishers.
Rockoff, H. T. (1975a) *The free banking era: a reexamination*, New York: Arno Press.
  (1975b) "Varieties of banking and regional economic development in the United States, 1840–1860," *Journal of Economic History*, 35(1).
Rogers, J. S. (1995) *The early history of the law of bills and notes. A study of the origins of Anglo-American commercial law*, Cambridge: Cambridge University Press.
Roosa, R. V. (1951) "The revival of monetary policy," *Review of Economics and Statistics*, 33(1).
Roover, R. de (1963) *The rise and decline of the Medici Bank, 1937–1494*, Cambridge, MA: Harvard University Press.
  (1974) "New interpretations of the history of banking," in J. Kirshner (ed.), *Business, banking and economic thought in late medieval and early modern Europe. Selected studies of Raymond de Roover*, London/Chicago: University of Chicago Press.

Rosenberg, E. S. (1985) "Foundations of United States international financial power: gold standard diplomacy, 1900–1905," *Business History Review*, 59(2).
  (1999) *Financial missionaries to the world. The politics and culture of dollar diplomacy, 1900–1930*, Cambridge, MA/London: Harvard University Press.
Rothenberg, W. B. (1992) *From market-places to a market economy. The transformation of rural Massachusetts, 1750–1850*, Chicago/London: University of Chicago Press.
Rousseau, P. L. (2002) "Jacksonian monetary policy, specie flows, and the panic of 1837," *Journal of Economic History*, 62(2).
Roy, W. G. (1991) "The organization of the corporate class segment of the U.S. capitalist class at the turn of this century," in S. G. McNall, R. F. Levine, and R. Fantasia (eds.), *Bringing class back in. Contemporary and historical perspectives*, Boulder: Westview Press.
  (1997) *Socializing capital. The rise of the large industrial corporation in America*, Princeton: Princeton University Press.
Rude, C. (2004) *The Volcker monetary policy shocks: a political-economic analysis*, unpublished paper, Department of Economics, New School University.
Ruggie, J. G. (1982) "International regimes, transactions and change: embedded liberalism in the post-war economic order," *International Organization*, 36(2).
  (2008) "Introduction: embedding global markets," in J. G. Ruggie (ed.), *Embedding global markets: an enduring challenge*, Aldershot/Burlington: Ashgate.
Sanders, E. (1999) *Roots of reform. Farmers, workers and the American state, 1877–1917*, Chicago/London: Chicago University Press.
Santiago-Valiente, W. (1988) "Historical background of the classical monetary theory and the "real-bills" banking tradition," *History of Political Economy*, 20(1).
Sarai, D. (2008) "US structural power and the internationalization of the Treasury," in L. Panitch and M. Konings (eds.), *American empire and the political economy of global finance*, New York: Palgrave.
Sassen, S. (1991) *The global city. New York, London, Tokyo*, Princeton, NJ: Princeton University Press.
Sassoon, D. (1996) *One hundred years of socialism: the West European left in the twentieth century*, New York: New Press.
Savage, M. and K. Williams (2008) "Elites: remembered in capitalism and forgotten by social sciences," *Sociological Review*, 56(s1).
Sayers, R. S. (1936) *Bank of England operations 1890–1914*, London: P.S. King & Son.
Scammell, W. M. (1968) *The London discount market*, London: Elek Books.
  (1985) "The working of the gold standard," in B. Eichengreen (ed.), *The gold standard in theory and history*, New York/London: Methuen.
Scheiber, Harry N. (1963) "The pet banks in Jacksonian politics and finance, 1833–1841," *Journal of Economic History*, 23(2).
Schenk, C. R. (1998) "The origins of the Eurodollar market in London: 1955–1963," *Explorations in Economic History*, 35(2).

Schlesinger, A. M. (1945) *The age of Jackson*, Boston: Little, Brown.
  (1957) *The colonial merchants and the American Revolution, 1763–1776*, New York: F. Ungar Publishing Co.
Schmidt, C. H. and E. J. Stockwell (1952) "The changing importance of institutional investors in the American capital market," *Law and Contemporary Problems*, 17(1).
Schwartz, H. M. (2009) *Subprime nation: American power, global capital, and the housing bubble*, Ithaca: Cornell University Press.
Schweikart, L. (1987) *Banking in the American South from the Age of Jackson to Reconstruction*, Baton Rouge: Louisiana State University Press.
Schweitzer, M. M. (1989) "State-issued currency and the ratification of the U.S. Constitution," *Journal of Economic History*, 49(2).
Scott, I. O. (1965) *Government securities market*, New York: McGraw-Hill.
Scranton, P. (1997) *Endless novelty: specialty production and American industrialization, 1865–1925*, Princeton, NJ: Princeton University Press.
Seabrooke, L. (2001) *US power in international finance. The victory of dividends*, New York: Palgrave.
  (2004) "The economic taproot of US imperialism: the Bush rentier shift," *International Politics*, 41(3).
Seavoy, R. E. (1972) "Laws to encourage manufacturing; New York policy and the 1811 General Incorporation Statute," *Business History Review*, 46(1).
  (1978) "The public service origins of the American business corporation," *Business History Review*, 52(1).
Selden, R. T. (1963) *Trends and cycles in the commercial paper market*, New York: National Bureau of Economic Research.
Seligman, E. R. A. (1927) *The economics of installment selling*, New York: Harpers & Brothers.
Seligman, J. (2003) *The transformation of Wall Street. A history of the Securities and Exchange Commission and modern corporate finance*, New York: Aspen Publishers.
Sellers, C. (1991) *The market revolution. Jacksonian America 1815–1846*, New York/Oxford: Oxford University Press.
Shade, W. G. (1972) *Banks or no banks. The money issue in Western politics 1832–1865*, Detroit: Wayne State University Press.
Sharkey, R. P. (1959) *Money, class, and party. An economic study of Civil War and Reconstruction*, Baltimore: Johns Hopkins University Press.
Shaw, E. R. (1978) *The London money market*, London: Heinemann.
Shultz, W. J. and M. R. Caine (1937) *Financial development of the United States*, New York: Prentice-Hall, Inc.
Silbey, J. H. (1991) *The American political nation, 1838–1893*, Stanford: Stanford University Press.
Silver, B. J. and G. Arrighi (2003) "Polanyi's 'double movement': The belle époques of British and U.S. hegemony compared," *Politics & Society*, 31(2).
Simmons, B. A. (2001) "The international politics of harmonization: the case of capital market regulation," *International Organization*, 55(3).
Simmons, E. C. (1951) "The structure of the postwar money market," *Southern Economic Journal*, 17(4).

Simpson, T. D. (1992) "Features of the new financial system in the United States," in H. Cavanna (ed.), *Financial innovation*, London/New York: Routledge.

Sinclair, T. J. (2005) *The new masters of capital. American bond rating agencies and the politics of creditworthiness*, Ithaca/London: Cornell University Press.

Singer, D. A. (2004) "Capital rules: the domestic politics of international regulatory harmonization," *International Organization*, 58(3).

Sklar, M. J. (1988) *The corporate reconstruction of American capitalism, 1890–1916. The market, the law and politics*, Cambridge: Cambridge University Press.

Skocpol, T. (1979) *States and social revolutions: a comparative analysis of France, Russia, and China*, Cambridge: Cambridge University Press.

—— (1985) "Bringing the state back in: strategies of analysis in current research," in P. B. Evans, D. Rueschemeyer, and T. Skocpol (eds.), *Bringing the state back in*, Cambridge: Cambridge University Press.

Skowronek, S. (1982) *Building a new American state. The expansion of national administrative capacities, 1877–1920*, Cambridge: Cambridge University Press.

Smiley, W. G. (1981) "The expansion of the New York securities market at the turn of the century," *Business History Review*, 55(1).

—— (1973) The evolution and structure of the national banking system, 1870–1913, PhD thesis, University of Iowa.

Smith, G. and D. Dyer (1996) "The rise and transformation of the American corporation," in C. Kaysen (ed.), *The changing American Corporation*, Oxford: Oxford University Press.

Smith, R. C. (2000) *The money wars: the rise and fall of the great buyout boom of the 1980s*, New York: Beard Books.

Smith, W. B. (1953) *Economic aspects of the Second Bank of the United States*, Cambridge: Harvard University Press.

Sobel, A. C. (1994) *Domestic choices, international markets. Dismantling national barriers and liberalizing securities markets*, Ann Arbor: University of Michigan Press.

Sobel, R. (1965) *The big board: a history of the New York stock market*, New York: Free Press of Glencoe.

Soederberg, S. (2004) *The politics of the new international financial architecture*, London/New York: Zed Books.

—— (2008) "Deconstructing the official treatment for 'enronitis': the Sarbanes-Oxley Act and the neoliberal governance of corporate America," *Critical Sociology*, 34(5).

Solomon, R. (1982) *The international monetary system, 1945–1981*, New York: Harper & Row.

—— (1999) *Money on the move. The revolution in international finance since 1980*, Princeton, NJ: Princeton University Press.

Sparks, E. S. (1932) *History and theory of agricultural credit in the United States*, New York: Thomas Y. Crowell.

Spong, K. (2003) "The US financial sector: regulatory issues," in A. M. Rugman and G. Boyd (eds.), *Alliance capitalism for the new American economy*, Cheltenham, UK/Northampton, MA: Edward Elgar.

Spufford, P. (1988) *Money and its use in medieval Europe*, Cambridge: Cambridge University Press.
Stanton, T. H. (2002) *Government-sponsored enterprises: mercantilist companies in the modern world*, Washington, DC: AEI Press.
Stern, S. (1951) *The United States in international banking*, New York: Oxford University Press.
Stiglitz, J. (2004) *The roaring nineties*, New York: W.W. Norton.
Stigum, M. (1990) *The money market*, Homewood, IL: Dow Jones-Irwin.
Strange, S. (1971) *Sterling and British policy. A political study of an international currency in decline*, London: Oxford University Press.
—— (1986) *Casino capitalism*, Manchester/New York: Manchester University Press.
—— (1988) *States and markets*, London: Pinter.
Stromquist, R. (2006) *Reinventing "the people": The Progressive movement, the class problem, and the origins of modern liberalism*. Champaign: University of Illinois Press.
Studenski, P. and H. E. Krooss (1963) *Financial history of the United States*, New York: McGraw-Hill.
Sylla, R. (1969) "Federal policy, banking market structure, and capital mobilization in the United States, 1863–1913," *Journal of Economic History*, 29(4).
—— (1998) "U.S. securities markets and the banking system," *Federal Reserve Bank of St. Louis Review*, May–June.
—— (1999) "Shaping the US financial system, 1690–1913: the dominant role of public finance," in R. Sylla, R. Tilly, and G. Tortella (eds.), *The state, the financial system and economic modernization*, Cambridge: Cambridge University Press.
—— (2002) "United States banks and Europe: strategy and attitudes," in S. Battilossi and Y. Cassis (eds.), *European banks and the American challenge. Competition and cooperation in international banking under Bretton Woods*, Oxford: Oxford University Press.
Tallman, E. W. and J. R. Moen (1995) "Private sector responses to the panic of 1907: a comparison of New York and Chicago," *Federal Reserve Bank of Atlanta Economic Review*, 80 (March–April).
Taus, E. R. (1943) *Central banking functions of the United States treasury: 1789–1941*, New York: Columbia University Press.
Temin, P. (1969) *The Jacksonian economy*, New York/London: W.W. Norton & Company.
—— (1976) *Did monetary forces cause the Great Depression?* New York: Norton.
Thayer, T. (1953) "The land bank system in the American colonies," *Journal of Economic History*, 13(2).
Thomasson, M. A. (2002) "From sickness to health: the twentieth-century development of U.S. health insurance," *Explorations in Economic History*, 39(3).
Tickell, A. (2000) "Dangerous derivatives: controlling and creating risks in international money," *Geoforum*, 31(1).
Timberlake, R. H. (1960a) "The independent treasury and monetary policy before the Civil War," *Southern Economic Journal*, 27(2).
—— (1960b) "The specie circular and the distribution of the surplus," *Journal of Political Economy*, 68(2).

(1978) *The origins of central banking in the United States*, Cambridge, MA: Harvard University Press.

(1984) "The central banking role of clearinghouse associations," *Journal of Money, Credit and Banking*, 16(1).

(1993) *Monetary policy in the United States: an intellectual and institutional history*, Chicago: University of Chicago Press.

Trescott, P. B. (1963) *Financing American enterprise. The story of commercial banking*, New York and Evanston: Harper & Row.

Triffin, R. (1961) *Gold and the dollar crisis*, New Haven: Yale University Press.

Tufano, P. (1997) "Business failure, judicial intervention, and financial innovation: restructuring U.S. railroads in the nineteenth century," *Business History Review*, 71(1).

Unger, I. (1964) *The greenback era: a social and political history of American finance, 1865–1879*, Princeton, NJ: Princeton University Press.

Useem, M. (1996) *Investor capitalism. How money managers are changing the face of corporate America*, New York: Basic Books.

Usher, A. P. (1914) "The origin of the bill of exchange," *Journal of Political Economy*, 22(6).

(1943) *The early history of deposit banking in Mediterranean Europe*, Cambridge, MA: Harvard University Press.

Vidger, L. P. (1961) "The Federal National Mortgage Association, 1938–57," *Journal of Finance*, 16(1).

Vitols, S. (1997) Modernizing capital: banks and the regulation of long-term finance in postwar Germany and the U.S., PhD thesis, University of Wisconsin–Madison.

Vittoz, S. (1987) *New Deal labor policy and the American industrial economy*, Chapel Hill: University of North Carolina Press.

Vogel, S. K. (1996) *Freer markets, more rules: Regulatory reform in advanced industrial countries*, Ithaca, NY: Cornell University Press.

Volcker, P. (2002) "Monetary policy transmission: past and future challenges," *Federal Reserve Bank of New York Economic Policy Review*, May.

Waddell, B. (2001) *The war against the New Deal. World War II and American democracy*, DeKalb: Illinois University Press.

Wade, R. (2008) "Financial regime change?," *New Left Review*, 53 (September–October).

Wagster, J. D. (1996) "Impact of the 1988 Basle Accord on International Banks," *Journal of Finance*, 51(4).

Wallison, P. J. and B. Ely (2000) *Nationalizing mortgage risk: The growth of Fannie Mae and Freddie Mac*, Washington, DC: AEI Press.

Walter, A. (1993) *World power and world money. The role of hegemony and international monetary order*, New York: Harvester Wheatsheaf.

Walters, R. (1945) "The origins of the Second Bank of the United States," *Journal of Political Economy*, 53(2).

Wang, J. (2005) "Imagining the administrative state: legal pragmatism, securities regulation, and New Deal liberalism," *Journal of Policy History*, 17(3).

Warwick Commission on International Financial Reform (2009) *In Praise of Unlevel Playing Fields*, Coventry: University of Warwick.
Watson, M. (2005) *Foundations of international political economy*, New York: Palgrave.
Weber, W. E. (2003) "Interbank payments relationships in the antebellum United States: evidence from Pennsylvania," *Federal Reserve Bank of Minneapolis Quarterly Review*, 27(3).
Wee, H. van der (1977) "Monetary, credit and banking systems," in E. E. Rich and C. H. Wilson (eds.), *The Cambridge Economic History of Europe Vol.5*, Cambridge: Cambridge University Press.
  (1997) "The influence of banking on the rise of capitalism in north-west Europe, fourteenth to nineteenth century," in A. Teichovia, G. K.-v. Hentenryk, and D. Ziegler (eds.), *Banking, trade and industry. Europe, America and Asia from the thirteenth to the twentieth century*, Cambridge: Cambridge University Press.
Weinstein, J. (1968) *The corporate ideal in the liberal state, 1900–1918*, Boston: Beacon Press.
Weldin, S. J. (2000) A.P. Giannini, Marriner Stoddard Eccles, and the changing landscape of American banking, PhD thesis, University of North Texas.
Wells, D. R. (2004) *The Federal Reserve System. A history*, Jefferson, North Carolina/London: McFarland & Company.
Wells, W. C. (1994) *Economist in an uncertain world. Arthur F. Burns and the Federal Reserve, 1970–78*, New York: Columbia University Press.
Werner, W. and S. T. Smith (1991) *Wall Street*, New York: Columbia University Press.
West, R. C. (1973) *Banking reform and the Federal Reserve, 1863–1923*, Ithaca: Cornell University Press.
Wheelock, D. C. (1989) "The strategy, effectiveness, and consistency of Federal Reserve monetary policy 1924–1933," *Explorations in Economic History*, 26.
  (1991) *The strategy and consistency of Federal Reserve monetary policy, 1924–1933*, Cambridge: Cambridge University Press.
White, A. M. (2004) "Risk-based mortgage pricing: Present and future research," *Housing Policy Debate*, 15(3).
White, E. N. (1983) *The regulation and reform of the American banking system, 1900–1929*, Princeton, NJ: Princeton University Press.
  (1990) "The stock market boom and crash of 1929 revisited," *Journal of Economic Perspectives*, 4(2).
  (1992a) *The Comptroller and the transformation of American banking 1960–1990*, Washington, DC: Comptroller of the Currency.
  (1992b) "The effects of bank regulation on the financing of American business, 1860–1960," in V. Zamagni (ed.), *Finance and the enterprise*, London: Academic Press.
  (1998) "Were banks special intermediaries in late nineteenth century America?" *Federal Reserve Bank of St. Louis Review*, 80(3).
Whitesell, W. E. (1964) "The Federal Reserve System's 'bills only' policy," *Journal of Finance*, 19(1).

Whitford, J. (2002) "Pragmatism and the untenable dualism of means and ends: why rational choice theory does not deserve paradigmatic privilege," *Theory & Society*, 31(3).

Whitley, R. (1986a) "The transformation of business finance into financial economics: the roles of academic expansion and changes in U.S. capital markets," *Accounting, Organizations and Society*, 11(2).

(1986b) "The rise of modern finance theory: its characteristics as a scientific field and connections to the changing structure of capital markets," *Research in the History of Economic Thought and Methodology*, 4.

Wicker, E. R. (1996) *The banking panics of the Great Depression*, New York: Cambridge University Press.

(1966) *Federal Reserve monetary policy 1917–1933*, New York: Random House.

Wiebe, R. H. (1962) *Businessmen and reform: a study of the Progressive movement*, Chicago: Quadrangle Books.

(1967) *The search for order, 1877–1920*, New York: Hill and Wang.

Wigmore, B. A. (1985) *The Crash and its aftermath: a history of securities markets in the United States, 1929–1933*, Greenwood Press: Westport.

(1997) *Securities market in the 1980s. Vol.1 The new regime, 1979–1984*, New York/Oxford: Oxford University Press.

Wilentz, S. (1984) *New York City and the rise of the American working class*, New York: Oxford University Press.

(1997) "Society, politics and the market revolution, 1815–1848," in E. Foner (ed.), *The new American history*, Philadelphia: Temple University Press.

Wilkins, M. (1974) *The maturing of multinational enterprise: American business abroad from 1914 to 1970*, Cambridge, MA/London: Harvard University Press.

(1999) "Cosmopolitan finance in the 1920s: New York's emergence as an international financial centre," in R. Sylla, R. Tilly, and G. Tortella (eds.), *The state, the financial system and economic modernization*, Cambridge: Cambridge University Press.

Williams, D. (1968) "The evolution of the sterling system," in C. R. Whittlesey and J. S. G. Wilson (eds.), *Essays in money and banking. In honour of R.S. Sayers*, Oxford: Clarendon Press.

Williams, W. A. (1959) *The tragedy of American diplomacy*, Cleveland/New York: World Publishing Company.

(1961) *The contours of American history*, Cleveland: World Publishing.

Wojnilower, A. M. (1987) "Financial change in the United States," in M. d. Cecco (ed.), *Changing money. Financial innovation in developed countries*, Oxford/New York: Basil Blackwell.

(1980) "The central role of credit crunches in recent financial history," *Brookings Papers on Economic Activity*, 2.

Wolfe, S. (2000) "Structural effects of asset-based securitization," *European Journal of Finance*, 6(4).

Wood, E. (1995) *Democracy against capitalism. Renewing historical materialism*, Cambridge: Cambridge University Press.

Wood, J. H. (2005) *A history of central banking in Great Britain and the United States*, New York: Cambridge University Press.
Woods, N. (2006) *The globalizers: the IMF, the World Bank, and their borrowers*, Ithaca: Cornell University Press.
Woods, R. B. (1990) *A changing of the guard: Anglo-American relations, 1941–1946*, Chapel Hill/London: University of North Carolina Press.
Woolley, J. T. (1984) *Monetary politics. The Federal Reserve and the politics of monetary policy*, Cambridge: Cambridge University Press.
Wray, L. R. (2009) "The rise and fall of money manager capitalism: a Minskian approach," *Cambridge Journal of Economics*, 33(4).
—— (1990) *Money and credit in capitalist economies*, Aldershot: Edward Elgar.
Wright, R. E. (2001) *Origins of commercial banking in America, 1750–1800*, Lanham: Rowman & Littlefield.
—— (2002) *The wealth of nations rediscovered: integration and expansion in American financial markets, 1780–1850*, Cambridge: Cambridge University Press.
—— (2005) *The first Wall Street. Chestnut Street, Philadelphia, and the birth of American finance*, Chicago: Chicago University Press.
Wyse, R. C. (1918) "The future of London as the world's money market," *Economic Journal*, 28 (December).
Youngman, A. (1906) "The growth of financial banking," *Journal of Political Economy*, 14(7).
Zweig, P. L. (1995) *Wriston. Walter Wriston, Citibank, and the rise and fall of American financial supremacy*, New York: Crown Publishers, Inc.
Zysman, J. (1983) *Governments, markets, and growth. Financial systems and the politics of industrial change*, Ithaca/London: Cornell University Press.

Index

agency, 4–6
American Dream, 82, 133, 156
American International Group (AIG), 156
American political development (literature), 7
Amsterdam, 19
Anglo-Saxon model, 9, 17, 26
antitrust legislation, 51
Antwerp, 18–19
Asian financial crisis, 148
asset inflation, 137, 139
asset-backed securities, 127, 147, 154–55
asset-based currency, 57

bailouts, 142, 158
balance of payments deficit, 12, 88, 95–97, 112, 120, 124
bank holding company, 113
Bank of England, 20, 28, 34, 56, 66, 71
Bank of North America, 24
bankers' balances, 36, 41–42
Basel Capital Accord, 144, 147
"benign neglect," 12–13, 97, 120
bilateral currency arrangements, 91–92
bills of credit, 21, 23, 25
bills of exchange, 18–19, 21, 23, 27, 30, 32, 34, 43, 58, 61, 72–73, 101
bills-only policy, 112–13
bimetallism, 49
branch banking, restrictions on, 30, 36, 42, 50, 106, 133
Bretton Woods, 12, 90, 92, 95, 97
  end of, 121–22
British colonial policies, 20, 23
British Treasury, 20
Bryan, William Jennings, 52
Bush, George W., 150, 154

call loans, 36, 44–46, 50, 52, 54–55, 62, 67, 101
capital controls, 90, 96–97, 117–18, 120
capital market, 31, 51, 59, 126, 138
capital requirements, 144, 147
Carter, James, 134
certificate of deposit (CD), 115
China, 154
Civil War, 34, 40–41
Civil War legislation, 40–41
Clinton, Bill, 147
commercial banking, 19, 23, 28–29, 31, 59, 62, 73, 80, 82, 100–02, 105, 126, 133
commercial paper, 43–44, 49, 61, 63, 72–73, 101, 107, 116, 125
commodity money, 21
Communism, 91
Community Reinvestment Act, 125, 147
Comptroller of the Currency, 113
concentration of banking sector, 145
Congress, 56, 103, 126, 128, 135, 144
Constitution, 24–25
Constitutional Convention, 24
consumer credit, 63, 83, 102, 105, 125
  as disciplinary institution, 64, 106
continental bills, 23–24
corporate charters, 29

195

corporate finance, 61, 105
corporate form, transformation of, 49
countercyclical policies, 65, 112
country banks, 31, 36, 46
crash of 1929, 10, 67, 73
credit cards, 106
credit-rating agencies, 52, 155
crisis of 1857, 37
crisis of 1873, 47
crisis of 1907, 55–56
Currency Act, 23
currency question, 49
cyclical model of capitalist development, 8, 10, 39, 70, 76

debt crisis of 1980s, 141
Democratic Party, 47, 79–80
deposit insurance, 105, 135
Depository Institutions Deregulation and Monetary Control Act, 135
derivatives, 123, 127, 138, 146
discount market, 23, 27, 30, 43, 72–73
discount window, 58–59, 66, 101
discounting, 19
disintermediation, 44, 50–51, 53, 61, 107, 124, 127
dollar
  as international currency, 12–13, 70, 73, 111, 123, 140, 157
  as reserve currency, 10, 71, 73–74, 88, 94
  as transactions currency, 75, 94
dollar diplomacy, 72, 74
dollar glut, 95, 117
dollar overhang, 12, 88, 118, 124
dollar shortage, 91–92
dollar standard, 121
double deficit, 142
dual banking system, 42, 127

endorsement, 18, 44
Eurodollar market, 13, 95–97, 111, 123, 127, 136, 154
  disintermediation, 107, 117
  Federal Reserve, 118–19
  inflation, 124
  liability management 118
  Treasury, 118–19
European Payments Union, 92
European reconstruction, 91

farmers, 9, 21–22, 27, 32–33, 40, 42, 47, 57

long-term credit, 22, 24, 30, 32
Federal Deposit Insurance Corporation, 82
federal funds market, 114, 119, 134, 136
federal funds rate, 114, 128, 134, 137, 149
Federal Home Loan Bank System, 83
Federal Home Loan Mortgage Corporation (Freddie Mac), 125, 156
Federal National Mortgage Association (Fannie Mae), 83, 125, 156
Federal Open Market Committee, 65, 119, 128
Federal Reserve, 10, 13–14, 57–61, 64, 67, 83–84, 107, 110–12, 115–16, 124, 127–28, 132, 135–36, 145, 148–49, 153–54, 156
  as bankers' bank, 60, 101, 112, 127
  Eurodollar market, 119
  money market strategy, 60, 65, 67, 112, 119, 127–28
  support for Treasury's debt-funding operations, 59, 94, 101, 111
Federal Reserve Act, 57, 66
Federal Reserve Bank of New York, 65–66, 80, 82
Federal Reserve Board, 59, 65–66, 83
Federal Reserve Reform Act, 129
Federalism, 27–28, 32
"financial banking," 9, 40, 51, 53
fictitious capital, 150
financial inclusion, 147
financialization, 124, 138
First Bank of the United States, 28
First World War, 10, 59, 71
fixed exchange rates, 90, 94
floating exchange rates, 122
Fordism, 79
foreign exchange, 73, 89, 94, 127
foreign investors, 138, 154, 157
fractional reserve banking, 18–19
fraud, 125, 142, 151
free banking, 35–36, 41–42
fund management, 146

Garn-St. Germain Depository Institutions Act, 135
Glass-Steagall Act, 82
  repeal of, 146
globalization, 2, 12, 39–40, 86, 109–10, 140
gold outflows, 96
gold standard, 20, 49, 52, 54, 57, 71, 74

Index

government debt, 14, 28, 34–35, 41, 59, 101–02, 105, 111, 139, 154
Government-Sponsored Enterprises, 125, 146–47
Great Depression, 10, 67, 73–74, 81
greenbacks, 43, 49
Greenspan, Alan, 148, 151

Hamilton, Alexander, 27
home ownership, 125
household debt, 14, 125

Independent Treasury, 34–35
inequality, 5–6, 56, 133–34, 138, 147, 153, 155, 158
informal credit, 21, 63
inside-out perspective, 89, 99, 109–10, 117, 141
insider trading, 125
institutional investors, 83, 104, 125, 145
institutional transplantation, 17, 23, 25, 39
institutions, 4–6
interlocking directorships, 52
internal improvements, 28
international banking, 62, 70, 73, 92, 96, 111, 116
international banking facilities, 136, 140
International Monetary Fund, 90, 95, 141–42, 148
international political economy (IPE), 7–8, 12, 16–17, 26, 39, 88, 110
   disembedding, 2–3, 55, 110, 121
   embedded liberalism, 2, 11–12, 70, 87, 100, 109
   hegemonic decline, 2–3, 14, 87, 109, 121, 131, 143, 150, 157
   hegemonic transition, 69, 76
   interpretation of interwar period, 10, 69
   interpretation of liberalism, 20, 54
   interpretation of neoliberalism, 2, 13, 131–32, 152
   interpretation of New Deal, 11, 77–78, 80
   interpretation of subprime crisis, 156
   market and state, 3, 109, 121, 129
   Polanyian perspective, 3, 77, 80, 87, 110, 131
Internet bubble, 151
investment banking, 31, 46, 50–51, 62, 66, 72, 80, 82, 100–04, 126
"irrational exuberance," 150
isolationism, 69, 84, 91

Jackson, Andrew, 32–34
Jacksonian coalition, 33–34
Japan, 143
Jefferson, Thomas, 28
junk bonds, 138, 142

Kennedy, Robert, 96
Keynesianism, 78, 81
Korean War, 111

labor unions, 124, 134
land banks, 22, 24
legitimacy, 5–6
Lehman Brothers, 156
lender of last resort, 32, 48, 60–61, 67, 83
leveraged buyout, 138, 142
liability management, 108, 114–16, 119, 127, 136, 144, 154
limits on bank loan size, 42, 44, 50, 107
loan sharks, 147
London, 54, 71–72, 96, 117
Louvre Accord, 142

market in corporate control, 126, 138
markets as institutional constructions, 3, 7
Marshall Aid, 91
Martin, William McChesney, 111
McKinley, William, 52
mercantilism, 21, 84
merchant banks, 31
merchants, 21, 24, 29, 43
Mergers and Acquisitions, 126, 138, 142
Merrill Lynch, 156
Mexico, 141
military spending, 133, 150, 154
misrepresentation, 5
monetarism, 14, 128, 131–32, 134, 136–37, 139, 151
monetary aggregates, 128, 137
money market, 19, 30, 51
   banks' changing relationship to, 114
money supply, 112, 119, 128, 132, 134, 136
Money Trust, 52, 55, 57, 59, 79–80
moral hazard, 142, 145
Morgan, John Pierpont, 55
mortgage credit, 63, 105–6, 125
mortgage-backed securities, 83, 113, 125, 154–55
mortgages, 22, 30, 83, 147
multilateralism, 11, 78, 84–85, 89
mutual funds, 125

National Bank Acts, 41–42
National Banking System, 36
national banks, 41, 49–50, 58
National Monetary Commission, 56
negotiability, 18
neoliberalism, 13–14, 131–32, 143, 151, 153, 157, 159
　as vortex-like process, 140
　disciplinary effects, 134
New Deal, 11, 77–78, 81–83, 100
　compared to European welfare states, 106
　foreign financial policy, 84–85
　integrative role of credit, 82
　shift in nature of economic policy, 80
New York
　as central reserve city, 36, 41
　as international financial center, 12, 70, 73, 88, 94, 96, 104, 117, 140, 154
New York Clearing House, 46, 50, 55
Nixon, Richard, 12–13, 88, 97, 111, 120

off-balance sheet securitization, 113, 155
Open Door policies, 74
open market operations, 65–66, 101, 112, 119
Operation Twist, 96, 113, 115

panic of 1837, 34–35
payday lending, 147
Pecora Commission, 79
pension funds, 82, 84, 107, 125
petrodollars, 123
Plaza Accord, 142
policy autonomy, 14, 97, 132
populism, 40, 47–48, 52, 57, 59, 63
　ideal of independent farmer, 22, 47
　transformation of, 53
postbellum political stalemate, 49, 52
power
　contradictions, 6–7
　network power, 37, 67, 100, 108, 139, 149
　structural power, 2, 4–7, 53, 68, 76, 81, 86, 98–99, 109–10, 121, 123, 129, 151
price inflation, 16, 20, 110, 112, 115–16, 120, 122, 124, 127, 133, 136
private equity, 138, 154

Progressivism, 55–56, 62–63, 78
promissory notes, 18, 30, 43
protectionism, 75, 85
Pujo Committee, 57, 62

railroads, 36, 45–46
Reagan, Ronald, 133, 138–39
real bills, 23, 44
real bills doctrine, 19, 24, 45, 57–60
Regulation Q, 82, 106, 114, 126, 133, 135
relationship banking, 104, 126
reparation payments, 73–74
Republican Party, 47, 52, 79
Republicanism, 28, 30, 32–33
repurchase agreements, 116
risk management, 122, 126, 150
risk-based pricing, 126, 147, 155
Roosevelt, Franklin, 75, 84, 89

Sarbanes-Oxley Act, 151
savings and loan crisis, 142
Second Bank of the United States, 32
Second World War, 89
securities affiliates, 50
Securities and Exchange Commission, 82, 100, 103, 125–26
securities industry, 103, 125, 133
securitization, 9, 11, 13, 51, 83, 107, 113–14, 125, 127, 146–47, 154–55
seigniorage, 12, 17, 88, 94, 97, 123
self-regulatory organizations, 103, 125, 133
September 11, 2001, 151
single-name promissory notes, 43
social finance (literature), 4
Specie Circular, 33
stagflation, 124
state
　infrastructural capacity, 6, 11, 14, 20, 25, 37, 55, 68, 78, 80, 82, 84–85, 88, 98, 108, 120, 122, 132, 139–40, 143, 152, 158
　integral state, 5–6, 68, 85, 103, 129–30, 132
　leverage, 5, 56, 77, 81, 84, 93, 120, 134, 140
state banks, 41, 49–50, 58
sterling as international currency, 71, 74–75, 94
sterling bloc, 72, 75, 89, 91
sterling crisis of 1947, 91

Index

stock market, 31, 36, 44–46, 50, 52, 54, 61, 63, 66–67, 74, 102, 125, 146
stock market crash of 1987, 142
Strong, Benjamin, 65
subprime crisis, 14, 153, 155, 157–58
subprime mortgage market, 153, 155
subsistence farming, 22
"System of 1896," 52, 73, 78, 84

taxes, 21, 23, 133, 150
term loan, 105
"too big to fail," 141, 145, 148, 156, 158
thrifts, 63, 83, 106–7, 115, 127, 142
total reserves, 119, 128, 134, 136
trade deficit, 142–43
Treasury, 27, 33–34, 41, 46, 55, 60, 95–97, 111, 118, 124, 139, 141, 145, 148
    Eurodollar market, 120
Treasury bills, 94, 96, 107, 112–13, 121, 144, 157

Troubled Asset Relief Program, 156
Truman, Harry, 90
trust companies, 50
trust funds, 49–50

unilateralism, 10

Volcker shock, 135, 141
Volcker, Paul, 134–36

war debts, 70, 73, 79
War of 1812, 30
War of Independence, 23
Washington consensus, 148
Whigs, 34
Working Group on Financial Markets, 144
World Bank, 90, 95, 141, 148